SEX, LIES AND TWO HINDU GURUS

Karen Jonson lived the life of a Hindu nun in the US ashram of two Hindu gurus, who turned out to be conmen dressed in saffron clothing. After this, she has been zealously working towards lifting the veil off the organization and the fake gurus. Her efforts to expose the con game included starting a blog (www.rishikaxcult.com) and a Facebook page (www.facebook.com/rishikaxcult) and culminated in the writing of this book. You can visit its official website at www.sexliesandtwohindugurus.com.

Karen is currently writing other books based on her experience of pursuing God while unknowingly living in a sex cult, including a book that deals with finding a guru-free path to inner wisdom (www.theinnerwisdomproject.com). She is based in Texas, USA.

Commentary on This Book

'*Sex, Lies and Two Hindu Gurus* is one of the most important books ever written on life inside of a cult by someone who lived it. Karen Jonson has made a substantial contribution to our understanding of cults. It is an insightful, even powerful account ... This I think is one of the strongest of various memoirs from former cult members. It is an excellent read.'
– Richard Schott, PhD, Professor of Public Affairs, University of Texas, Austin

'When friends or my child asks me about my life in this cult, I can show them this book. Karen's story perfectly captures the twisted, insular and secretive world in which we all lived.'
– Kate Tonnessen, child victim, Washington

'I was one of the people who gave all of my life energy to this organization for six years. I am grateful to Karen for her brave pursuit of the truth, her wonderful memory, wry sense of humor and great literary talent in making transparent the "business" of a corrupt cult. Truth can be stranger than fiction, but it is also stronger than fiction.'
– Suzy Parker, ex-JKP devotee, Connecticut

'After spending many years involved in this corrupt religious organization, I would like to acknowledge the author for taking on the painstaking task of systematically writing the true story of the series of events that took place. I feel it is important to record the story of what happened in the form of this book because, if the story isn't told, it can eventually be forgotten ... I commend her once again for her excellent organization of the series of events that led up to the trial, conviction and disappearance of Prakashanand Saraswati. Her painstaking documentation and writing took place at a time when she was in the middle of rebuilding her own life and reclaiming her soul.'
– Kathi K., ex-JKP devotee, California

'*Sex, Lies and Two Hindu Gurus* exposes a world that few have ever seen and that many deny even exists. It's a world where corruption and deceit run free, and where people's vulnerabilities are preyed upon and used against them – all in the name of religion. It's a world that was run by two men and supported by a bevy of followers, who sadly in their search for enlightenment, have been elevated to

merely the position of pawns in a game of sociopathy. Karen, the author, shows great courage throughout the entire book, as she reveals the truths behind the countless lies that she and many others lived with and around for significant portions of their lives.'
– Sheridan B., friend of ex-JKP devotees, Texas

'The author recounts the unraveling of this sex and money scam with unflinching honesty. By telling this difficult story in a personal way, she draws us in and helps us understand. I found the story, the way it was written, very, very compelling.'
– Karen Roller, friend, Austin

'This is really heavy-duty stuff ... I do lose sleep over Hindu dharma being dragged into mud because of the actions of these people.'
– Milan P., USA

'With each new revelation in your book, I get more angry and more determined to do something to cripple this corrupt organization.'
– Raj S., India

'All I can say is wow ... and amazing. You have clearly exposed the inner dealings of JKP, and the true personalities of Prakashanand and Kripalu. As you say in your book, they are truly rakshasas, demonic entities who have manifested in this age of darkness to feed upon the innocent minds and faith of countless people. I applaud you for this. By exposing them and publishing this book, you've clearly illustrated that they could never break you. Instead, you have broken them.'
– Suren Pandya, ex-devotee, California

'If it wasn't for your book and your Facebook page, I am not sure I would be healing as quickly as I am.'
– Jai Hari, ex-devotee, Oregon

'Your narrative is very, very gripping. Excellent stuff! I like your honesty and truthfulness.'
– Sandeep S., USA

'Wow! I just finished your book and want to tell you how much I enjoyed it. It was just as good as any other true-crime drama I've ever read in its attention to

detail and writing style. I couldn't put it down. Also I have read a lot of books written by people who have been involved in abusive cults and I rank your book as being among the best, most definitely. You shared your evolving beliefs in a way that shows the maturity of your current state of mind ... I admire your bravery in bringing this story to light.'
– Holly June Graves, ex-devotee, Missouri

'Thank you for writing this book and exposing these people. There are way too many lives destroyed in JKP. There are kids who were involved with their parents who ended up with drinking, drug and gang problems. This has to STOP. I spite people who do ANY harm to children, especially. I was 22 when I was molested by Kripalu for the second time. My husband asked me, "How can you let it happen to you a second time?" My answer was, "I was brainwashed." After reading *Sex, Lies and Two Hindu Gurus*, I am getting some closure and want to start my life again. I just hope now to get my family and extended family out of this organization. It is an uphill battle.'
– Kailasa, ex-devotee, California

'I enjoyed reading the book. It is a great expose of these two "holy crooks". If someone with an open mind at JKP/Radha Madhav Dham reads this book, it should be a wake-up call for him or her to leave that cult. They were running an age-old scam with their preaching based on two principles: making it attractive and scaring people with tall tales of their supreme spiritual powers and credentials. There were a lot of suckers to fall into their "gopi" trap. You did cover very well the way they swindle their disciples of their innocence and their wealth.'
– Rahul, husband of devotee

SEX, LIES AND TWO HINDU GURUS

My Journey to Hell and Back

KAREN JONSON

HarperCollins *Publishers* India

First published in the United States in 2012 by
Rishika Books

First published in India in 2014 by
HarperCollins *Publishers* India

Building 10, Tower A, 4th Floor, DLF Cyber II,
Gurugram Haryana - 122002, India
www.harpercollins.co.in

P-ISBN: 978-93-5136-291-3
E-ISBN: 978-93-5136-292-0

2 4 6 8 10 9 7 5 3 1

Typeset in 11/14 Minion Pro by
R. Ajith Kumar

Printed and bound at
MicroPrints India, New Delhi

This book is dedicated to all of the people, anonymous and otherwise, who were willing to stand up and expose the nearly lost secrets of this organization. Without so many voices telling their stories, I would not have learned the truth and been able to tell mine. Thank you to each and every one of you – you know who you are.

Contents

Part 2: In the Ashram – The Razor's Edge

Part 3: In the Dark – Curiouser and Curiouser

Part 5: In the World – Divine Intervention

Part 6: In the Trial – Truth and Consequences

PROLOGUE

The Case of the Disappearing Swami

Whereabouts Unknown

MONDAY, 7 MARCH 2011, Hays County courtroom.

At 9:10 a.m., I noticed that Swami Prakashanand Saraswati (aka Prakash), my former guru, was not in the courtroom for the sentencing phase of his criminal trial and that there were far fewer of his devotees in the courtroom than usual. Though all the seats were filled, the crowd of his faithful followers was not spilling out into the courthouse hallway as it had during the previous ten days of his trial. Most of the people were chit-chatting as we waited, including the lawyers.

By 9:20 a.m., I began watching the devotees more closely. Some were talking to each other, some were sitting quietly, a few were reading. Overall, their demeanour seemed odd, considering that today the fate of their guru, including the number of years he might spend in a state penitentiary, would be decided.

At 9:35 a.m., the lawyers on the prosecution team started looking around the courtroom and realized that the defendant hadn't shown up yet.

By 9:40 a.m., it was clear that Prakash was not coming that day. Cathy, the lead prosecution attorney, walked over to me and said, 'It looks like we are missing one swami.'

Hays County officials kicked into high gear, following their procedure for finding a missing convicted felon, including calling all the area hospitals and putting out a warrant for his arrest.

While we were waiting for Judge Charles Ramsay, I called Eric Dexheimer, the journalist covering the case from Austin's daily newspaper. He was not in the court that day either, though he'd been at the trial on every other day.

'Hello, this is Eric.'

'Eric, it's Karen. I noticed you aren't here today.'

'No, my editor thought that two weeks was enough for one story.'

'Oh, because something is happening.'

'What?'

'Prakash is not here. He didn't show up this morning and no one seems to know where he is.'

'Wow, you really know how to bury the lede! What's going on there?'

'We're waiting for the judge to arrive and make a decision.'

'Okay. Keep me posted.'

Then I called my main 'inside' source, who told me that there had been a meeting the night before at the house where Prakash had been staying. All the devotees had gone to his dinner at about 5:00 p.m. I passed this information on to the prosecution. This titbit became a critical piece in the puzzle of his disappearance because it provided his last known location.

Many times during the three-year wait for his criminal trial, I had imagined Prakash not showing up. And now, on the tenth day of his trial, when he was a convicted felon, he was on the run from justice. Prakash had nine lawyers and a private investigator on his team. Curiously, none of them or any of his devotees seemed to know anything about his whereabouts. Moreover, no one seemed to care that he was missing. I thought that was very strange – and very telling.

Early on in the search for Prakash, the US marshals had evidence that he had crossed the border into Mexico at Nuevo Laredo after his dinner on Sunday evening and that he was neither alone, nor broke.

Several of his devotees were known to have accompanied him into his Mexican hiding place. And then his trail went cold.

As of the time when the book is being sent to press, the self-proclaimed 'saint' remains a fugitive from justice for the sex crimes for which he was convicted in a Texas courtroom. All that is known now is that he escaped from Mexico to India, probably in disguise and with a fake passport. He is now living in and around Delhi – hiding in plain sight.

Although he was convicted on twenty counts of indecency with children by sexual contact, those crimes were only a fraction of the ones he had committed in his five-decade reign as a saffron-clad 'guru' from India. He had come to the US in the 1970s 'to help deserving souls achieve God realization' through a style of Hinduism he called raganuga bhakti (which he translated as 'divine-love consciousness').

In contrast to his public life as a renounced, God-realized spiritual master, Prakash led a private life that only his inner circle of followers knew about. In that secret world, he enjoyed several perks, including unlimited access to some of his female followers, occasional intimate encounters with underage girls and massive amounts of tax-free money through an international moneymaking operation involving a network of devotees who were sworn to secrecy. It was as though he existed in two parallel worlds – in public he appeared as a God-loving, soul-saving saint; in private he was a key player in an international spiritual con game.

He wore the orange colours of a Hindu sanyasi and painted a tilak down the middle of his forehead. In true sanyasi fashion, Prakash claimed to carry no money. During his early days in the US, before he had a place of his own, he stayed in Hindu temples and people's homes for free, from New York City to Los Angeles, as he sought followers. He hit the jackpot in a small town in the middle of nowhere called

Fairfield, in Iowa, where he founded and converted many members of Transcendental Meditation™, the organization found by Maharishi Mahesh Yogi who rose to fame in the 1970s after the Beatles met him.

Prakash travelled in and out of Fairfield for a few years until he accumulated a core base of followers. Many of them formed the nucleus of his tribe of devotees for the next three decades. These people and others, whom he gathered from around the country, committed their lives to serving him and his mission. His dream was to build a Hindu temple of his own in the United States and he took a major step towards achieving that goal in 1990 with the purchase of 200 acres in the far south-west city limits of Austin, Texas.

Ranch Road 1826 snakes over and around the foothills of the Texas Hill country for fourteen miles, starting in the Austin suburb of Oak Hill to the east and ending in tiny Driftwood to the west. About halfway along the curvy, two-lane road, just after it passes into Hays County, a stone-and-wrought-iron gate marks the main entrance into what was called the Barsana Dham Ashram for twenty-one years (the name was changed to Radha Madhav Dham after Prakash's conviction and disappearance).

All you can see from the road are trees. But once you drive through the main gates and down into the ashram, a 90-foot-high pink-and-grey temple steeple rises up through the surrounding oaks and cedars like an oversized fire hydrant. This is the centrepiece of the two-storey, 40,000-square-foot temple that Prakash built to glorify his guru.

Prakash ruled his US kingdom from 1990 until 2011 with the autocratic zeal of a dictator, operating under the umbrella of an even more corrupt guru in India – Kripalu Maharaj (aka Ram Tripathi) – just seven years his senior. Kripalu, who had thousands of followers compared to Prakash's hundreds, committed many indecent acts similar to those committed by his protégé for at least sixty years in India, but on an even grander scale. In fact, the extent of this man's sex and money-collection activities, conducted under the guise of a saint, was so voluminous and horrendous that it remains unimaginable to normal human beings – a fact that serves him well in keeping his non-spiritual activities a secret.

For more than six decades, neither man had ever been held accountable for his reprehensible actions. Thanks to a wide net of believers with blind faith, significant stores of cash and mafia-worthy intimidation tactics, they had been able to keep secret the inner workings of their international spiritual scam.

Until now.

PART ONE

In the Beginning

For the Love of God

'Memory is the scribe of the soul.'
– Aristotle, Greek philosopher and scientist

'How the Soule dischargeth her Passions upon false objects, when the true faile it.'
– Lord Michel Eyquem de Montaigne,
Essays, The First Book

Ask and You Will Be Given

Seek and You Shall Find

BY EARLY 1991, my eleven-year spiritual journey was going nowhere.

I was thirty-three years old, not happy with my life, and desperately seeking God. My freelance writing career had stalled after a near-nervous breakdown when a series of family tragedies caught up with me. My boyfriend, Roy, was nice but not fulfilling. I loved him, but I was not in love with him. We were living in a dreary apartment in a run-down neighbourhood and he seemed to have little ambition to strive for a better life for himself or me, despite having recently asked me to marry him.

One Sunday, after I had returned home from yet another disappointing spiritual programme, Roy and I went to a local Wallingford cafe for breakfast. As I ate scrambled eggs, bacon and a large cinnamon roll, I discussed my despair over not having found a spiritual path to call my own.

'I don't think I'm ever going to find what I'm looking for,' I said.

'Well, maybe it doesn't exist.'

Since Roy was not spiritual, he could not comfort me the way I would have liked to be comforted.

I had moved from Atlanta to Seattle in 1989 and, after the limited options in the south-eastern Bible belt, found the West Coast to be a spiritual smorgasbord of unlimited opportunities. I feasted like a woman starved, attending talks on everything from shamanism to goddess worship at a wide range of organizations, from a small Buddhist temple to New Age bookshops. I read voraciously, including books like *The Autobiography of a Yogi*. But every workshop I attended, lecture I heard or book I read held my interest only momentarily. Nothing resonated completely with my spiritual desires.

In July, Roy went on a weekend hiking trip with his friends to the Cascade mountains. On Saturday morning, lying alone in our apartment reading the newspaper, I read an article about a Hindu preacher who was in town to give a three-night lecture at the University of Washington. That night was the final talk in the series. With nothing else to do, I decided to go.

I knew almost nothing about Hinduism and had no idea what to expect. As I sat in the small auditorium on the college campus, a woman took the stage to introduce the speaker who, she said, was a guru. He walked onstage dressed from head to toe in saffron. In his talk, he gave many reasons why God exists, reciting verse after verse from Hindu scriptures as proof.

Enchanted by the profound discussion, I left the lecture feeling buoyant and longing to hear more about this religion that I had never studied.

A couple of months later, I opened the local New Age newspaper to find the beatific photograph of another Indian man dressed in saffron. His head was slightly cocked to one side, his white, wavy hair falling on his shoulders. His white beard was short and shaped smoothly around his face, and his plump lips were curled up in a charming smile. His dark eyes looked wise. The accompanying article talked about the spiritual message he preached around the world and mentioned a series of lectures being given in the Seattle area in the following two weeks.

Excited by the chance to hear another Hindu guru speak, I called the contact number. The woman on the other end told me: 'The guru is not coming to Seattle. One of his preachers is.' I was disappointed.

'Okay, never mind,' I said. I wanted to hear the man himself, not his preacher.

'But you must come,' the woman implored. 'Priya Dasi (later renamed Prabhakari) has been taught by the guru himself. She's a gifted speaker. I'm sure you'll enjoy her lectures.'

Still unsure, I nonetheless wrote down the dates and times of the lectures, scribbling on the margins of the newspaper as I balanced the receiver to my ear. As I wrote, I noticed a small advertisement about the lectures under the article. It included a photo of a Western woman who looked to be in her early twenties, with long, wavy, blondish hair.

Nothing in the woman inspired in me the desire to hear her speak.

Desperately Seeking God

Fateful Attraction

I DECIDED AT the last minute to attend the lecture while eating dinner with Roy at a Mexican restaurant – it sounded better than sitting around. I dropped Roy off at our home in Fremont and drove to the nearby New Age bookshop.

The bookshop was the smallest I'd ever seen. The back right-hand corner had been walled off to make a tiny, windowless meeting room. There were a couple of people and twenty or so folding chairs positioned in two semicircles, pointing towards a slightly raised platform supporting a large, fabric-covered ottoman-type bench. Two middle-aged Western women dressed in prim mid-calf skirts and blazers were walking back and forth between the shop and the meeting room.

As I waited for the speaker, more people entered the room and sat down. Several minutes passed. Then I overheard one of the organizers ask the other: 'Where is she?'

The second woman rolled her eyes and said in a low tone, 'She's in the car, praying.'

They exchanged frustrated glances.

About five minutes later, one of the women stepped up and welcomed us to the meeting: 'We are pleased to present a preacher from a religious organization called the International Society for Divine Love (ISDL, later renamed Jagadguru Kripalu Parishat) here tonight to talk about the path of divine-love–consciousness. Priya Dasi is one of the few Western women to have taken the order of sanyasi, which means a person who has renounced worldly attachments and dedicated her or his life to God. You can think of her as a Hindu nun. The programme will include a few minutes of chanting the divine names of God in Sanskrit, a short lecture, then a few more minutes of chanting.'

The woman took a seat and we sat in complete silence for a minute.

Suddenly, a tall, twenty-something woman dressed in a bright orange sari and shawl wrapped tightly around her shoulders entered the room with quick, graceful strides. Her long, wavy, dishwater-blond hair fell around her shoulders and down her back. I noticed a red mark in the shape of an inverted exclamation point in the middle of her forehead, just like the one I had seen in the photo of the guru. She paused before the platform for a second to slip off her orange Birkenstock sandals.

She sat on the ottoman, pulled her legs up into a relaxed yoga lotus pose, clipped a small microphone to the edge of her shawl and began to speak. 'I'll start with a prayer, then we'll sing a simple chant for a few minutes. You can either repeat the line after me or listen silently. Then I'll give a short talk about God realization and end with a few more minutes of chanting.'

She instructed us to close our eyes, and began reciting a prayer in a language I'd never heard. The acoustic two-minute prayer was enchanting, with several dramatic flourishes. Then she began to chant in Hindi, singing one line and waiting for the audience to repeat it. Only the two female event organizers and a man in the audience seemed to be familiar with the ritual and sang along with every verse. I just listened, since I couldn't understand the foreign words.

After a few minutes, I found the chanting tedious. Restless, I opened my eyes and tried to gauge the possibility of a quiet exit. But there was no graceful way out without disturbing the proceedings, so I sat with growing impatience, waiting for the chanting to end.

After a few minutes, Prabhakari started to speak and I perked up. Her spiritual message immediately captured my attention. It was simple, but profound.

'There are only three places a human soul can hope to go: to hell, back to this world in a reincarnated physical form, or to ascend to the divine world and live in bliss with God forever. Hell is not even worth talking about, and this world is the realm of pain and suffering. This leaves the divine world as the only worthwhile goal for a soul.'

She added that every soul longs for complete and permanent happiness, which is only available with God. She explained that to gain entrance into God's divine world was easy and required only three things: 'a human body, desire and a qualified teacher'. I already had the body and the desire, but I had never heard until that moment that I also needed a teacher.

The spiritual philosophy she described seemed magical and resonated with my spiritual desires more fully than anything else I'd heard. Like precision missiles entering the gaping wounds of my heart, her words and simple speech brought hope to my troubled mind. For years I had felt a pressing need to find God. And now, with renewed hope, I believed that this woman was opening a door to a path that would finally lead me there.

Halfway through her speech, I had a profound experience. I felt that the information she was delivering was the 'inner circle' spiritual teaching that, for years, I had hoped to find on my spiritual journey. I had once read in an esoteric book that Jesus had delivered a secret inner-circle message to his disciples who were qualified to hear it. At that time, I hoped to one day receive my own secret divine lessons that would accelerate my spiritual advancement.

Now, sitting in this tiny bookshop, listening to this young sanyasin, in the company of a few lucky people, I felt that God had finally sent me my inner-circle message.

Irresistible

Did I Even Have a Prayer?

CAPTIVATED BY HER first lecture, I attended Prabhakari's next lecture a few days later at another bookshop in my neighbourhood.

After that second presentation, when people lined up to ask her questions, I got in line. When it was my turn, I had two questions. I asked about Buddhism as a way to God. 'Buddhists don't believe in God,' she replied dismissively.

I then asked what specifically I could do to speed up my progress towards reaching God. Glancing at the line of people still waiting, she said, 'Why don't you call me to talk further?' I was surprised, but honoured, by her offer.

The next day, I was nervous about speaking one-on-one to this uber-religious person. I was self-conscious about my mundane life. But I phoned her anyway. She invited me to meet her at the organization's Seattle centre in the home of a married couple, both followers of this spiritual path. The wife was the woman who had originally encouraged me to attend the first lecture and one of the female organizers at the lectures. We set a time to meet for the next day in the afternoon.

Sitting in the quiet, orderly kitchen, talking with her, I was enthralled by her spiritual appearance, authoritative demeanour and self-assured answers to my questions. She was tall and extremely thin.

I could see her flat stomach in the inch or so of space between her hip-hugging saffron sari and midriff-baring blouse. Despite her young age (she looked to be about twenty-four), she seemed uncommonly confident with herself and her scriptural knowledge.

For several minutes, we talked casually about our lives and spiritual longings. Then we moved into the questions

'Why are there so many gods in Hinduism?' I asked.

'Why not?' she quickly retorted.

I was surprised and impressed by the simplicity of her answer. Why not indeed? After all, it is God. This was an 'aha' moment for me in my spiritual journey.

I also asked her about Jesus: 'Was he a true spiritual guide?'

Without any hesitation, she responded, 'He was a good teacher, but *you need a living saint to find God*.' Her emphasis was so specific that I can still hear her utter the words.

In eleven years of intense spiritual searching, I had never heard or read that I needed a spiritual teacher to find God, let alone a 'living saint'. I'd already tried and rejected Western organized religion and had concluded that connecting to the divine must be a solo journey. I believed that if I tried hard enough, God would eventually impart to me directly the critical missing links in my spiritual evolution. I believed that once I had the mysterious missing information, spiritual awareness would wash over me in an instant.

Yet, for some reason still not entirely clear to me, I believed this young, thin, Western woman dressed in saffron. Perhaps I was desperate to settle down into a spiritual path that I could call my own, after having dabbled in so many that just did not fit. Or perhaps I was intrigued by the unique persona of this woman who oozed spiritual confidence. Prabhakari had the kind of attitude you encounter with the most popular person in high school. It's that intangible 'I-don't-care-if-you-like-me-or-not-because-I'm-the-centre-of-the-universe-and-I-have-all-the-answers' attitude.

I could not resist the allure of a spiritual path that had created such a confident young spokesperson.

Hear No Evil

The Guru's Gospel

FROM THE FIRST videotaped lecture I ever heard by Swami Prakashanand Saraswati (called 'Swamiji', meaning, respected spiritual teacher), I was riveted.

I couldn't wait to get to the twice-weekly prayer meetings at the Seattle centre to hear Swamiji give his views on God, souls and divine love. His lectures were much more detailed than the earlier two given by his disciple, Prabhakari.

Every Wednesday and Sunday night, I joined six to twelve others to stare up at a tiny TV screen with dogged devotion, completely taken by the words of the man of about sixty years sitting cross-legged on a raised platform.

He radiated an uncommon self-assuredness and superiority. His deep, authoritative voice, with only a modest Indian accent and near-perfect diction, was reassuring. His immense confidence as he spoke was calming. Listening to him, I felt safe and secure, like a child hearing her father deliver sage wisdom. Swamiji seemed as dedicated to God and to spiritual knowledge as his saffron clothing and the tilak mark on his forehead indicated. (I would learn much later that orange is a common colour worn by spiritual people in India and that the shape of the tilak signifies a particular Hindu sect.)

The programme periodically cut away from Swamiji to shots of his audience, a group of serious, mostly Western people, sitting cross-legged on the floor facing him in perfect rows. They would occasionally smile or laugh at something he said, but otherwise were quietly, but intently, focused on him.

At every prayer meeting (called satsang), I basked in his spiritual discourse like a leaf steeping in sunshine. His teachings seemed to crystallize many of the ideas I already believed to be true and brought additional insight to many of my nagging spiritual questions, filling in the blank spots in my understanding of God.

His basic philosophy was that we are here on earth to learn about God's love, because that's what all souls long for. We do not actually long for material love, which makes us both happy and unhappy, but for love that is everlasting. And that can only come from God. Otherwise we are never truly content in the world.

In every thirty-minute speech, Swamiji made profound statements that resonated deep inside my mind, such as: 'God is just waiting to grace his selfless devotees' and 'God's grace is easily attainable through love and faithful surrender to a God-realized saint.'

As much as I was obsessed with Swamiji's speeches, the ninety-minute prayer meetings were far from perfect experiences. Much to my distress, I had little affinity to the chanting sessions that bookended the videotaped lectures. In each chanting, either live or on video, a lead singer played the harmonium and sang a spiritual chant while a drummer marked the beat.

The lead singer would sing one line of the chant, which would then be repeated back by the audience, such as 'Jai Shree Krishna', 'Jai Shree Radhey' and 'Jai Shree Vrindavan'. The first line was often repeated several times before the hymn moved on. All the chants were in Hindi, and we used chanting sheets or booklets to read the translations as we sang.

The chants typically started out slowly, picking up steam about two-thirds of the way through. Then, as the chanter and drummer became more animated, the devotees would begin to clap and sing more loudly. After fifteen minutes, everyone would calm down and end with several slow stanzas.

I often thought I would go mad waiting for the repetitive chanting to end.

To make things worse, only a few of the singers had decent voices, and the guru was not one of them. In contrast to his pleasant speaking voice, Swamiji's singing was nearly intolerable. Because Swamiji stressed that chanting God's name was one of the most essential components of 'purifying your heart for God realization', I considered my lack of affinity a serious defect. Other devotees seemed to love the chanting, many swooning with eyes closed, others softly crying.

I simply assumed that I was at a lower devotional level than the others and hoped that my aversion to chanting was temporary. I wanted to be as enraptured as most of the other devotees appeared to be.

In the meantime, I decided to just grit my teeth and tolerate it.

Fork in the Road

A Spiritual Seduction

I CAN'T REMEMBER a time in my life when I was not longing for God.

Even as young as five, I realized that life was difficult and potentially sorrow inducing. But I always counted on there being a final destination, some place free from pain, where each day was as idyllic as the day I rode in a convertible with my best friend and her family to pick strawberries at a farm in the warm Vermont sunshine.

My childhood was rough – a dysfunctional family, family illnesses and money problems. By the time I was a teenager, I was witness to the cruelty of the world in multiple ways. My family seemed to suffer one financial hardship after the other – shortage of food and clothing, mother worrying about paying the monthly bills, and parents fighting over endless money issues.

Being a highly sensitive child didn't help. For example, one of my aunts was severely deformed by rheumatoid arthritis. This made an enormous impression on my young mind. She was one of the nicest people on earth and I wondered why she had to suffer when so many horrible people were not in chronic pain.

I would often sit and stare at a picture of Jesus that my grandmother had given us. My parents were not religious at all, but no matter where we lived during our many moves around the country, that picture hung on our living room wall. Affixed to an oval piece of wood with tree bark along the edges, the image had Jesus sitting on a large boulder at twilight with a small village lit up in the background. Despite being alone, he seemed content. My young mind concluded that his apparent solitary contentment must be because he possessed the love of God. I longed to be as at peace as Jesus appeared to be in that image.

During my teen years, I worried about typical religious issues, like 'why are we here?' The traditional Christian notion of spending our brief earthly lives earning either an eternity in heaven or hell never sounded reasonable to me. Life was too random, with some people born into poverty and pain, and others into wealth and luxury.

There had to be another answer.

At twenty-five, after attending a two-year Bible study course, I finally rejected Christianity outright. I came away from the course with a deep respect for Jesus as a spiritual teacher, but came to the conclusion that, the way it was practised, Christianity was greatly flawed. The final blow for me was the expulsion of a truly Christian minister from a Presbyterian church I had been attending while living in Atlanta. He was forced out because, according to his conservative parishioners, his beliefs were too avant-garde and not in keeping with their comfortable status quo.

I walked away disgusted with the entire belief system.

During my first job out of college, I was given a book called *There is a River: The Life of Edgar Cayce*, about the life and revelations of a twentieth-century mystic reputed to have channelled knowledge from multiple sources, including many of the world's religions.

'Here. Read this book. It might answer some of your questions,' said a co-worker after I had quizzed her extensively the previous day about her non-traditional spiritual beliefs. She was the first person I'd ever met who did not think Christianity was the only option.

I was mesmerized by the life story of this man and by the spiritual knowledge he revealed in his trance-like states. Cayce's explanation of reincarnation changed the course of my spiritual journey. He described how we are repeatedly reborn in this world based on our karmas from past lives, and how the cycle continues until we advance spiritually and leave the cycle of rebirth forever when we finally reach God.

What a revelation!

At last, I had found a logical explanation for why we are born into our particular circumstances. I could finally see a system of justice in the world. We aren't just born once and subsequently thrust into heaven or hell for all eternity. We are born uncountable times and each life is dictated by our past actions. As we sow, so shall we reap. During the ongoing cycle of birth, life and death, we each have endless opportunities to grow spiritually. And by evolving high enough, we would eventually gain entrance into the divine world for eternity.

My grandmother's sister once called me an 'old soul'. This was an unusual comment from a strict Christian, but I had always felt the heaviness of having lived many lives. It was not a Shirley MacLaine kind of thing – I didn't claim to have been a princess or a warrior or Buddha in my past lives. It was more like a *Groundhog's Day* type repetitiveness: I felt a weariness in my soul, as though I had made the same mistakes over and over and never learnt my lessons. I felt that spiritually, for innumerable lifetimes, I had been endlessly taking one step forward and two steps backward.

Now I was exhausted from my endless journey in this world. I wanted the cycle of life and death to be over, preferably with my soul residing permanently in the divine world, never to darken the doorstep of the material world again. I was desperate to find the path that would accelerate my transcendence into the divine realm.

Could a Hindu guru hold the key?

Intense Longing

A Trip to Texas

MY LONGING TO meet Swamiji came on suddenly and powerfully three months after I heard Prabhakari speak.

I had been attending satsang regularly for only a few weeks in late 1991 when the centre manager announced that the organization's annual Fall Intensive programme would be held in early October at its new US ashram – called Barsana Dham – in Austin, Texas. The event was for 'life members' only, but new people could attend the three final days of the two-week event. I stopped listening after the word 'intensive'. I was attracted to the path, but, at that moment, didn't feel ready for a gathering with such a severe-sounding title.

The couple who ran the Seattle centre, Carla and Michael, went to the ashram for the entire programme. Later, Michael told me how rewarding it was to spend time there and 'do service for the guru'. I had no idea what he was talking about.

In their absence, local devotees stood in for them at the satsang meetings. When I arrived at the centre in the second week, I was greeted by a young Western woman named Christi. Dressed in a pretty pastel sari, she said that she had just returned from a week at the Intensive.

Up to that point, I had not questioned any of the devotees about the guru. But now I was growing increasingly curious and asked her a few questions.

'What is he like in person?'

She lit up, smiled broadly and gushed: 'He's wonderful!'

'Is he tall or short?'

'He's on the short side, but seems larger than life when you are with him.'

'Is he funny or serious?'

'He can be both. Sometimes he's funny, and quiet and reserved at other times.'

I had never heard anyone describe another person with such love and tenderness. Noting her happiness as she talked about her guru made me a little jealous. It also awakened in me the desire to meet him personally.

One night after satsang, while carpooling home with Richard, one of the other devotees, I decided to find out if he was as smitten with the guru as Christi was. I asked him question after question until, finally, he said, 'You understand that he's a God-realized saint, don't you? He has the power to grace souls and make them divine.'

His words startled me. I had not heard the word 'saint' uttered since the day Prabhakari told me that everyone needs a living saint to find God.

I considered the enormity of this reality on the drive home across Lake Washington. What Richard was telling me, basically, was that this man was equivalent to God – and that we had a rare opportunity to know him in human form. I was entranced.

I arrived home eager to share my new-found understanding with Roy. I told him with complete conviction: 'You've got to get on board with this swami before it's too late and you're trapped here in this world forever.'

His eyes narrowed to slivers as he grimaced and said, 'I was worried this would happen.'

I recoiled at his scepticism and realized then and there that he was a lost cause. He would never join me on my spiritual journey, no matter how profound. I realized that I had to distance myself from him. He had been my best friend and the only person who truly cared about me. But I did not want to be bogged down by somebody who did not support me in my quest for spiritual fulfilment. I had to embrace this path to God fully.

I learnt that the guru was staying at his new ashram in Austin until late December, after which he would return to India for several months. Deciding that I had to meet him before he left the US, I booked a trip to Austin for five days in early December 1991.

I suffered from occasional bouts of agoraphobia and the thought of flying so far from home terrified me. But the thought of missing my chance of meeting the guru scared me even more. I conquered my fears with the hope that this could be a soul-changing trip if Swamiji really was a saint.

To divert my mind and tamp down my panic on the flight from Seattle to Austin, I listened to one tape over and over. It was the soundtrack to *Godspell.* One song in particular calmed me: '*By My Side*'. The lyrics spoke to my belief that I was going to meet a living saint who could heal my wounded life and direct me on the surest path to God. I cried softly every time the singer sang about asking Jesus where he was going and begging him to 'please take me with you'.

As far as I was concerned, this was the only request I had of the saint I was about to meet: *Take me with you to the divine world.*

The Guru's Darshan

Meeting Swamiji

ALTHOUGH I DESIRED to know him, I was petrified at the thought of actually meeting Swamiji.

I could not even imagine the moment I would see him for the first time. What would happen? Would I feel a rush of bliss? Would I faint? I had no idea what to expect.

I arrived in Austin after a long flight and hired a cab to take me to the Barsana Dham Ashram, located about twenty-three miles from the city's former airport. We reached the ashram's front gates at about dinner time. A semi-paved road wound through the property, passing fields and oak trees and a few run-down houses, finally ending at a two-storey white limestone building.

A female devotee in a long skirt, cotton blouse and sweater greeted me at the door. She led me to a large room with several bunk beds at the end of the building. This was where I would be sleeping. After I dropped off my suitcases, she escorted me through a hallway at the centre of the building into a cavernous dining hall. Following her lead, I picked up a metal plate and bowl and helped myself to dal, rice and carrots, which were served from large pots along a serving line between the dining room and the kitchen.

The woman sat down with me at one of several long, rectangular folding tables that filled the room. I chatted nervously with her, both excited and scared to be in such an unusual place. She explained the ashram's daily schedule.

'Morning satsang is at 7:30 a.m., breakfast is at 8:30, Swamiji's breakfast is at 9:00 a.m. …' She rattled off the day's schedule. But I was confused by the exacting routine.

As I was finishing my meal, she looked out of a window and smiled. I followed her gaze and, there, just on the other side of a pane of glass, was a short man with a pot belly in flowing bright saffron clothing, flanked by two Western women wearing orange saris and sweaters.

'There's Swamiji,' she said as he entered the dining hall through a side door.

'What do I do?' I whispered self-consciously.

'Just smile,' she said reassuringly.

All the diners stopped what they were doing to watch Swamiji in silence as he bustled through the room with his preachers following close behind. He walked down the hallway and disappeared up a flight of stairs. I later learnt that he spent the majority of his time in his bedroom on the second floor.

I experienced no shock wave of rapture or heated rush of bliss, but just curiosity. I was disappointed, but assumed my lack of devotional thrill to be due to something missing inside *me*. I assumed that I was not elevated enough to appreciate his immense spirituality.

The next time I saw Swamiji was at the evening satsang programme, held in a long, narrow room located on the second floor of the building. After the first chant and a videotaped speech, we started the evening's second chant. About ten minutes into the music, Swamiji entered the room from a side door. He walked straight to the front of the room and climbed up onto a single bed positioned next to an ornately decorated altar. The same two women in saffron whom I'd seen him with earlier followed him through the door. One of them carried a garland of fresh flowers, which she placed around his neck once he sat down. Both women sat down on a small carpet in the front row, where other preachers were already seated.

As Swamiji took his seat, everyone in the room bowed from their sitting positions, most touching their foreheads to the floor. Called pranam, bowing is a form of showing respect to an individual, especially a spiritual leader, and the devotees offered their pranam every time he entered or exited a room.

Swamiji sat quietly on his elevated platform, leaning back on several pillows with his arms resting on two identical tube-shaped pillows. We watched him intently as he sat in silence. (Viewing the guru is called 'having his darshan'. Darshan literally means an auspicious viewing of a guru or deity, who blesses those viewing him or her.)

After a few minutes, Swamiji made a gesture and everyone rose in unison for the arti which was performed at the altar. Then the arti tray was offered to everyone present for the people to wave their hands over the flame and touch their foreheads to receive a blessing. Alongside, small plates of food, such as nuts and fruit, were offered at the altar and then distributed to everyone as prasad.

After the arti, we sat on the floor, staring up at the guru. After about five minutes, Swamiji rose from his couch and walked out of the room.

As he departed, I offered my pranam to him along with everyone else.

It's the Guru's World

Learning the Ropes

DURING MY FIVE days in the ashram, there were many hours of boredom.

Apart from morning and evening satsang and the three daily meals served in the community dining hall, there were few activities to keep ashram guests occupied. I had heard that devotees often did physical seva while at the ashram, such as gardening, cleaning or other tasks. But since it was nearly winter and raining while I was there, not much was going on. The only seva to be done was in the kitchen. So, in the afternoons, I would chop vegetables to help prepare the simple vegetarian meals served to everyone at dinner.

Most of the devotees who lived in the ashram at that time had their own businesses or were employed in a business operated on the ashram property, owned by a devotee from California. A few people had jobs in town and a few were 'on staff', including two accountants and a kitchen manager. So I hardly saw anyone during normal working hours.

To pass the time, I took long walks around the large, undeveloped property. It was mostly flat, but featured one prominent hill, which had formerly been called Friday Mountain but was renamed Barsana Hill by Swamiji. A dirt path curved up the hill to the top, which offered a view of the 200-acre ashram property and beyond. A small creek ran through the property, more or less bisecting it. It had been called Onion Creek, but Swamiji had renamed it Kalindi River. These names, as well as the name of the ashram itself, were from places in India that he said were exceptionally holy.

At that time, the ashram was just a muddy enclave with a few dilapidated buildings housing approximately thirty people, including several children. The two-storey limestone building and the small houses in which the devotees lived were clustered together in the front section of the property. No one seemed to mind the pioneer-like hardships, because they were all focused on one thing – the guru. They talked about him all the time, quoting his teachings and displaying his photographs in their homes. They stared at him adoringly whenever he was present, and continually asked him personal questions about their devotions, lives and work.

We saw Swamiji several times a day. At the end of the morning and evening satsang meetings, he would either sit quietly on his raised platform as we sat on the floor gazing up at him, or he would chat casually with various devotees.

Most of his devotees also sat with him during his morning and evening meals each day at 9:00 a.m. and 5:00 p.m. Each 'viewing time' typically lasted fifteen to thirty minutes.

Swamiji's actions dictated the mood at these times. Few addressed him directly without being spoken to first. When the guru did speak, one found him to be a gifted storyteller and mimic. However, he could be quite gruff when displeased, even with something quite minor. I witnessed his temper for the first time one morning when a devotee was removing his folding tray table after his breakfast. When she accidentally tilted the table, tipping stray food particles onto his bed, he scowled at her clumsiness and abruptly pushed the table upright. Her face turned red as she put the table away, apologizing softly and dropping her head in shame.

During these tense incidents, everyone would hang their heads and wait for the moment to pass.

In addition to the main times for his darshan, there were also impromptu times to glimpse the guru if you were lucky enough to be around as he went about his daily routine. Swamiji's habitual activities included several daily golf-cart rides around his property. He always had at least one saffron-sari–clad woman with him. His main companion was Vishwambhari Devi (originally named Ranjana), a short Indian woman who was about my age. Her duties included cooking his meals, washing his clothes and being on call to attend to any other physical needs he might have. In those days, Vishwambhari Devi (formerly named Ranjana, now called Vishi for short) travelled with him on his many trips between the US and India.

During my visit to the ashram, all four female preachers were also in residence. More than once did I see Swamiji driving around his golf cart with all the preachers as well as Vishwambhari Devi squeezed onto the front and back seats. Often he would accelerate suddenly, causing the cart to rocket forward and the women to scream in giddy delight. Any devotees in the vicinity would gaze after them. Watching them, I felt an odd mixture of happiness at witnessing the scene and jealousy at not being one of the lucky few to join him on his thrill rides.

I received his direct attention twice during my visit and, in those moments, I understood why people were addicted to him. Although I didn't feel any thrill of divine love, I did feel bathed in the warm glow of his charismatic personality. The first occasion was during my first morning in satsang. From his cushioned platform, he suddenly started asking me questions.

'What's your name?'

'Karen,' I replied nervously. I could feel that every eye in the room was on me.

'Where are you from?'

'Seattle.' I began to perspire from nerves despite the chill in the room.

'Oh, rain country,' he responded and chuckled.

Everyone giggled.

'What do you do?'

'I'm a writer.'

'What do you write?'

'Mostly articles and marketing material.'

'Oh.' He nodded.

We all stared at him intently, awaiting his next utterance. But he sat quietly for a few more minutes, our exchange clearly over. I left the prayer hall feeling elated to have been singled out and validated as a new devotee.

Later that day, I was once again the object of his attention. This time, I choked under the pressure. When he started his morning meal, I was not there yet. He told one of the female devotees to 'go get the new girl'. She bolted into the dorm room and told me in a rush that Swamiji wanted me at his meal.

I quickly followed her to his room, where everyone was sitting on the floor around his bed. He was sitting cross-legged, learning forward over a folding tray that held several small plates of food. As he ate, he was chattering about something and the devotees were laughing. He looked up at me as I bowed to him. He picked up a piece of bread from his plate and held it towards me. I looked at him, unsure what to do. Another devotee quietly indicated for me to take it from him. I leaned forward and took the piece of bread from his hand. I felt many eyes on me and self-consciously started nibbling on the bread. As a natural wallflower, I was embarrassed by the special attention.

Then he picked up a samosa from another plate and tossed it to me. I caught it just in time. With both hands filled with food, I was even more embarrassed. The envy among the devotees was palpable. Out of sheer nervousness, I asked the woman next to me if she wanted a bite of the samosa. She took the dumpling and, to my shock, ate the whole thing.

I later got to know that it was considered an extreme grace for the guru to give a devotee food directly from his plate. Eating the guru's leftover food, also called prasad, is among the more cherished experiences in a devotee's life. Internally, I kicked myself for my lack of knowledge about the significance of the guru's offer and was horrified that I had missed a chance to benefit from his intended grace – and disturbed by the woman taking advantage of my naivety.

Despite my awkward and confusing experiences in the ashram, by the time I packed my bags to leave, I believed that Swamiji was a true saint.

I was confident that I would one day gain entrance into the divine world by faithfully following his directions.

Swami Dearest

Hooked on the Guru

WHEN THE STUDENT is ready, the teacher appears.

I took this expression to heart after meeting Swamiji in his Barsana Dham ashram. I felt more than ready for my spiritual teacher to appear in my life – and I wanted him to know how happy I was that I had finally found him. As soon as I returned home, I wrote him the first of many letters.

Dear Swamiji,

Words cannot fully describe how wonderful it was to meet you. While I was with you, something within me awakened and connected to you as if something deep inside of me had always known that I would find you.

I am happy and relieved that I did find you, because I was drowning in maya. I felt that life must have some purpose, but no matter where I looked, I couldn't find any meaning. I had searched for answers to my questions about God, and found nothing satisfying. But you have lightened the darkness of my life. The pains I suffered before I found you no longer cause me anxiety and unhappiness. And now I see that my whole spiritual search, every step I took, was leading me to you.

While with you, I got a peek into what it means to enter into 'divine-love-consciousness'. It is so wonderful and comforting to think of God first, and not be totally trapped in material consciousness. I am longing to expand my divine-love-consciousness. I long to experience God.

Before finding you, I had thought that I could find God on

my own. I'm glad that I no longer live in ignorance. I'm looking forward to seeing you again. You have stolen my heart.

Your devotee,
Karen

Roy Adored Me

A Shot at Worldly Love

ROY ADORED ME, and that was a feeling worth its weight in gold – at least before I found my spiritual teacher.

I met Roy in a chance encounter two months after moving to Seattle from Atlanta, and he probably saved my life. I had been suffering from extreme bouts of grief and depression as I finally started to feel the effects of having lost my brother and mother in my early twenties. When my mother killed herself just eight months after my brother committed suicide, I had gone into shock and never fully grieved for either of them.

My path to meeting Roy began to be laid eight weeks before I moved to Seattle, during a vacation with a friend from Atlanta. Caroline was originally from Canada, and one of her sisters lived in Vancouver with her husband. In addition to a vacation, this trip gave me the opportunity to check out Seattle as a potential place to live.

After living in Atlanta for nine years, I was tired of the place. Too many bad memories were weighing me down, suffocating me, including a divorce on top of the two deaths in the family. I was more than ready for a change of scenery. One day I was so depressed that I imagined the city was a king-size hypodermic needle sucking the life force out of me. I knew it was time to leave and start over somewhere new and far away.

I had moved to Atlanta from upstate New York in 1980, right out of college. Curiously, the idea of moving to the south-east was first suggested to me by my college journalism advisor.

'It's growing fast and there is a lot of opportunity,' he had said. 'Plus, a new all-news television station called CNN just opened there and they'll need a lot of writers.'

I didn't understand why he was telling me this. Surely he knew that I was not training to be a news writer. I was a features writer, for print features at that. There were plenty of other students majoring in television news at Fredonia State University.

But this sixty-plus curmudgeon, straight out of a 1940s film noir about the newspaper business, could not have been more clairvoyant. One month later I met a man named Tommy from Atlanta, who would become my next boyfriend. He was the drummer in a two-man band that showed up at the Holiday Inn where I worked to play a two-week gig. I'd been working there as a bartender and cocktail waitress to earn money for college. Tommy and his band mate were travelling up and down the east coast, playing at any hotel or dive bar that would have them. We dated the entire two weeks. Then, with few other options, I decided to follow him to Atlanta.

With all my worldly possessions in the back seat and boot, and my cat in a cardboard box on the passenger seat, I drove due south and took up residence with him in a small apartment. But I figured out pretty quickly that Tommy and I were not a love match. Luckily, he was on the road a lot, so I had plenty of time to think about what I was going to do next. I contemplated leaving Atlanta altogether, maybe going to Denver or Phoenix – two popular destinations in the early 1980s.

When I told a friend about my dilemma, she had an easy solution: 'Why leave Atlanta? Just leave Tommy. You and I can get an apartment in a cool neighbourhood.'

I accepted her offer. She and I moved into a hipper neighbourhood just north of Atlanta.

Five months later, I met the man I would marry in a neighbourhood bar. It was the first time I had ever fallen head over heels in love. David was smart and very funny – my favourite combination. He was also creative. He had wanted to study photography, but his father insisted he attend college for engineering. David compromised and studied architecture. But his heart was never in it and he could never seem to gain any traction in his career, a fact that depressed him.

We married in January of 1982, in a small ceremony in some random church, and honeymooned in Charlotte, South Carolina. I was crazy about him, but over our five years of marriage, he never quite settled into the notion of being a husband and I'd had no role model for being a good wife. It was as if we were merely best friends. One day I discovered that he had been frequenting some of the 'lingerie stores' that dotted the shadier parts of town. It broke my heart, but I ended our union a few months later. I didn't want a male room-mate – I wanted a lover and life partner.

I lived in Atlanta for almost two more years, dating a few men. I had a rebound relationship with a recovering alcoholic hired to paint the house David and I had shared before we sold it. I lived in a dysfunctional on-again off-again relationship with Tim over the next year and a half. I felt the only way to get over him once and for all was to leave Atlanta. That's when Caroline and I planned our vacation to Seattle.

I had passed through Seattle the summer before with a friend and knew how beautiful it was, tucked between mountains and the sea. By the end of my first day back, I had decided that it would be my next home. I told Caroline's sister and brother-in-law while we were in Vancouver.

'My brother's room-mate's girlfriend, Elizabeth, lives in Seattle. She's an airline stewardess and just got transferred from Washington DC to live closer to her boyfriend. I'll get her phone number for you. You should call her when you move there.'

'Thanks so much,' I said.

Before Caroline and I boarded the plane back to Atlanta, I had rented an apartment.

Six weeks later, I was in Seattle. Along with being scenically gorgeous compared to Atlanta, the area was also a cultural and spiritual smorgasbord. Plus, the cooler weather was a relief from the unrelenting heat of southern summers.

I revelled in my new home and fresh start. But the euphoria didn't last.

Without the structure of my former life to hold me up, all the trauma and turmoil of the previous nine years caught up with me. I began to crash hard. I felt myself sliding downhill and couldn't stop my descent. The worst times were at night. I would dream about my brother, who had shot himself in the head at twenty-two after living five years with schizophrenia.

The nightmares were mired in grief and guilt. I had never properly grieved for my brother, because nine months after he took his life, my mother had taken hers with an overdose, sending me into deeper shock.

In Seattle, the shock began to wear off and I didn't know what to do about the flood of grief descending on me. I tried to find new freelance clients, but suddenly I found the normal rejection associated with finding freelance clients unbearable. The rain and darkness of my first winter in Seattle did not help my state of mind.

I was in this downward spiral when I remembered Elizabeth's phone number in my wallet. I called her and left a message. To my surprise, she called back a day later. She was bubbly and uber-friendly: 'Hi, it's great to meet you. Do you like Thai food? It's my favourite.'

Elizabeth and I met for dinner at a Thai restaurant on Capitol Hill. She was outgoing and entertaining, full of stories about flying around the country and meeting her Canadian boyfriend in South America.

'I just moved here three months ago and haven't had time to make new friends,' she said. 'One of my old friends from DC lives here, though. We could all go out sometime.'

'Great,' I said.

She called the next day, 'Hey, let's go ice skating.'

That's when I met Roy, a quiet, sweet guy, who began pursuing me feverishly. We began dating, but more as friends than lovers. Shy and nerdy, he didn't seem at all my type, but I continued seeing him platonically. Then one day I realized how much he loved me and realized that I really needed someone to love me. He would do anything for me, I thought. This feels really good.

Over the next two years, we lived together and occasionally talked about marriage. I wasn't crazy about the idea, but I didn't want to hurt his feelings. Our relationship was always unbalanced. I loved him in a best friend sort of way. He loved me romantically and wanted to marry me. However, he was fully aware of my passion for God. He always said, 'I accept that I will always be number two in your life.'

A few months before I attended Prabhakari's lecture, he awkwardly asked me to marry him. It wasn't the least bit romantic. We were just sitting in some average local restaurant. I said 'yes' for all the wrong reasons.

So when push came to shove a few months later regarding my spiritual pursuits, Roy didn't stand a chance.

Guru Preparations

The Teacher Visits

I LEARNT WHAT 'seva to the guru' meant when Swamiji decided to visit Seattle in June 1992 – hours of dedicated service with no complaining.

We got the news in March that Swamiji would be visiting for eight days. This announcement kicked off a whirlwind of activity among our group of devotees. I soon understood how much preparation was required for his visits. For his personal comfort, there was no detail too insignificant for consideration – from the china he ate in to the mattress he slept on. I was surprised at the levels of manpower and expense required to serve a sanyasi, one who had renounced earthly attachments.

Besides buying everything from new sheets to tea towels, we set up a public lecture site, rearranged the prayer hall to accommodate more people, ran ads in the local New Age publications, hung posters all over town, made lists of groceries for his meals and to feed the devotees who would come to see him, landscaped the yard of the home where he would stay, and cleaned every crack and crevice of the house, especially his bedroom and bathroom.

One of my assignments was to clean his bathroom, but nothing was ever good enough for Carla.

'Get those streaks off the shower tiles and mirror,' she said for the third time.

Carla and Karen L., who organized Prabhakari's lectures, also organized the guru's visit. They were a maniacal pair, seemingly trying to outdo each other to win the 'fanatic of the year' title. Only the best was good enough for them. But their lavish spending had made money an issue. They asked us each to give as much as we could of both time and donations. At one point, they decided that Carla's TV would not be good enough for Swamiji. But they could not afford to purchase a new one. So they asked if any of us had a nice TV and VCR we could loan for his visit. I did, and was thrilled at the idea of Swamiji using them. Even though I had been involved for only six months, I too wanted to do whatever I could to make him happy.

During the two months of preparation, I put my personal life on hold. Roy and I had made travel plans for that spring, including finally getting to the Mount Rainier National Park, one of the highest peaks in America with enough snow in April to ride inner tubes and sledges.

But I never made it to Mt Rainier, and many other places, because very soon Swamiji became the primary focus of my existence.

Total Immersion

For the Guru's Pleasure

LIKE ALL DEVOTEES, I longed for more physical proximity to Swamiji.

When he arrived in Seattle in June 1992, I was unable to go to the airport to greet him with the other devotees because my boss had scheduled a meeting for the exact time that his plane landed at Sea-Tac Airport. I considered this schedule conflict an extreme karmic injustice.

I fantasized about having that first glimpse of him as he emerged from the airplane, smiling playfully at everyone who greeted him. Imagining the devotees following him through the airport, I longed to be among them.

My meeting dragged on past normal work hours. It was torture, and took every ounce of my patience to not just stand up and walk out. I suffered silently as the seconds ticked by. Finally, the meeting ended at 5:30 p.m. I ran out of the building and sped to Carla's house.

As I entered, the devotees were getting ready to eat a simple meal of white rice, toor dal and some type of Indian spiced vegetable. Though I had eaten it before, I was not yet used to Indian cuisine and found the meal strange and unappetizing. It didn't help that the devotees who prepared the food were not good cooks. Perhaps they were just more focused on Swamiji than on providing a good meal to the devotees. They had not even made enough rice to go around. But that night my focus was on hearing about Swamiji's arrival, not on filling my belly.

After dinner, I faced the unexpected challenge of dressing in a sari for the first time. I had learned in Barsana Dham that Swamiji liked his female devotees to wear these flowing outfits. Of course I didn't own one, but Carla had recently received a shipment of saris from another devotee. After the other female devotees had picked the ones they wanted, there were just two saris left: a brown-and-tan flowered print for me, and a solid blue cotton one for the other new woman in our group, Gloria.

Putting on a sari for the first time is no easy feat. It requires a precise process of tucking and folding the fabric to wear it so that it falls to your ankle and drapes over your shoulder correctly. An experienced sari wearer can get one on in just a few minutes. But it took me over thirty minutes to wear mine as I folded, wrapped, refolded and rewrapped the fabric numerous times. But once I finally got it on, I felt surprisingly comfortable in my new outfit.

I wore my sari every night. On the fourth night, after satsang was over and all the non-devotee visitors had departed, Swamiji was lounging on the couch, with the rest of us sitting on the floor around him.

Noticing Gloria and me sitting side by side, he said, 'Their saris each match their hair.' I was a blonde and she a brunette.

Delighted, both of us grinned shyly at the attention.

'How many saris do you each have?' he asked.

'We each only have one,' I said quietly.

'One's enough,' he said, and everyone laughed.

After Swamiji departed for his bedroom, two of the other devotees convinced us to play a little playful trick on the guru.

The next night, Gloria and I made sure we got to the prayer room before the satsang began so we could sit together in the first row, closest to Swamiji's couch, with me in her blue sari and she in my brown one. When the guru saw us, he noticed immediately and chuckled softly.

We giggled, enjoying our little secret with Swamiji.

Speak No Evil

Father Knows Best

'DON'T ASK SWAMIJI for advice unless you intend to follow his instructions fully.' This was the firm instruction to any devotee requesting permission to speak personally with Swamiji. Devotees were constantly seeking his advice on everything under the sun – from which job to pursue and what school to make their children attend, to how to surrender to God more completely.

People were so addicted to his advice that whenever they faced a dilemma they encouraged each other to 'ask Swamiji'. But this encouragement came with a cautionary footnote: 'Just be prepared to do exactly as he tells you to do.'

I was not privy to this insider directive when I first asked Swamiji a question about my life. I just formulated my query and hoped for the opportunity to ask him while he was in Seattle. The question regarded a single sentence I'd read in a little booklet created for new members, which included short excerpts from Swamiji's speeches. One of the excerpts stated: 'It's easier to follow this path if you are single.'

This worried me. After all, I was in a relationship with a man who had become my best friend and was going to be my husband. I became concerned that my relationship with Roy might be a hindrance on my path to God realization. I desperately wanted to ask Swamiji about it. I felt sure that he would understand my predicament and reassure me that everything was fine, that I didn't need to be technically single to find God. I assumed that his response, whatever it was, would improve my devotional life. I didn't realize that his answer would completely upend my life as I knew it.

I had planned to explain to Swamiji that my boyfriend was not just my future husband, but also my best friend and, effectively, the only family I had left on earth. I would tell him that my mother and one of my two brothers had died and that I was estranged from my father and second brother. I needed Roy. He was all I had.

My chance to address this issue with Swamiji came when I was invited up to his bedroom while he was in Seattle. The minute I was told that Swamiji wanted to see me in his room, I became nervous. My heart raced as I climbed the stairs and entered his inner sanctum, the largest room in the house. He was half sitting, half lying on the bed, resting against a pile of pillows.

I was surprised that I was not alone with him. In my mind, I had seen myself delivering my little speech to him in private. But he had also invited Gloria to see him at the same time. His assistant and Christi were there as well. All three women were sitting on the floor around him, gazing up at him lovingly. I sat down on the floor near his feet.

As he chatted first with Gloria, I reconsidered what I had planned to say to him. During a lull in the conversation, I made my move.

'Swamiji, can I ask you a question?'

He turned and looked down at me as if he just remembered that I was there. 'Yes,' he said, with a hint of amusement in his tone.

My mind went blank just then. Rendered mute, I looked down and stared at the edge of his bedspread for a few seconds. To my surprise, I blurted out: 'I read that it's easier on this path if you are single.'

Without missing a beat and with the timing of a seasoned entertainer, Swamiji replied: 'You are single.'

His response startled me in its simplicity. I managed a simple reply: 'Yes, but my boyfriend wants to get married.'

Again, without a moment's hesitation, he responded: 'Don't get married. You'll just get divorced again, and what's the use of that?'

His reply was not at all what I was expecting. I was ready for assurances that we all need someone to help us through the difficult ups and downs of life, and that I could be in a worldly relationship and still find God. I thought he would tell me that God understands that a material relationship is only temporary and that what we really want is to be with Him forever. There's no sense in living completely alone in the world until that time comes. Certainly, marry your boyfriend, love him and love God too.

I couldn't have been more wrong. Instead of giving me his blessing to marry Roy, he asked me to make the ultimate sacrifice, telling me that I should abandon my only friend on earth and set off on a journey to seek God completely alone. But none of that mattered now.

I decided in that moment that I would not marry Roy.

Blindsided

The Price of Devotion

MONEY HAD BEEN a huge concern for me since childhood and if the guru had asked me for my life savings right from the start, I would have bolted.

I was a sensitive child and my parents' constant fights about money made an enormous impression on my young mind. I was acutely aware that we typically did not have money for frivolous things or even, quite often, for necessary expenditures. That's why when Valentine's Day rolled around in first grade, I did not ask my mother to buy me valentines to give to the other kids.

Mrs Bledsoe, our teacher, showed us how to make big heart-shaped pockets, which she then hung around the room. Every day, during the week before the holiday, the kids in my class came into the room with handfuls of tiny Valentine's Day cards. They walked around the room placing a card in each heart-shaped pocket. As I watched our little 'mailbags' puff up with valentines, I knew that I would not be able to add my own envelopes to those pockets.

When my mother saw the pile of red and pink notes decorated with hearts I had brought home, she asked me why I hadn't told her that the class was exchanging valentines. In my six-year-old innocence I said simply, 'Because we don't have any money.' She assured me that money could be found for school activities, but I had already learnt a different lesson from her: *Money doesn't grow on trees.*

To compensate for growing up poor, I became frugal once I started earning. I was more of a saver than a spender, and felt safer when I had money in the bank. I worried constantly about money, fearing a grim future as a bag lady living on the streets all alone.

The one thing I would never have done was join an organization that asked for my hard-earned savings. So the fact that this group had not emphasized on donations gave me great relief and reinforced my impression that it had honourable intentions.

My first personal money-related experience with Swamiji was a small matter, but it made me confident that he would never expect me to drain my bank account for him.

While he was in Seattle, we went on several shopping trips. On one such trip, our mission was to find bread-making machines for Barsana Dham and the other centres he visited across the country.

While we were shopping, Swamiji wandered out of the mall hallway and into a bookshop. I followed him while the others headed into Penney's. Suddenly I was alone with him. I followed and watched his every move as he looked at various books. Then he picked up the smallest dictionary I'd ever seen, handed it to me and said, 'I'll take this.'

Because it was one of the cheapest items in the store, it didn't set off any warning bells in my money-cautious mind. But a few days later, Carla told me that Swamiji had asked if I wanted to become a life member.

When she told me that the donation for that privilege was $1,000, my deep-rooted money fears flared up immediately. But when I responded saying that I would think about it, Carla backed off, with no hint of pressure whatsoever. No one else brought up the subject again. A few months later, I happily handed over my $1,000 to become a life member of Swamiji's organization.

See No Evil

The Guru Plays Favourites

AFTER BECOMING PART of Swamiji's group of followers, I realized that they were not like the people I'd met in churches.

Here, there was a constant air of competition among his followers to seem the most holy of the lot. This rivalry was palpable as we prepared for his visit. The 'top-dog' climate went into overdrive once Swamiji arrived. Everything was fair game, from a person's proximity to him in the prayer hall to being chosen to personally serve him in his bedroom.

Every evening, there was a race to secure the most coveted seats right in front of and closest to his couch on the floor of the prayer room. Serving him personally was not as egalitarian. Karen L. dominated on that front for three reasons: she had gained the upper hand due to her senior status among the new devotees; the fact that Carla was busy dealing with everything else; and, probably most importantly, her daughter, Christi, was Swamiji's undisputed favourite.

Christi had recently started studying to become one of his preachers, joining the ranks of the other women who wore saffron and proselytized his message of divine-love-consciousness. Swamiji fawned over her constantly. Whenever he was driven anywhere in Michael's BMW, he always singled her out to ride with him. I longed to hear Swamiji call my name to join him, just once.

He also called Christi into his bedroom on a regular basis, especially in the evenings, after the rest of us left for home. Karen L. would often join them, watching movies, eating snacks and generally having a grand time with Swamiji. One morning I noticed Karen L. and Christi bustling around the kitchen, secure in their roles as teacher's pets. Their smug happiness felt like a swift kick of rejection.

Swamiji's personal assistant, Vishi, also spent a lot of time alone with him. One day as I passed by his open bedroom door, I saw Vishi standing next to his bed. He had one hand on her body in what looked like an intimate touch of some sort. Her back was to me, however, so I could not see clearly what was going on without stopping to stare.

The fleeting image startled me. Later that night when I was alone in bed, I felt a niggling suspicion: 'Is this really the spiritual path I think it is, or something else?' I felt a bit sick. But I tamped down my negative thoughts and reassured myself that whatever I had seen was innocent.

After all, Swamiji was a saint, right?

A Sacrifice

The Turning Point

AFTER EIGHT DAYS of existing in close proximity to the jockeying-for-position devotees, I had had enough and needed a break.

The minute Swamiji left Seattle for his next destination, I wanted to get back to normal life as fast as possible. I asked Carla for my TV and VCR, but she was going in several different directions at once and I had to wait to get her attention. Finally, impatient, I went to the second floor to get them myself. As I struggled to carry the TV down the stairs, Michael came rushing to me.

'Here, let me help you.'

'Okay, thanks,' I said, barely containing my irritation.

'Is everything okay?' he asked, ever the most upbeat member of the group.

'Yes,' I lied. 'I'm just tired and want to get home.' We placed the TV in the back seat of my Honda Civic and I hurried back upstairs for my VCR and practically threw it on my passenger seat as Michael looked on, concerned.

'See you later,' I called out, then closed the car door. I could not back out of his long driveway fast enough. I wanted to go far away from all of those people.

As I drove home across the long, low bridge spanning Washington Lake, I breathed in relief. My muscles, which had tightened into knots over the past week, finally started to relax. I couldn't wait to see Roy.

Life fell back into a familiar, comfortable pre-Swamiji routine. We hadn't spent much time together in a couple of months, so we celebrated by going to the coast for the weekend. On the winding road to the ocean, I felt free. I savoured the feeling of walking along driftwood-dotted beaches, dining on fresh seafood, and lying in each other's arms in our B&B that overlooked the forest.

We were also making plans with Roy's five siblings to celebrate their parents' upcoming fortieth wedding anniversary, which was to be a three-day extravaganza. We decided to spend an additional two days camping with one of Roy's brothers and his wife. Meanwhile, I was still doing my daily devotions at a little makeshift altar tucked in a corner of our bedroom. But I wasn't going to satsang.

About three weeks later, Prabhakari surprised me at work, calling to say that Swamiji was asking for me. 'He wants you to come to the ashram for guru poornima,' she said.

Swamiji was asking for me, I thought joyously. I wasn't even sure what guru poornima was, but if Swamiji was asking for me directly, I wanted to be there.

When she told me the date, my stomach muscles tightened. It was the weekend of the anniversary celebration. My euphoria turned to anxiety as I told her of my plans.

Clearly uncomfortable with my reluctance, Prabhakari played the trump card. 'The more you do what the guru says, the faster you'll reach God.'

With that, I felt the stress drain out of me. My decision was made. Swamiji wanted me – Roy and his feelings came second.

Needless to say, Roy did not take the news well. He yelled and screamed in rage and frustration, 'Now I'm even questioning if we should get married, because Swamiji might call you at the last minute and you'll leave me standing at the altar.'

I had not yet told him that Swamiji had already instructed me not to marry him.

Roy left for Oregon as I returned to Barsana Dham the following day. I was excited to see Swamiji.

One afternoon, a group of women from the ashram walked the dirt path down to the creek that snaked through the property. It formed several swimming holes along its route. While cooling off in the water, Carla said: 'Tell them your story.' The women were delighted and congratulated me on my wise decision to choose Swamiji over Roy.

The tale of my 'surrender' to my guru became something of a badge of honour.

A Leap of Faith

Ashram-Bound

IN AUGUST, I broke the news to Roy that I would not be marrying him.

He was resigned to the fact. We planned an amicable split. In September, I moved into a small one-bedroom apartment next to the Seattle zoo. My only long-range plan at that time was to devote my life to 'God realization'. At the time, it did not occur to me to ask to live in the ashram. I was happy with my solitary existence in Seattle, away from the other devotees.

In fact, every time I visited Barsana Dham, I was happy to leave. I did not feel cut out for living in cramped quarters with so many people. I had always been a loner and cherished my privacy and solitude. Plus, the people at the ashram were different. Even though I was becoming more dedicated to Swamiji, there were still some whose level of devotion made me uncomfortable.

Nonetheless, I woke up one day during a visit to Barsana Dham and suddenly realized that I did not want to leave the ashram. I decided that if I was going to dedicate myself to this spiritual path, I might as well commit fully – like a good Catholic girl who decides to become a nun. I believed that the ashram lifestyle would facilitate my goal of achieving God realization by making me fall in line with everything from the daily schedule of devotion to the minimalist living conditions and even help me deal with the melting pot of personalities.

One afternoon, I scoured the 'help wanted' ads in an Austin newspaper and also thumbed through the Yellow Pages to see how many advertising agencies and public relations firms were in town. Austin wasn't as big as Atlanta or Seattle, but it looked like it was just big enough to support my career as a marketing writer.

On the morning I was scheduled to leave for Seattle, I went to bid goodbye to Swamiji. I blurted out: 'I love Barsana Dham, Swamiji. I never want to leave.'

To my surprise, he encouraged me to stay and look for a job near the ashram. 'Can you change your flight and stay two more days?'

My mind raced. Could I? Should I? 'I'll try, Swamiji.'

I left his room in a state of bewilderment and panic. Was this a gift from God, or a totally crazy lark? I ran down to the kitchen to get my plane ticket out of my luggage. My suitcases were packed and standing like two soldiers in the dining hall outside the women's dormitory. Karen L., who was supposed to fly back to Seattle with me that afternoon, was sitting in the dining hall, having tea with Christi.

They could tell that something big had transpired. I was clearly radiating a 'you'll never guess what just happened to me!' devotee giddiness. Grinning widely, I announced my change of plans: 'I'm not going back to Seattle today. Swamiji told me to stay here and look for a job in Austin.'

Karen L. frowned. She had been a devotee for two years and desperately wanted to move into the ashram. However, she was married to a man who was not a devotee, and so would not be allowed to move into the ashram with him. Christi had recently moved in full-time to further her studies to become a preacher. Most devotees believed that living in Barsana Dham was the greatest opportunity a devotee could receive.

I was able to get a seat on a flight leaving two days later. Once that chore was accomplished, I went to the satsang hall just as the morning prayer service was starting. My mind raced with job-searching plans. I could not calm down enough even to pray.

As always, Swamiji entered the prayer hall a few minutes before satsang ended, two ladies in orange trailing after him. As soon as he entered, all eyes were on him and all ears ready to hear any words of wisdom he might utter.

But today, after crossing his legs on his decorated bed and leaning back on his pillows, he looked right at me and asked: 'Did you change your flight?'

I grew warm at the attention. I could sense the curiosity of the other devotees.

'Yes, Swamiji,' I said, nerves audible in my shaky voice.

'When are you leaving?'

'In two days, on Wednesday.'

'Good. What will you do now?'

'I'll apply for jobs around town today.'

Christi, who had offered earlier to ask Swamiji for permission to take me out job hunting, was sitting next to me. 'Swamiji, can I take Kare ...'

'Take care of her?' Swamiji said, cutting her off.

Laughter bubbled around the prayer hall.

'Yes, you can take care of her.'

Christi cocked her head and smiled coyly at him. 'Can I take Karen around Austin to apply for jobs?'

'Yes,' he said.

At that moment I did, indeed, feel taken care of – by God himself in the form of my spiritual master.

PART TWO

In the Ashram

The Razor's Edge

'Arise, awake, and learn by approaching the exalted ones,
For the path to salvation is as sharp as a razor's edge,
Impassable, and hard to go by, say the wise.'
– *Katha Upanishad*, 1-III-14

'Hope springs eternal in the human breast; Man never is,
But always to be blest: The soul, uneasy and confin'd
From home, rests and expatiates in a life to come.'
– Alexander Pope, *An Essay on Man*, Epistle I

Journey's End

Abandoning the World

ON TUESDAY, 13 April 1993, I moved into the Barsana Dham ashram, south-west of Austin, Texas, with no fanfare.

I drove through the gates with the last of my remaining possessions squeezed into my car. I had shipped eleven boxes from Seattle the week prior, but had given away everything else. At thirty-five, my personal possessions were reduced to just my clothes, business files, computer, sewing machine and photographs.

It had been a challenge to pare my stuff down to these bare essentials. But I had done exactly what my new guru instructed me to do. Some of my 'non-essentials' included a prized collection of art deco antique furniture, which I'd purchased piece by piece over the years.

When I first broached the subject of living in the ashram with Swamiji, I didn't know where I would live in the ashram – and I didn't care. At that point, my desire to find God at the feet of Swamiji was so intense that I believed I would happily live in a tent in the woods if it meant I could spend the rest of my life worshipping Him in close proximity to my guru.

As it turned out, I didn't have to live in a tent. Swamiji assigned me to one of the eight bedrooms in what he called 'The Girls' House'. The Girls' House sat on a small hill facing the new temple construction site. The house had been completed a few months earlier and, when I arrived, only five women lived there: an elderly woman who had donated most of the money for the building's construction, two women my age, and a mother and daughter who shared a 200-square-foot bedroom and bathroom.

During my previous visit, I had been asked to help clean the building to get it ready for the first residents. At that time I had no idea that I would be one of them. As I wiped up drywall dust from the windowsills and vacuumed the floors, I admired the simplicity of the building's design: each bedroom had a compact walk-in closet and shared a bathroom with a neighbouring bedroom.

A shared living room, a small kitchen and a laundry room formed the centre of the house. Both sides of the building housed four bedrooms, effectively creating west and east wings. Each 12×8-foot bedroom had just enough space for a twin bed, desk, nightstand and a bookcase. Not exactly a spacious place to showcase my eclectic collection of antique furniture.

But Swamiji had told me, 'Don't bring your furniture, just your personal items.'

I loved my furniture. But Swamiji taught us that, to find God, we had to loosen our grip on our material possessions and attachments in the world in any and all forms. Giving up my beloved furniture was a small price to pay for reaching the divine world, I thought.

I placed a classified ad in the newspaper. By chance, I received a call from a man who had just opened a new antique store in a hip part of Seattle.

'I'll take it all,' he said upon seeing my cherished collection.

It couldn't have been easier. Surely, I thought, this was too miraculous to be a coincidence.

I believed that my guru had orchestrated a miracle for me.

Living the Dream

Settling into Ashram Life

IT WAS MORE challenging than I expected to live in such close proximity to so many different personalities in the ashram. There were conflicts in every corner – from whether to serve rice or potatoes for dinner to how to dig a hole. Also, the lack of control over most aspects of my life was unsettling. The sun-up to sun-down schedule was exhausting, while the noise from the ashram's nearly non-stop construction projects was irritating.

When I complained to a fellow devotee about the challenges of ashram life, she tried to reassure me by telling me that Swamiji said it takes two years to adjust to ashram living. This news was not encouraging.

In April of 1993 there were already about fifty people living in the ashram: a mix of single men and women, married couples and about a dozen children. Within a few years, the population would reach its height of about seventy adults. While the property was 200 acres, we all resided in small houses or group-living situations within about one square mile.

Our proximity was a snug living situation by US standards. But The Girls' House was probably the most tightly packed 3,000 square feet on the property. It was not fun, sharing a small living space with eight adult women. With all the ensuing cliques and conflicts, it was basically high school all over again.

I am not, by nature, a person who travels in packs. For most of my life, I had two or three carefully chosen friends at a time. In the ashram, I was suddenly living with seven other women whom I had not chosen as friends, let alone housemates.

I did, however, make friends with two female devotees who did not live in The Girls' House. We would take little breaks from ashram life for some shopping, a movie or just a quick lunch somewhere.

I learnt to circumvent many of the struggles of ashram life by focusing on my career. In fact, my work became my refuge. It's where I felt normal, competent and self-sufficient. I had been a freelance writer in magazines, and for marketing and public relations for eleven years prior to moving to the ashram. I planned to resume my career in Austin. But during my first year, I worked mostly for two businesses on the property – by chance, not by design.

I soon realized that I did not want to live with and work with the same people forever. So I ventured off on my own and found some freelance clients in Austin in the health-care and high-tech industries. I eventually rode the wave of the tech boom, finding more work than I could take on.

During all of the years that I worked for Austin companies, I never once revealed my place of residence to anybody I worked for. I decided that it would be easier to keep my work life and religious affiliation separate – especially since I lived in a highly unusual situation.

It was a challenge to fit my work around the ashram's daily religious activities, and to find enough time for exercise, relaxation and sleep. Soon after I moved there, I began to wonder if I'd made the right decision. Then I had two dreams.

In the first one, I dreamt that in a past life, I had been on a spiritual path, but I left it because I fell in love with an extremely handsome man. One night, during a gathering outdoors with a group of people, he grabbed my hand and pulled me away from the group. We looked deeply into each other's eyes. I was mad with desire for him. We started running away. He guided me along a winding trail up a hill through a thickly wooded area. I was wearing a long, flowing dress and my long, blonde hair was swaying in the wind. He had black, wavy hair that fell to his broad shoulders.

We entered a circular clearing under a canopy of trees and stopped. He pulled me into an embrace with his muscled arms, and I began to melt into his broad chest. Just before our lips touched in a kiss, a giant hand as tall as our bodies came out of nowhere. Like a snowplough, it pushed us. Suddenly I was falling off a cliff. My would-be lover and I were instantly separated and I was falling into a black abyss, alone. I knew it was the hand of God.

When I woke up from my lost-lover dream, the emotional loss I felt was as if it had actually happened. But I believed the dream was a warning that I had wasted too many past lives chasing worldly love. By dramatically ending my romance, God was telling me that it was time to give up the pursuit of worldly love. It was time for me to devote my life to God and guru.

In the second dream, I was kneeling on the floor next to Swamiji, gazing up at him with great love and devotion. Suddenly, the rug underneath us lifted off the ground and we were flying off into the sky. Sailing swiftly through the air, it was clear that we were headed straight for the divine world. Ecstatic that I was one of the chosen few leaving this earthly world with Swamiji, I felt completely happy, grateful and already divine.

When I remembered this dream later, I was sure that it was only a matter of time before Swamiji literally took me with him to the divine world from which, I believed, he had directly descended.

Life was far from perfect in the ashram – but I believed that my endurance would pay off in the end.

Inside the Gates

Steering Clear of 'The World'

INSIDE THE GATES of Barsana Dham's 200 acres, we lived in a self-contained world created by our guru.

We had roofs over our heads, three meals a day in the community dining room, a daily devotional programme and the occasional holiday or special programme for entertainment.

We also had an 'us versus the world' attitude. In devotee-speak, 'the world' was physically any place outside of Barsana Dham, its centres around the world, or the guru's ashrams in India. Among devotees, 'the world' was a place to be feared and shunned. Swamiji told us repeatedly: 'Don't waste your life pursuing the material world.'

If we were not with the programme – in other words, living our lives according to the guru's guidelines – we were often accused of 'being in the world'. It was the worst insult a devotee could receive.

Whenever a follower left the organization, those of us still in lockstep with the guru's world view would shake our heads, look at each other knowingly and make comments such as 'He (or she) is back in the world'. You could feel a there-but-for-the-grace-of-the-guru-go-I shudder as we acknowledged that soul's tragic misstep outside of the guru's protection.

Swamiji handpicked every person who lived in the ashram. In addition to The Girls' House, there were several other living situations on the property, including some other group quarters, bedrooms in the main buildings for single people and small houses for families. Some families had built their own homes or remodelled existing structures left over from the property's former existence as a boys' camp.

As per our guru's instructions, our meals were prepared in the community kitchen by a rotating schedule of devotees. As dictated by Swamiji, the ashram was completely vegetarian, which meant no meat of any kind, nor eggs. However, we did eat milk products. Typical meals included toast and cereal for breakfast, soup and sandwiches for lunch, and some type of bean dish, vegetables and rice for dinner.

Every day was bookended by satsang in the prayer hall. From 7:30 to 8:15 a.m., we'd say our prayers, chant and sit in silent meditation, women sitting on the left and men to the right. In the evening, from 7:30 to 9:00, we would pray, chant and watch a video speech. We sat on the floor of the prayer hall cross-legged, facing an altar. All satsang meetings ended with the distribution of prasad.

Some of the devotees in Barsana Dham worked full-time for the ashram: at that time, it was two accountants and a construction manager. The staff devotees were not paid, but were supported with room, board and expenses. Some of the devotees moved to the ashram to work for a devotee-owned business on the property. Others found their own jobs in town or as self-employed practitioners of some sort.

All of the work we did in the ashram was volunteer labour, or seva, without payment. Doing seva is one of the essential components of achieving God realization, along with chanting, offering gifts and remembrance. We were constantly guided by one of Swamiji's key messages: 'Seva quickly purifies your heart and mind, and brings you closer to the master and Radha–Krishna.'

When not working, in satsang, our life was dedicated to serving the guru's divine mission on earth. We engaged in a wide range of activities to keep the ashram running. My regular sevas were cooking, cleaning, and and preparing the prasad for the evening satsang. Those with certain skills had other specialized sevas, such as editing video speeches, translating speeches, decorating and building new structures.

We even had our own forms of entertainment, including celebrations for Swamiji's birthdays and Hindu holidays like Holi, Krishna Janmashtami and Diwali. Swamiji taught the Western devotees all the essential components of each holiday, including what food to cook, which sweets to serve, how to string flower garlands and decorate the prayer hall, and which religious skits to perform during the events. Over the years, the holidays became public events that attracted hundreds and even thousands of people.

Swamiji flew back and forth from India to the US several times a year. When he was in residence, which was generally about half the time, we spent time with him during his morning and afternoon meals and sometimes assisted him in special events or projects.

Early in my spiritual search, long before finding Swamiji, I had come across Scott Peck's iconic book, *The Road Less Travelled*. His first line struck a chord with me: 'Life is difficult.' I believed this wholeheartedly, because that's exactly what I had experienced in my youth. Now I was hoping for an existence that would eradicate the difficulty of the world as I knew it. I thought I had found in it Barsana Dham under the tutelage of Swamiji.

I felt safe in the ashram. Many nights, on the way to satsang or heading back to The Girls' House, I would look up at the dark Texas sky, gaze at the moon and stars, and thank God that I was safely ensconced in this island of devotion.

I counted my blessings that I was no longer alone out in the big, bad world without a divine guide.

Hinduism Light

The Western-Friendly Dogma

IN THE EARLY days, Swamiji played down the fact that we were Hindus.

Actually, I didn't even know I was a Hindu until I'd been a devotee in his organization for over a year. When I found the path, I assumed that it was not affiliated with any specific religion, because no one ever mentioned the words Hinduism or Hindu in the beginning.

In hindsight, I assumed that this was because Swamiji did not want to risk scaring off Western devotees with traditional aspects of Hinduism, such as worshipping Lord Hanuman, who takes the form of a monkey, or Lord Ganesha, who takes the form of an elephant. He also left out many common Hindu rituals, such as fire ceremonies and fasting. People in the Western side of the world like things with a more 'New Age' packaging. Swamiji's brand of Hinduism fit in well – and was, in fact, carefully packaged to fit – within that milieu.

During my pre-Swamiji years, I had read only one book on Hinduism and heard only one lecture given by a Hindu monk.

Neither the book nor the monk mentioned the divine-love concepts of Hinduism espoused by Swamiji and his preachers.

Intrinsic to Swamiji's philosophy of divine-love-consciousness is the form of God called Radha–Krishna, which is one God in two forms: male and female. However, unlike any other branch of Hinduism, Swamiji emphasized the female form as being supreme. He taught us that Radha is, in fact, the highest form of God, but that few know this secret even among Hindus, for Radha is commonly believed to be just a 'consort' or the primary love interest of Krishna.

However, Swamiji's comments on the subject were vague. For example, he wrote that the saints of Vrindavan revealed, through their writings, the 'Divine secrets' of Radha's personality and her superiority in all aspects during the leelas, which were held in 'Divine Vrindavan', one of the highest 'abodes' of God.

The hallmark of Radha–Krishna is the countless divine loving activities they engage in with each other and their 'playmates', the young cow-herding maidens, called gopis. Their divine actions are called leelas, and include everything from dancing to eating to performing loving actions in worship of God. We were instructed to meditate on leelas in satsang – even to envision ourselves actually participating in divine leelas.

As Swamiji wrote in one of his books, Radha–Krishna descend on the earth and grace souls 'by revealing their love and leelas for them.'

Swamiji said that the more we meditated on Radha–Krishna, the quicker we would purify our material hearts, become divine like him, and attain our spiritual goal. But we were also supposed to imagine that we were engaging in leelas with Radha–Krishna as we carried out our tasks around the ashram, for thinking devotional thoughts while doing work was 'direct service to God' and would speed up our spiritual progress. For the same reason, we were told to do our work in the world with our thoughts constantly on the divine, because our jobs afforded us the opportunity to 'financially support God's mission'. As a result, our jobs were also a form of seva.

One way to meditate on these leelas, as well as the forms of God, was to recite God's many names over and over. The common way to do this was in kirtan – chanting or singing, which is always part of satsang. We were supposed to remember the chants and sing them in our minds after we left the prayer hall. In fact, we were instructed to strive to remember God's name even while sleeping. Swamiji assured us that the only sure-fire way to purify our worldly hearts and minds was through constant 'remembrance'.

While striving to achieve divinity, devotees sometimes experienced the ecstatic state of bhao – a transcendental hypnotic mental state where a person feels God's presence within himself – during satsang. When a person 'goes into bhao', he might feel tingly or warm, sway uncontrollably, or even pass out. It's basically a deep dive into the subconscious mind where a person temporarily loses touch with the conscious world and enters an ecstatic state of mind, envisioning God with him, in him and around him.

Devotees craved this experience. If they achieved bhao once, they wanted it again and again, the way a junkie craves a fix. Some devotees claimed to have experienced many bouts of bhao. I was not one of them. Because I never went into bhao, I doubted its existence and felt that the devotees' claims of bhao were more likely self-induced states of forced euphoria. After all, the mind can imagine all kinds of things, given enough desire and suggestion. But I kept this non-devotional thought to myself.

The goal of all of this focus on God was to divinize our minds so that we could achieve union with Radha–Krishna – ideally in the form of a gopi. According to Swamiji, becoming a gopi was the most coveted of all divine states that a human could achieve. Living eternally in the divine world in this form gives souls the opportunity to participate in many 'intimate divine activities' with Krishna, such as the mystical divine dance called maharas in which it appears that He is dancing with each gopi individually.

Swamiji taught us that there was a downside to not following the spiritual path he propagated: Our souls would be trapped in maya (the world) for uncountable lifetimes. He said that if we missed this rare chance offered through his guidance now, we could be reborn over and over again. And not necessarily as humans, but as every conceivable form of life: plants, bugs or animals.

He once told us: 'Being on the path to God is like climbing a tree. If you let go, you fall to earth. The higher you climb, the greater the damage will be if you fall, because you'll break more bones. Once you fall, you might never get the opportunity to find such a rare spiritual path and master again.'

There were many obstacles on the path to God realization, including our own bad sanskars (past-life actions), committing new transgressions, and our attachments to anything in the world. Attachments to any 'worldly' person, object or activity were to be avoided at all cost. This included our family members, our possessions and our pride.

Regarding sanskars, he said, 'Sometimes strong bad sanskars of our past lives influence our actions in this lifetime and affect the dedication of the mind. When such things happen, he should know that his old sanskars are playing with his mind. He must then, firmly keep doing his devotions and service, and pray [sic] Radha Krishn and his Master to overcome this situation and to improve his faith and dedication.'

Transgression came in many forms, but the worst was harbouring a negative thought against the guru. This was an almost unforgivable offence. Swamiji cautioned: 'Even God himself might not be able to free a soul from the karma acquired from this mistake.'

Also working against us mere mortals in our pursuit of the divine was the current period of time we live in. According to Hindu scriptures, we are living in the age of Kaliyug, the darkest of the four periods in the world's cycle of existence. Kaliyug started about 5,000 years ago and is going to last for about 400,000 more years. Swamiji said that this age will get much darker, more evil and more painful as it progresses.

One aspect of the faith that Swamiji was never vague about was the idea that none of us could reach God without the assistance of a God-realized saint, such as himself. He would say things like, 'God is omnipresent, but we can't find him. He's in our hearts, but we can't feel him. So, to help the souls, he sends saints to earth to teach them the path to Radha–Krishna.'

In the beginning, I knew nothing about Hinduism except what Swamiji taught us. I accepted his version of the religion without question and didn't explore it further, because to question the guru would have been an unforgivable transgression. He even warned us against reading the scriptures or the writings of any other guru. 'You do not have the capacity to understand the scriptures on your own,' he said, 'and other people's writings could be incorrect and poison your mind.'

Swamiji's emphasis on Radha, gopis and an amorous Krishna would take on a new meaning for me years later.

The Tea Towel Incident

A Ritual Restored

SWAMIJI ESCHEWED MOST traditional Hindu rituals. In fact, he would often mock the sacred religious customs of the different branches of his faith, such as praying with japa (prayer) beads and worshiping multiple forms of God, but only in private. However, he had his own rituals that required exacting execution.

On my first visit to Barsana Dham, Swamiji did not appear to have much to do, but what he did do seemed to be on a generally predictable schedule. He spent the majority of each day in his bedroom with a few devotees, including his assistant, Vishi, and his first preacher, Sureshwari (originally named Meera Devi). I later learnt that he watched a lot of TV and movies, especially Hindi films. He also had several favourite American TV shows, like *Gilligan's Island* and *Columbo*.

Twice a day, he walked down the hallway to make an appearance for the last few minutes of satsang. Typically, Vishi and Sureshwari would enter the prayer hall with him. He also came down to the breezeway on the first floor twice a day for his meals, during which time devotees would gather around him and have his darshan while he ate. A few times a day, he would ride around the property in his golf cart.

Whenever he entered a room, all eyes were on him. Devotees would sit on the floor facing him, focused. Swamiji would either sit quietly 'in his own devotional bhao', as we were told, or would give some short spiritual message, ask people questions, or entertain his captivated students with amusing stories, which were often his own version of some recent or past incident.

While his daily patterns looked relaxed to the casual observer, in reality, his life was extremely ritualized. Each of his daily habits required precise execution, even when he was served a cup of tea or a bowl of fruit. His food had to be cooked and served in a specific manner. For example, his rice had to be skimmed off the top of the pot, because he preferred the perfectly cooked rice on top, rather than the more moist rice underneath. All of his food had to be served in precise proportions and on fine china. His clothing had to be sewn in a specific fashion. His living quarters had to be cleaned a certain way.

Also during his meals, everything had to be just so, including the size and height of his custom-made folding table, the pile of small pillows placed behind him, the position of the package of toothpicks he used after every meal, as well as the placement of the tea towel he used to cover his lap while he ate. I learnt the hard way how grave a mistake it was to mess up any of his requirements. I was the target of a severe lesson one day when he sat down on his couch for dinner and there was no tea towel beside him.

As I sat on the floor staring up at him, he seemed agitated. I knew from experience that it was just a waiting game until he blew up. This was not unusual, because he would often become upset over little, unremarkable things. Like the time he threw a fit because he could smell room freshener that had been sprayed in another room about 200 yards away. He said, 'It hurt my nose' (meaning it smelled badly). For a while after that, canned air fresheners were banned from public places in the ashram.

However, the tea towel incident still took me by surprise.

'Where's my towel?' he barked. In his anger, it was difficult to understand him. His accent was always thickest when he was mad, because he slurred his words. Everyone sat frozen, not knowing what to do.

'My towel, my towel. Where is it?' he growled, gesturing to the place on the couch where his tea towel normally sat. Unfortunately, that day I was sitting closest to the stairs up to his kitchen where his towels and other belongings were stored.

'I'll go find it, Swamiji,' I said jumping up and running up the stairs two at a time.

Vishi was in the little kitchen in the old stone building where she prepared Swamiji's meals. She was serving his freshly cooked rice, dal and vegetables on a set of china placed just so on his oversized serving tray.

'Swamiji needs a towel,' I said frantically. 'There's none on his couch and he wants it *now*.'

She set the pot down and hurried to the storage area, grabbed a towel and held it out to me, fear clearly evident on her face. I ran back down the stairs.

'Here, Swamiji,' I said, placing the cloth on his couch. I sat back down on the floor. He continued to fume.

Shortly, Vishi came down the stairs carrying his tray. She placed it cautiously in front of him, careful not to make any other slip-up.

'My towel wasn't here,' he snapped at her.

She looked around at us. 'Who's responsible for Swamiji's towel?' she asked.

No one said anything.

'Someone has to take responsibility and make sure Swamiji's towel is there every time,' she ordered, sounding disgusted.

It turned out that no one was in charge of this particular seva. But after this incident, an older devotee woman was given the responsibility of preparing Swamiji's sitting area for his meals.

From that day on, he never sat down to eat without his tea towel sitting beside him in the exact right spot.

The Guru's Playground

Life on His Golf Cart

SWAMIJI LOVED HIS golf cart – and every devotee loved to ride with him.

Right after ISDL purchased the 200 acres of land for the ashram, Swamiji drove around the property in an old van. One day, someone suggested getting him a golf cart. From the minute he hit the gas on his first 'trolley' (as he called them), he could regularly be seen driving on and off the dirt roads that circumnavigated the property, or racing the cart across a field, crushing weeds, flowers and small shrubs as he drove as fast as the cart would allow, bumps be damned. I'm sure at some point over the years, most of the accessible ground on the property had felt the weight of his golf cart's four stubby wheels crunching the earth as he barrelled over it.

One day in late 1992, he told his followers to build a hill behind the site for the new temple. He said it was going to be a replica of Govardhan Hill. Govardhan Hill is a place of worship in northern India because, according to Hindu scriptures, Krishna convinced the locals to worship the hill instead of Indra, the god of thunder and rain. Krishna had seen the villagers making regular offerings to Indra and told them that they should concentrate on farming and protecting their cattle, not worshipping gods of natural phenomena.

When the villagers did not proceed with the next special prayer service to Indra, the god in his fury made it rain for seven days and seven nights until it flooded the region. In response, Krishna lifted Govardhan Hill up into the air, giving shelter to all the animals and people from the rain. Indra finally accepted defeat and recognized Krishna as the supreme form of God. The point of this fable is that people should divert their senses away from the world and towards Krishna – and he will protect them.

Govardhan Hill is roughly shaped like a long, fat, hand-rolled cigarette – wide in the middle and tapered at the ends. While the actual Govardhan Hill is several miles long, Barsana Dham's replica was only about twenty yards long. To build it, boulders from around the property were moved onto the hill's location (selected by Swamiji), and then dirt was hauled in to cover the rocks. Next, a wide variety of flowers and bushes were planted over the mound of dirt.

Whenever there was a project under way, Swamiji always showed up at the scene several times to survey the progress and bark orders from his perch behind the wheel of his golf cart. He was usually accompanied by two or three of his preachers or his favourite female devotees.

A seat on Swamiji's golf cart was a coveted position. There was room for three passengers, but people would often crowd in, sitting on each other's laps or standing while holding onto the sides or roof. Sometimes he would take off in a flourish, flooring the gas pedal and causing everyone on board to scream with delight. Many times he would load up all the children present – as many as one dozen at a time, some barely hanging on – and take off, the cart rocking and wheezing from the weight. Many devotees would stand gazing at the joyous scene. I longed to be with him on his cart, and other devotees told me they did too. Most of us only got a precious few opportunities.

One of mine occurred one evening as I was walking around the ashram in the dark after satsang, Swamiji pulled up beside me with one of his favourite female devotees. 'Who's that?' he asked.

'It's me, Karen, Swamiji,' I said sheepishly.

'Oh. Get on.'

I jumped into the back next to Jennifer, not believing my luck for being in that place and time at the right moment. He drove down to the river, where he commented on a few fireflies flitting about.

'Look at the lightning bugs,' he said. We all laughed. 'I want to see more,' he demanded, somewhat petulant.

'They might be closer to the water, Swamiji,' Jennifer said.

He started driving along the riverbank.

'I don't see any,' he pouted.

We all frantically searched the darkness, hoping to be the one to make him happy by finding more fireflies. Then I remembered having seen several the night before during my walk. 'Swamiji, there were a bunch of fireflies up by the front gate the other night,' I said, nervously.

'Where?' he demanded.

'Near the entrance to the ashram.'

He stepped on the gas pedal, spun the cart in the opposite direction, and suddenly we were sailing through the warm night air, giddy with the wind whipping our hair. We were all alone in the dark with our guru at the wheel – just the three of us – and it was glorious. I was drunk with happiness.

As we approached the area, I directed him to the place where I'd seen the fireflies the previous night. I was fearful that the trip would not be fruitful and I might get in trouble. But we were not disappointed. There were several dozen fireflies darting about under the oak and cedar trees, their tails luminous in the darkness.

Swamiji was happy and all was right with the world at that moment.

The Temple

Witnessing a 'Divine' Creation

JUST BEFORE I moved to Barsana Dham, they had broken ground on the enormous temple that would one day be the central focus of the ashram.

A devotee showed me a photo she took of the first shovelful of dirt being scooped from the earth with a large backhoe. It was a dramatic scene with the metal claw of the massive piece of machinery ripping and shredding the hard ground. A cylindrical cloud of dust circled up from the bone-dry Texas hardpan, swirling around like a dust devil. I felt a rush of pride that I was one of the select few mortals on earth who would be witness to the creation of what we all believed would be one of the most important spiritual structures in the US – if not the most important.

We were all excited to watch the progress of the building – from a hole in the ground to a slab of cement to a steel beam skeleton to a finished building and finally an ornately decorated edifice. During the two years of its construction, we were all excited by the prospect of one day doing devotions in the temple. I imagined myself sitting in the prayer hall of the massive building, staring up at the life-size deity of Radha–Krishna and weeping with joy at my great luck to have found such a special spiritual path.

Swamiji told us that this temple would play a vital role in the spread of his teachings. 'It will be a divine light for true devotees for generations to come. We're building it to last a thousand years.' Devotees revelled in his pronouncements, believing themselves to be the lucky ones chosen to participate in something rare and divine.

By this time, Swamiji had become more visible in Barsana Dham, staying for longer periods of time instead of hurrying back to India.

Rather than staying tucked away in his bedroom for most of the day, he regularly visited the temple worksite to oversee the building's progress and view the architectural drawings. After his morning and evening meals, he would often sit in the breezeway, studying blueprints and discussing issues with the construction team. I was fascinated by the temple project and watched in awe as Swamiji oversaw every decision, no matter how seemingly inconsequential. He said that the building's design was a mixture of ancient and modern Indian architecture, and that it came to him in a dream.

The largest and most labour-intensive part of the construction was a 90-foot-high pink-and-grey granite tower which would rise above the surrounding oak and cedar trees, and sit over the shrine. Once finished, the tower was visible from a couple of miles in all directions. But I always thought it looked out of place amidst the rolling hills of the Texas Hill country, where barbeque restaurants and country stores were the norm.

When the construction was halfway finished, Swamiji asked the devotees to submit suggestions for the name of the temple. The devotees came up with a wide range of options but, in the end, he chose it himself: Shree Raseshwari Radha Rani Temple. I assumed he knew all along what he was going to call it, but had generously given us a chance to feel involved in the project that, otherwise, most of us had very little to do with.

Raseshwari is one of the names of Radha, derived from the fact that she initiates the sacred maharas leela between Krishna and the gopis.

In October 1995, Barsana Dham hosted an elaborate show for the temple's establishment ceremony. Several gurus from around the world were invited to attend as guest speakers. A helicopter was hired to drop dozens of bags of marigolds grown on the property onto the temple's steeple. Hours of dances and skits were performed by groups of children and adults. A devotional procession from the front gates of the ashram to the temple doors kicked off the event. When it reached the front of the temple, Swamiji and the other gurus danced in a circle as devotees crowded around. One of my proudest mementos from the event was a photograph of this dance from overhead, with me dancing right behind Swamiji, wearing a pink sari.

Just prior to the ceremony, I was asked by one of the preachers to write an article about Barsana Dham for *Hinduism Today*. At one point, I quoted Swamiji: 'The time has now come when faithful souls will receive the path of Krishna-love, provided they are not possessed with the intellectual fancy of instant enlightenment and keep their hearts and minds open to receive this message. Krishna-*ras* is bliss. Just drink.'

I believed his words with all my heart and was thrilled that I was one of the few souls present in the place where the divine ras seemed to be pouring down on us.

The Guru's Rules

Law of the Land

IN THE ASHRAM, women were not allowed to show their legs or the top of their arms. It was just one of Swamiji's many rules. We had to wear skirts or dresses that fell at least to the middle of our calves. No sleeveless tops were allowed. Also, our skirts could not be see-through. As a result, most women wore slips – an unwelcome extra layer on many hot, steamy Texas summer days. Shorts were not allowed either. When we went swimming, we had to wear T-shirts and long pants. We could wear pants around the ashram, but not into the prayer hall. Men also did not wear shorts or sleeveless shirts. It was all part of a forced modesty to promote pure spiritual living and discourage sexual energy.

This dress code was not cited in Swamiji's 'Guidelines and Disciplines for a Devotee of Radha–Krishna', yet was most definitely part of the law of the land governed by the guru. In an effort to further reduce sexual excitement among followers, he instructed that single women and men were not to talk to each other or engage in work projects around the ashram together. This rule was documented, for Rule 24 stated that single devotees were particularly likely to be distracted from their devotions when sexual attraction came into play. The rule prohibited men and women from sharing ashram work with members of the opposite sex.

Some of us made an effort to abide by this rule. But, practically speaking, it was impossible to uphold. Among the fifty or so adults, there were about a dozen single women and eight single men. As much as we tried, we could not live in such close quarters without coming into verbal contact with members of the opposite sex. So most of us just did the best we could to limit our interaction.

Other rules included Rule 9 which warned against sloth, Rule 18 that encouraged us to be more accommodating towards fellow ashram dwellers, and Rule 23 which asked devotees to come clean about their 'mistakes' to the 'Master' before the problem got out of hand.

Like the clothing rule, there were many other rules not listed on the official list, like 'silent dining'. Swamiji instructed us to eat our meals without talking, so that we could use the time to meditate on God. Signs were placed all over the dining hall to remind us. Over the years, the devotees tried to follow this rule, but could rarely make it stick. Periodically the preachers would remind us that we needed to work harder to maintain silent dining and the devotees would spend a week or two trying, but our resolve would break down and we would revert back to our old habits. Not even the preachers ate in silence all the time.

Another unwritten rule, which I personally found difficult to abide by, was to get up every morning at 6:00 a.m. Swamiji said that this helped prevent slothfulness. My best effort was 7:00 a.m. But I suffered from guilt over this lapse. One day when he came to The Girls' House, I decided to seek his advice.

'Swamiji, I'm having a hard time getting up at six. What should I do?'

'What time do you wake up?'

'At seven.'

'That's okay,' he said with an approving tilt of his head.

I couldn't believe it was that easy to get permission to break one of his rules. From that day on, I slept happily and guilt-free until 7:00 a.m.

Most of Swamiji's rules were nearly impossible to follow, but that did not stop him from trying. Over and over, in multiple tirades over the years, he told us that we were the luckiest people on the planet because we lived in his ashram, and if we didn't sincerely follow his rules, we were wasting a precious opportunity to achieve God realization in this lifetime and committing a grave disservice to him, to God and to our souls.

I struggled for years to follow all of his rules and always felt lacking in my ability to follow them perfectly.

The Ladies in Saffron

Holier than Thou

THERE WAS AN absolute hierarchy in the ashram, with Swamiji at the top and his sanyasi preachers directly below him.

The preachers were the primary upholders of his rules. As sanyasis, they had ostensibly 'given up their lives' to serve God and the guru full-time. They were supposedly no longer engaged in 'worldly activities' of any sort. Swamiji told us that his preachers were 'examples of dedication and devotion' for the rest of us and that we were to show them the utmost respect, no matter what. In particular, we could not talk back or argue with them without incurring the guru's wrath.

Swamiji's twenty-ninth rule for living in the ashram was for them: 'A sanyasi sets the example of renunciation, devotion, discipline and loving, devotional humbleness for others. He must be aware of that, and maintain it in his behaviour.'

I think most of them struggled with this rule.

When I moved to the ashram, there were four preachers – all female and all westerners, ranging in age from twenty-two to thirty-seven. Swamiji had given them all their first Hindi names. But his guru renamed them in the early 2000s. They were Meera Devi (renamed Sureshwari Devi), Priya Dasi (renamed Prabhakari Devi), Hari Dasi (renamed Nikhileshwari Devi) and Krishna Dasi (renamed Janeshwari Devi). The fifth woman who wore saffron was not a preacher. Originally named Ranjana (renamed Vishwambhari Devi, and whom I call 'Vishi' in this book for short), she was Swamiji's full-time cook, laundress and travel companion. Later, he would ordain four other women, one westerner (Christi) and three Indians.

Each of the preachers had spent about two years studying Hindi, Sanskrit, scriptures like the Bhagavadgita and the *Bhagavatam*, chanting with a harmonium and drum and memorizing a batch of prepared speeches.

When I moved to the ashram, all five women in saffron lived together in a single rectangular room next to Swamiji's bedroom. Their room contained five single beds, two desks and a few end tables. They shared two closets. After the temple was built, they each got their own tiny bedroom near Swamiji's suite. I was always jealous of their proximity to the guru. One night, as I was walking past their bedroom, the door opened and they all came out wearing thin cotton nightgowns that he had bought for them that day. Giggling like schoolgirls, they ran out of their bedroom and into his, closing the door behind them.

I knew it was a strange scene, but all I could feel at the time was jealousy. I learnt later that they all went into his bedroom every evening. I wondered what they did in there with him. At the time, I didn't think too much about the polygamous overtones of the women's relationship with Swamiji.

These women lived a highly unusual lifestyle, one that most people unaffiliated with the organization could not imagine. Even though I was a devotee and watched from a front-row seat, I still could not really imagine what it must be like to be in your early twenties and elevated to a status position that put you above everyone around you, including, in the case of one of the preachers, her own parents. Some devotees treated the preachers like they were princesses, catering to their every whim, including doing their laundry, buying them special things or taking them shopping.

Meanwhile, the preachers typically exuded an air of superiority and entitlement and enforced Swamiji's edict to treat them as special. One devotee told me that to be on the safe side she just treated them all 'as if they have come directly from God's divine world'.

The preachers stood out from the regular devotees because they dressed head-to-toe in bright saffron like the guru, from their saris to their socks to their jackets and even their shoes. Saffron is one of the colours that represent renunciation in Hinduism and, while wearing orange is common for Indians, it is not so for westerners. After travelling on a plane for the first time dressed in saffron, one of the preachers said, 'I felt like a gigantic carrot.'

Also, like Swamiji, the preachers wore tilaks and gold-and-black beaded necklaces. Their primary role was to go out preaching across the US. When they weren't doing that, they engaged in various activities around the ashram. For example, Prabhakari worked on videos, and Nikhileshwari worked on the computer and baked bread.

With their monochrome costumes, they definitely looked the part of renounced spiritual teachers – but they did not always act the part. For example, there was the day when Prabhakari came into the dining room, took one look at the food set out for lunch and said snidely, 'Aren't these just leftovers from last night?'

After spending three exhausting hours in the kitchen cooking lunch for sixty people, I couldn't hide my irritation at her meanness. 'We made a fresh dish, but it ran out. What else are we supposed to serve?'

Without missing a beat, she straightened her spine and snapped, 'You can't talk to me like that. You have to show me respect.'

I made a mental note on that day not to respect her, but to avoid her.

When Swamiji was out of the ashram, the preachers were in charge, their power struggles and rivalries out in the open.

In the late 1990s, Swamiji announced that he was stepping down from his role as president and appointing his oldest preacher, Sureshwari, in his stead. Prabhakari would be the vice-president. At first, some of the devotees rebelled against the new leaders. Then one day Swamiji gathered us together for an 'important meeting' and told us sternly: 'You must treat anything Sureshwari and Prabhakari say as if their instructions are coming from me directly.'

We immediately felt the shift of power, especially from Prabhakari, who began inserting her will all over the ashram. She became a power-monger to the point of misery for many devotees.

My only saving grace was Sureshwari. When the going got rough, I knew I could go to her for some measure of protection from Prabhakari's megalomania. However, Sureshwari was also suffering under Prabhakari's power plays. Rumours swirled that the two regularly engaged in very un-sanyasi-like arguments, some even bordering on all-out 'knock down, drag out fights', one man who witnessed them fight told me.

The preachers were most definitely not divine beings but experts at myth-making – appearing on the surface to be a unified front, far higher in devotional accomplishment than the rest of us mere minions. But under the saffron clothing, they were all just human beings. Once I realized this, it was a relief. It allowed me to see their ministrations in perspective and take their attitudes in my stride.

In the end, I did learn one important lesson from them that helped me navigate ashram life in the years ahead – the guru's rules were made to be broken.

Missed Connections

Outside Looking In

SWAMIJI LIKED TO be surrounded by female devotees and, when his preachers were not available, he always found other female companionship. He could always be assured of an adoring group of women at The Girls' House. In the early days, he visited on a regular basis. This turned into a misery for me, because I seemed to never be around when he showed up, which was usually at odd hours, like early in the morning or late at night. I was always either taking an early morning walk or working late in my office.

Once I'd return home, one or more of the women would tell me about Swamiji's visit to the house, making my heart break. They would retell the funny things he said or did, like the time he made one of the women dress up in various costumes that were being prepared for an upcoming celebration. The tales were always filled with laughter and swooning from the smitten women, who seemed to savour the pain I was in.

I took my missed connections with him personally. After all, we believed he knew everything, so he must have known when I wasn't in the house. He also taught us that everything that happened to us was the result of our karma. Clearly, my karma caused me to miss out on an abundance of fun time with my guru.

One evening, the pain became unbearable. I was in the community kitchen after satsang preparing food for the next day. One of The Girls' House residents came into the kitchen. 'Swamiji was just at our house,' she chirped. My heart sank. I'd missed him again.

'What did he do?' I asked, sick with the loss.

'Oh, my gosh, he was so funny. He went into everyone's bedroom looking to see how many saris each of us has. He started pulling saris off the hangers and giving them away. Then he wrapped a sari around me.'

As I walked home in the dark, I ruminated on my continuing bad luck. I desperately needed a fun experience with Swamiji to lift my spirits.

As I walked past the temple construction site in the dark, I heard laughter. I slowed my pace to try and figure out who was having such a grand old time. Then I heard Swamiji's voice, followed by peals of girlish giggling. I looked towards the temple and could make out four or five figures in saffron sitting on the temple's front steps. I stood silently for a few minutes and realized that Swamiji was there with his preachers, regaling them with funny stories.

I felt the sting of being an outsider looking in at his inner circle of women. My already depressed state darkened even more. I believed more than ever that I was not good enough to be one of the lucky devotees to receive entry into the guru's intimate world.

When I got to my bedroom, the pain and isolation overwhelmed me. As I stood in front of my bathroom sink, brushing my teeth, tears started flowing. Soon, I was weeping loudly, with jagged sobs that ripped at my heart and stomach. I dropped to the floor and wept until all my energy was exhausted.

My head ached as I got up from the floor, took a shower and got into bed – lonelier and more dejected than I'd ever felt in my life.

'One Big Family'

Big Fish in a Little Pond

SWAMIJI OFTEN TOLD us that those of us living in the ashram were 'one big family'.

This was a happy thought, but not the reality. We were just a large group of very different people from very different backgrounds who had been brought together by a shared interest – worshipping God by serving our guru.

There were occasional group activities such as picking beans, canning peaches, preparing for a celebration, or having a picnic, where we would feel the bond of camaraderie for an afternoon or so.

Once, Swamiji gathered us together after evening satsang to pick beans in the moonlight. We worked happily side by side under the guru's approving gaze. When we were almost finished, he directed some of us to go fetch some home-made bread and lemonade. We ate our bread and butter in the dark, feeling like the most blessed people in the whole wide world.

But day-to-day life was not a big happy family existence, to say the least.

None of us *chose* to live with each other. Swamiji alone determined who lived in the ashram and who did not. And he did not justify his decisions. The only comment he ever made about whom he chose is: 'People who live here have reached a particular level of devotion to God.'

Comments like that gave us all a certain cache among devotees who merely visited the ashram. Some of them treated us like we were special. Many of us believed we were. I definitely felt arrogant about my status as an ashram resident. But the reality was that most of us struggled mightily with our devotions, with one another and with ourselves – wondering if we had made the right decision to move into such a cloistered, high-pressure living situation.

One of the most frequent ongoing problems was the power struggle. The preachers were not the only people in the ashram who craved power. There were conflicts at every level – primarily, turf battles over areas of responsibility such as the ashram kitchen or the construction department. People wanted control, because being in charge of something usually gave them greater proximity to the guru – and that was the Holy Grail of living in the ashram. No position of authority was too small to give one person an edge over another. Whenever two devotees worked together, a struggle for dominance was inevitable.

For me, living in the ashram required a Teflon exterior to deflect the constant barrage of spiteful barbs frequently shot at me. Either I didn't clean up after myself well enough, or someone had a complaint about a meal I cooked, or a preacher chastised me for being able see my underwear through the fabric of my skirt.

I felt like there were always eyes on me, that someone was always poised to judge my actions or tell me how to do something differently. I sometimes joked about it, asking the others: 'Is there a target painted on my back?'

The ashram was a prime example of the classic 'big fish in a small pond' syndrome – and we had a very small pond with far too many wanting to be the big fish.

Ashram Seva

Damned if You Do, Damned if You Don't

AMONG THE CHALLENGES of ashram life was doing seva under the rule of the devotees in charge. The scriptures say that this type of volunteer work should not be a tool for making one feel superior or to receive rewards. Seva, like charity, should be done with a pure and undemanding heart.

But in the ashram, most seva turned into a damned-if-you-do-and-damned-if-you-don't stranglehold – and nowhere was this truer than in the ashram kitchen, which generated an exceptionally high degree of conflict because of the woman in charge. Swamiji gave Prabhakari's mother Sondra Tonnessen the position of kitchen manager. When it comes to power-mongering, the tree was not far from the fruit.

She became a kitchen dictator. The worst part of her totalitarian management style was that she ruled from a core of incompetence.

'How could someone so incompetent be so arrogant?' another devotee once said.

Her ineptitude led to chronic problems that would turn even the most saintly person into a raving shrew. For example, she planned the menus on a weekly basis, but would often change them at the last minute, sending the cooks into a tailspin.

On a typical day, a rotating team of two devotees would prepare both lunch and dinner for forty to sixty people. One person would be the lead cook, the other the helper. I started out as a helper, but out of sheer frustration, I pushed to be a lead cook. The first meal I served was ripped apart by several devotees, who complained to Sondra. It was an unpleasant experience, but it spurred me to work harder to prepare better meals.

I started out as just an average cook with only a few simple dishes in my repertoire. And my former meat-based specialities were not going to fly in a vegetarian ashram.

What's more, Swamiji pushed us to try more Indian recipes, rather than the spaghetti, tacos and veggie burgers we all craved. But we were all westerners and did not know how to cook Indian food. I certainly did not know the first thing about Indian cuisine, but became very interested after my first demonstration on using traditional Indian spices like mustard seeds and freshly grated ginger. I started shadowing the Indian cooks who visited Barsana Dham and got them to show me how to correctly spice each dish, when to add ingredients to a pot, and how to finish off a dish to maximize flavour.

They encouraged me to bring my own personality to the cooking process and make every dish my own, which I am proud to say I did. I turned a peas-and-paneer recipe, with its complicated steps, into a delicious dish that I could whip up for fifty people in an hour and a half. I worked on perfecting my pau bhaji for over one year until it was a rich and complex stew of vegetables and spices that many devotees craved.

To my relief, and to the gastronomic delight of many of the other devotees, my cooking skills blossomed. I found it thrilling to toss a handful of mustard seeds into a pot of smoking hot oil and let them dance and pop, then toss in a handful of grated ginger to 'cool' the cooking process. As the spices sizzled in oil, the kitchen filled with the most amazing aromas.

I began to receive compliments from westerners and Indians alike. My new-found proficiency bolstered my confidence. And on the days I made the devotees happy by preparing delicious, wholesome vegetarian meals, it almost felt like we were a family at last.

Ashram Children

The Guru's 'Grandkids'

I HAD NEVER wanted children of my own and, at first, did not appreciate living in such close proximity to the kids in the ashram.

When I first moved to Barsana Dham, it already housed eleven children between the ages of three and fourteen. When the ashram population reached its peak a few years later, there were sixteen children, plus the kids visiting with their devotee parents for the day or weekend. As children do, they were always running around, getting in the way and making noise. They received the lion's share of Swamiji's attention, particularly at mealtimes. The kids would usually sit up close to him, huddled around his folding TV table. As he ate, he would often toss them little morsels, such as pieces of bread or carrot sticks.

He called the kids his 'grandchildren' and would often give them bear hugs. If there was more than one around, they'd end up in a group hug. Occasionally, he took them on golf-cart rides, with as many bodies as could fit on the vehicle. He would drive off with the children hanging on for dear life, screaming in delight.

Kids played a big part in all the celebrations at Barsana Dham. There were always roles for children in the dances and performances, which depicted stories from the Hindu scriptures related to whatever holiday was being celebrated.

In general, I kept my distance from the young ones. Sometimes they would play in a large field outside my bedroom after evening satsang. When I could not take their screaming any longer, I would go out in my pyjamas and tell them that it was time for bed. Naturally, the parents did not appreciate me shushing their kids. I developed a reputation as a curmudgeon and, for the most part, the kids stayed clear of me.

One of the little girls lived in The Girls' House with her mother across the hall from me. Shyama and I had made bad first impressions on each other.

During one of my visits, before I moved to the ashram, I was instructed to clean the kitchen pantry. Nancy told me that Shyama was supposed to help me. 'She'll try to get out of it, but make sure she does her share.'

I went to the prasad room and started cleaning. Within ten minutes, a young girl with thick, long, brown hair walked in.

'Are you Shyama?' I asked.

'Yeah,' she said, looking at me with suspicion.

'Oh, good. Can you start sweeping over in that corner?'

She gave me a disgusted look, turned around and walked out.

Years later I learnt from her that her first impression of me was equally bad. During a particularly busy visit, when I occupied the makeshift girls' dormitory, which was just a part of the temporarily walled-off section of the dining hall, my head was pounding from lack of sleep. The women were all at work one afternoon, so after lunch I retreated to the relatively quiet space, closed all the blinds, climbed on one of the empty top bunks and began to fall asleep. Just as I was finally nodding off, the door opened, letting in all the jarring light and noise.

I bolted up from the pillow to see who was intruding on my peace and quiet. It was Shyama. 'Can you please be quiet? I'm trying to sleep,' I grumbled at her.

Years later, she told me she had thought I was mean. We laughed at our first impressions of each other.

Many devotees believed that the children living in the ashram were special, because they got the chance to worship Swamiji from such a young age – something most adults wished for themselves. Some of the parents, especially the women, used their children as conduits for proximity to the guru. Several of them assumed that their kids were going to become preachers and so instructed them to do seva for the guru and his preachers.

In the end, only one of the children ever became a preacher, but not a very good one and only for a short time. Other than that, only one other child even went on to became an adult devotee, to my knowledge.

To my surprise, I eventually warmed up to some of the children. One little boy was particularly charming. I had thought him a spoilt brat and had avoided direct contact. Then one day I noticed that he was alone in the dining hall, eating one of the particularly spicy dishes – fiery hot pakoras. The boy was popping them into his mouth like M&Ms. I went up to him and said, 'Isn't that a little hot for you?'

He looked up at me with big, blue eyes and round, chubby cheeks and said sweetly, 'Not so far.' I actually felt a rush of tenderness towards him. It was one of the first times I ever felt anything close to a motherly concern for a child.

In that moment, my opinion of him as a precocious brat changed. I started talking to him more often and found him delightful. He was just starved for attention and affection. So one day I took him with me to a bookshop. As we sat on a bench perusing books, he leaned into my back and we read quietly together in the middle of the bookshop.

I also became close to the oldest girl in the ashram, Kate. In fact, she and I became good friends and started talking and sharing our thoughts on the frustrations of ashram life. We began going out together for lunches, coffee, hiking and swimming. Despite a twenty-year age difference, we shared surprisingly similar views on what constituted proper behaviour and opinions on the various personalities that existed inside the ashram gates. Needless to say, I thought her quite level-headed and mature for her age. Little did I know then how that friendship would endure over the years – or the impact it would have on our lives years later.

The Birthday Cake Miracle

Saving the Day

ONE AFTERNOON, SONDRA, the kitchen control freak, called me in a panic.

'Can you bake a cake?' she asked me in a frantic tone.

'No,' I replied, truthfully.

She ignored my answer. 'We need a cake tonight. There's no one else around. It's Swamiji's birthday today.' I could feel her distress rise with each sentence. I was miffed that she even called me, because even though I worked from home, I was still working.

Plus, I was no baker. When I was in high school I made boxed cakes and brownies. But every time I tried to bake anything from scratch, I failed stupendously. No matter how hard I tried, or how carefully I measured and mixed, the result was usually the same: something completely inedible. I was like Ellie May Clampett on *The Beverly Hillbillies* when it came to baking.

I once made peanut butter cookies that tasted like sawdust. 'There's something wrong with these cookies,' my youngest brother said about the round discs I'd thrown on the table in disgust. Then there were the biscuits that even the ducks in the local pond wouldn't eat. There was also the blueberry pie with the partially cooked dough and runny berries that my boyfriend pretended was delicious.

Now I was being cornered into certain failure, because everything in the ashram was made from scratch.

'You're the only one I could find,' Sondra insisted. 'Adolph and I have to run an errand for Swamiji. Everyone else is busy or at work.'

I remained silent with dread.

'Ellen usually bakes his birthday cakes, but she's at work.'

I realized that she wasn't going to give up. Maybe I could save the day, I thought, and relented. 'Okay, I'll bake the cake.'

'Great,' said Sondra. 'We have a recipe book,' she said, leading me to the cabinet. 'There's one for chocolate, vanilla, and zucchini. Pick what you want.'

I wasn't a fan of chocolate, and vanilla seemed boring. So I opted for the zucchini cake.

'Okay,' Sondra said, 'but make sure you cut back on the cinnamon. Swamiji doesn't like it.'

Swamiji had a long list of very particular likes and dislikes which, to be honest, was a little annoying. For example, he always wanted (and always got) only the middle part of a watermelon – the sweetest portion and the only part without seeds. Or the most tender, centre leaves of lettuce.

The thought of leaving the cinnamon out of a spiced cake was too much. I thought to myself that I might *accidentally* use the right amount of the spice.

In the ashram, baking a cake (or anything else for that matter) was not like baking in the normal world. For one thing, everything was oversized. After all, in the ashram we typically cooked meals for forty to fifty people. Everything was built or purchased to accommodate cooking large quantities of food, from the number of stove tops (four), to the size of the bowls and pots (huge), to the quantity of supplies (abundant).

I surveyed the large kitchen, which felt titanic with no one else there but me. I began to panic. But there was no backing out now. A cake had to be baked and I had to make it. I studied the recipe.

There were three lists of ingredients for the zucchini cake, based on quantity: forty, seventy-five and 110 people. Sondra had told me to make a medium-sized cake for seventy-five.

I started carefully measuring out ingredients: twenty-two cups of flour, sixteen cups of sugar and four cups of grated zucchini, for starters. But it was difficult to maintain my focus, because it seemed like every few minutes a curious devotee would come in to get a cup of tea, a cheese sandwich or whatever.

'What are you making?' each one asked, and got excited at the prospect of a cake since we didn't have them that often.

The interruptions with the same questions were making me tense. 'Please. I have to concentrate,' I told the others who trooped in hearing the news.

I was so anxious that I had to check and recheck the directions several times, so it took me twice as long to make the cake.

Finally, I poured the oversized bowl of batter in the 24" x 36"-deep dish baking pan and heaved it into the oven. While it baked, I made the cream cheese icing.

I couldn't wait to taste my creation – I needed to make sure it was edible. I cut off a small piece on the edge and blew on it until the steam disappeared. I popped it into my mouth. The spicy richness flooded my taste buds. It was delicious, with just the right balance of spice and sweetness. It was even light and moist. That night everyone agreed that it was an exceptionally delicious cake.

That day, I became the official baker of Swamiji's birthday cakes for the next fifteen years.

Cooking Halva

Trial by Fire

ALL DEVOTEES IN Barsana Dham eagerly ate the leftovers on the guru's plate or in his cooking vessels, believing it to be blessed food. We also enthusiastically ate any food he tossed to us. If Swamiji walked through the kitchen and touched anything, say a banana or a slice of bread, a nearby devotee would grab the item and quickly consume it. Once I saw Swamiji pick up a loaf of bread I had just purchased, look at it and keep it back. I ate that loaf over the next several days with special delight, simply because he had touched it.

At Barsana Dham, the typical prasad served consisted of nuts, raisins and chopped fruit. When we offered the prasad bowls to Swamiji for his blessing, he typically just laid one finger on the side of each bowl for a second or two. Occasionally, he would be more playful, picking up an almond or grape and putting it into someone's mouth. On other occasions he'd pick out several pieces and toss them to his preachers. From time to time, he would take the entire bowl and throw handfuls of the contents out into the prayer hall among the devotees. Fruit would roll over the carpet, with devotees diving for pieces, snatching up as many as they could, squealing with laughter the whole time. They would eat the fruit right off the floor, seeking the guru's grace as they chewed and swallowed each piece.

Thanks to my daily prasad seva, I received a few nanoseconds of one-on-one interaction with Swamiji each day when I offered him one of the prasad bowls. At one point, he developed a habit of dropping one of the many fresh flowers placed on his couch into the bowl. I always retrieved the flowers and saved them in glass jars. After fifteen years, I had five jars filled with flowers, which became, for me, a visual symbol of the grace that my guru was showering on me.

On Wednesday, Saturday and Sunday nights, a sweet was added to the prasad offering, such as small cookies or a piece of cake. On these occasions, the prasad was distributed in paper bowls. Before the temple was built, Swamiji decreed that halva would be the Saturday night sweet at Barsana Dham. In the ashram, it was made from semolina and chana flour.

Although there are only a handful of ingredients in halva, it can be difficult to make. It requires special instruction from an experienced halva maker to learn the exacting steps of the process. Lois, the person in charge of prasad at Barsana Dham, had learnt to make halva to Swamiji's liking from Vishi. As Lois's assistant in prasad preparation, I had watched her make it a couple of times, but was never officially taught how to do it.

One day, Lois left for a business trip. Neither she nor I had thought about the halva preparation in advance. On Saturday, I realized that someone had to make it. I assumed that Vishi would do it, but wanted to make sure she had planned it into her busy schedule of taking care of Swamiji. I knew she was probably with Swamiji in his bedroom, but was too timid to go upstairs and ask her myself. As I was fretting over my predicament, Brenda walked into the kitchen.

'Lois is gone,' I said, 'and I don't know who's going to make halva tonight. Will you please go up and ask Vishi if she can make it?'

Brenda seemed to have no fear of Swamiji the way I did. Either that, or she relished having a legitimate excuse to go up to his bedroom.

She finally returned with a mischievous grin on her face.

'Well? Is Vishi going to make it?'

'No. You have to make it yourself,' she stated bluntly. 'I asked her and she asked Swamiji. He said, "Tell her to make it. There's a first time for everything."'

I was horrified. 'I don't know how to make it.'

'Well, it's always trial by fire around here,' she said blithely. Then she laughed as she walked out of the room. 'Good luck!' she called out from the breezeway.

I walked into the kitchen and found the ashram recipe book. There was a partial recipe for halva, but it only listed the ingredients. There were no cooking instructions whatsoever. All I had to go on was my memory of watching Lois make it a couple of times. But I had no choice except to figure it out.

I started gathering the six ingredients: sooji, besan, butter, water, milk and sugar. I got out a large, shallow saucepan from the pot room, placed it on the stove and dropped in ten sticks of butter. As the butter melted, I stirred the milk, water and sugar and turned up the heat.

From watching Lois, I remembered that she continually stirred the sooji as it cooked. She added the flour at some halfway point, then cooked both until they turned a shade of deep golden brown. At that point, she added the sugary milk mixture, which she had first boiled. When the liquid was added to the dry ingredients, it would bubble and sputter like molten lava. Then it was done.

It was a slow, tedious process.

I poured the cracked wheat into the butter and started stirring, wondering when to add the flour. Just then, Don, the ashram accountant, walked into the kitchen. 'What are you cooking?' he asked.

'Halva. Do you know how to make it?'

He stared into the pot. 'All I know is that you cook it until it gets really, really brown.'

'Thanks.'

At that point, I would take whatever extra information I could get. I cooked and stirred, cooked and stirred, and watched its colour turn from a yellow tan to a slightly darker yellow tan, but not to the deep brown hue I knew it needed to be.

Suddenly, Prabhakari entered the kitchen from one of the back doors. 'Have you ever made halva?' I asked, hopeful. 'Swamiji said I have to make it tonight and I don't know how.'

She walked over and looked into the pot. 'Not really. But that looks like too much butter.'

I peeped into the pot and realized that the sooji was swimming in butter. I grabbed the recipe to check the ingredients. The recipe said five *sticks* of butter and I had put in five *cups,* which was double the correct amount.

I felt queasy.

What was I going to do now? My panicked brain raced for a solution. Either I had to start over or find some way to drain the excess butter from the large pot. I carried it over to the metal sink and began skimming off the butter. When most of the excess butter had been taken out, I placed the vessel back on the stove.

Without all the extra butter, the sooji browned quickly. I sifted in the flour and stirred. Finally, the mixture reached a deep shade of brown.

I put on two large cloth mitts, picked up the saucepan and poured the syrupy sweet liquid into the pot. Steam shot up into the air. I felt moist heat sting my face as the gooey mass sputtered, spit and boiled. I turned off the heat and stirred the mixture. The consistency seemed perfect. Of course, now I had to taste it to make sure it had turned out right.

Just as I was getting a spoon, another devotee barrelled into the kitchen. 'Swamiji wants to know if the halva is done. He asked you to bring him some.'

My stomach clenched and nerve endings buzzed.

'Right now,' Dan barked. 'He's sitting in the breezeway.'

I knew better than to keep Swamiji waiting. I grabbed a metal bowl, ladled an ice-cream-scoop-sized portion into the bowl and carried it into the breezeway, my body shaking and heavy with dread.

Swamiji looked up at me as I walked towards him.

'Is it ready?' he asked. The devotees sitting around him glanced up at me, no doubt wondering what he was talking about.

'I just finished it, Swamiji. I was just going to taste it.'

'I'll taste it.'

I placed the bowl on the edge of his wooden dining table with a trembling hand. Then I sat on the floor a few feet away, struggling to breathe. Swamiji glanced at the halva.

'It looks like it's cooked correctly.'

I relaxed a tiny bit.

He picked it up and took a whiff. 'It smells right.'

I breathed again, but was still nervous. I just needed him to taste it and get it over with. But he set the bowl on the corner of his table and leaned back onto his pillows. I sat stiffly, ramrod straight. I could have dropped through the floor as I waited for his verdict. A few minutes later, Vishi brought his meal on a plastic tray. He started eating his food in his typical ritualistic style. I thought he would never finish.

Finally, he finished and Vishi took his tray away. He turned his attention back to the halva and scooped out a spoonful. Slowly, he put it in his mouth and chewed. He swallowed and looked at me. With his free hand, he gave me a thumbs up and everyone laughed. My whole body slumped in relief. I could not have been happier in that moment. He continued eating until the bowl was empty.

I had made it through this trial by fire – and relatively unscathed.

Barsana Dham in the News

Rolling with the Punches

WHEN I ARRIVED at the ashram in early 1993, there was an undercurrent of hush-hush scuttlebutt about an article that had appeared a few months earlier in the local daily.

It was only by chance that I got to know about the existence of the newspaper article, since Swamiji had strictly forbidden the devotees from talking about it.

'What's it about?' I asked one of my ashram friends.

'We were told not to talk about it. But it was pretty negative,' she said conspiratorially. 'Some former devotees from Philly turned on Swamiji. One of them had some mental problems.'

Naturally, I was curious, so I asked some of the other devotees.

But no one would share any details. They just said 'You don't want to know' or 'They can't hurt Swamiji; they are only hurting themselves' or 'It's a *transgression* to talk about it'.

As luck would have it, my public relations service projects for the ashram provided me with access to the computer room, where all of the media files were stored. One day, while looking for something else in the large, four-drawer filing cabinet, I found the article in the *Austin American-Statesman*. Titled 'Swami's Planned Hindu Temple Is Centre of Speculation', the article cited three former followers who claimed to have had bad experiences with the organization back when it was headquartered in Philadelphia in the 1980s.

There were comments from former devotee Joe Kelly, who started an anti-cult organization after leaving Swamiji: 'My involvement, in some ways, was one of the most devastating experiences of my life. I'm very suspicious of this organization as a benign religious group. I was frightened by what I saw around me, which was people giving up their total will to the system. I consider it very much a cultic group.'

Former devotee Diane H. likened her year with the society to spiritual rape. 'He told me that if I ever left him, I would spend the next 500 lifetimes as an insect,' she said. 'It's funny now, but it wasn't then. I actually had nightmares about that for a while. He had a hold on me.'

The reporter of this story mentioned a woman quoted in a *Miami Herald* article from 6 July 1989. Cassandra T. says that during her two-year experience with the organization, 'it controlled her mind and almost ruined her marriage to a non-member'.

Swamiji was defended in the article by three of his followers, including his main preacher at the time, Sureshwari Devi: 'He's so inspiring. To us, his whole life is dedicated to God. He's very much a fatherly figure in a spiritual sense. He guides us to God. We've never been perceived as a cult by any people I know. We're teaching a very traditional path. Any group has disgruntled former members.'

Swamiji devotee Raj Goel said that the ex-devotees 'misunderstood the guru–disciple relationship, mistaking advice for commands'. He added, 'To run any organization you need money, and this is all pure charity. But Swamiji would never force how much you give and what you give. I give whatever I can afford and what I think needs to be given at the right time.'

In the article, Swamiji's responses seemed evasive. On why he chose to build his ashram in Austin, he said simply: 'Austin chose us.' When asked about his detractors, he was quoted as saying, 'Ridiculous. All ridiculous statements.' He also commented that his critics 'are very prejudiced people'.

Despite the revelations, the only negative impact the article seemed to have on Barsana Dham was lower attendance at the organization's first public event – the ceremony in which we broke ground for the temple – which was held in 1992, just before I arrived. However, the number of visitors increased steadily over the years.

After that article, Barsana Dham worked proactively on its media image. The work paid off when Austin's alternative weekly paper, *The Austin Chronicle*, ran an article on 9 December 1994, with a photo of the temple even making it to the cover. The article, written by Bill Crawford, was positive. The only negative comment was when the reporter stated that the people living in the ashram looked like 'dorks', no doubt referring to the residents' drab, boxy attire.

We revelled in the good publicity and rolled with the one negative comment. After all, one devotee pointed out that 'DORK' stood for: Devotees of Radha–Krishna.

It was easy for us to recast every seemingly negative comment or event into a devotional context, for we believed that people out in the world could never understand the divine work that was going on inside the ashram gates. Our party line was that other people just didn't 'get it'. Meanwhile, we staunchly believed that Swamiji possessed the power to override the effects of any such negative publicity and criticism of detractors.

He successfully convinced his followers that negative reactions were part of the whole package of following a true God-realized saint. As he often said, 'There will always be negative forces at work against the divine ones.'

RV Rides Come

And Go

DAILY LIFE IN the ashram was mostly boring, but Swamiji liked to have fun and, when he was in residence, often created amusing diversions that charmed us.

There were occasional picnics all over Barsana Dham, such as by the river that ran through the property or near a field of bluebonnets in the spring. Occasionally, we'd have impromptu ice-cream-and-potato-chip parties after evening satsang outside the temple to celebrate some small event, such as the completion of some milestone in the temple-building project.

There were larger celebrations, such as for his birthday, with music, dance and drama performances by talented devotees. At my first ashram 'party', I remember thinking, 'Wow, this place has everything, including entertainment, all contained within 200 acres.' It was strange to think of us enjoying our own private corner while the rest of the world carried on as usual outside of our gates.

Several times we even slept outside with Swamiji, Boy Scout style. When he announced we were having a sleep-out, the devotees would spring to action, setting up a bed outside for him, usually on the cement slab we used as a patio, called a mandala, located behind the dining hall. We would lay our sleeping bags, blankets and pillows around his bed, women on one side and men on the other and jockey for positions closest to our guru. He would arrive late and climb onto his plush bed, then begin regaling us with commentary and stories. Someone would bring us freshly popped popcorn and lemonade. Finally, he'd say, 'Okay, time to sleep.'

The sun would not even be up when Swamiji would wake up, climb off the bed and depart for his bedroom. The rest of us would either go back to our rooms or continue sleeping outside until it was time for the satsang.

Of all the fun things we did with Swamiji, there was nothing better than when he purchased an old recreational vehicle (RV) to transform into a chariot for his new idea – the annual parade of the deity of Radha. The plan was to tear off the RV's roof, walls and guts, and build a float-type structure on the chassis. But that came later.

The minute the RV was on the property, Swamiji began taking groups of devotees for joy rides around the property in it. We would all squeeze into every available nook and cranny inside the vehicle, bodies smashed together, and shriek and laugh with delight throughout the ride, which lasted fifteen to twenty minutes.

The rides became a daily adventure and Swamiji always added some new twist. When the inside of the cabin got too crowded, he had the men make more room by ripping out the guts of the cabin, including the built-in table and seats, and the cupboards. Soon, it was just a large, rectangular shell with beat-up, patchy carpet.

When he saw that everyone was falling all over each other as he manoeuvred the vehicle around tight corners at high speeds, he told the men to nail wooden beams across the cabin, so that people would have something to hang on to.

One day he started driving into dead branches, knocking them off trees. The crash and crunch of the wood thrilled everyone. We started scouting for them. When a devotee spotted a dead branch that needed trimming, he or she would yell out, 'Swamiji, there's one to the left (or right).' He would turn on a dime and aim dead centre for the branch, often rocking the entire van on the bumpy ground underneath. We would laugh and scream all the way as we tilted and swayed and hung on for dear life.

One day the ladder on the back of the van was ripped off by a particularly stubborn branch. Someone yelled out that we had lost the RV's ladder. As we looked at the spot, we could see it dangling from a branch, swaying in the breeze. It was a particularly ludicrous and hysterical sight, apropos of the entire unusual adventure.

When he returned to the front of the temple, we would all file out in a stream of humanity. One time we looked up and found dead branches sticking out all over the vehicle, including a large one lodged in the roof's air vent. Another time the windshield cracked from the impact.

That was the end of the RV rides, because it became too dangerous even by Swamiji's standards. Soon the van was retired as a source of amusement and put to its intended purpose. A few devotees stripped it down to the bare metal and built an ornamental structure on top. From then on, we brought the 'chariot' out of storage once a year and decorated it with flowers and fabric for the annual 'chariot procession'.

For this event, the former RV was driven around the property in a more dignified fashion – a single entity in a one-float parade – with devotees chanting and dancing around it.

Waiting for Grace

Hope Springs Eternal

WE WERE ALL waiting to be graced by Swamiji. It was the carrot at the end of the stick that kept us all going in an otherwise brutal environment. Every devotee yearned to receive the grace required to enter the divine world for eternity.

Our belief that we would soon receive Swamiji's grace gave most of us the strength to endure any and all challenges we encountered on the path. But along the way, some gave up the ghost and left the ashram, usually disappearing, belongings and all, in the middle of the night, never to be seen again. Eventually, even three of Prakash's ordained preachers disappeared, every one of them with little or no explanation.

The 'true believers' stayed, accepting that Swamiji was gracing us in innumerable little ways all the time. When he talked to us, touched us, fed us his leftovers, gave us instructions or made us laugh – all of these were flashes of grace. However, these fleeting blessings were only a temporary high, like a shot of whiskey or a hit of cocaine. But the feeling would fade all too quickly.

I might have felt terribly guilty about my lack of sustained happiness from Swamiji's ongoing benevolent gestures if it wasn't so obvious that no one else was retaining that loving feeling either. Even people who seemed to be showered with his attention on a regular basis, ultimately appeared to be as bereft of grace as the rest of us.

Yet, most of us persevered, living in hope.

It wasn't for lack of trying on the guru's part – at least not according to him. Swamiji told us over and over: 'The guru is always gracing. Receiving grace is your own effort. You only need a pure heart to scoop it up. The purer your devotional heart, the more grace you can receive.'

He often used the analogy of going to a river to collect water. If you took a teacup along, that's the amount of water you could collect, but if you took a barrel, you could collect much more. 'Your devotional heart is the vessel. However pure it is, is how much grace you can receive.'

He told us that a receptive heart that could hold an unlimited amount of grace was one that had surrendered completely to the guru. So naturally, if the grace didn't seem to stick, it was our own fault.

Under Swamiji's tutelage, I lived in the belief that my devotional heart was a sun-baked stone – incapable of retaining even the smallest drops of his grace.

Guru Bonding

Fear and Longing

UNLIKE MANY OF the other devotees, I rarely had a problem understanding Swamiji's English, despite his moderate Indian accent – something that I took as a badge of honour. I also had an unusual ability to remember things he said nearly verbatim.

I was always surprised by how many devotees misunderstood him when he gave us some bit of wisdom, instruction or scolding. I became known for my unique skill and some devotees regularly relied on me for clarification on what Swamiji had said, especially if there was more than one version making the rounds.

While my special gift garnered me some small level of notoriety, by no means did it get me any closer to Swamiji. That was the primary desire of all devotees: to have something, *anything*, that gave them a reason to talk to him, personally serve him, or get them the ultimate prize – spend time with him in his bedroom, his inner sanctum. The people who spent time close to the guru were the envy of the ashram.

Swamiji's favourite devotees, besides the preachers, included a small group of people who ran businesses that supported him and his organization – wealthy and generous devotees, and followers who had special skills such as construction and sewing.

During my fifteen years in the ashram, my one-on-one interactions with him were like crumbs: I would hungrily gobble up each one and eagerly wait for the next morsel. Few and far between, these little nuggets never satisfied fully. Nonetheless, I savoured my moments with him.

One day Prabhakari asked me to edit Swamiji's next book, an encyclopaedia, as he called it, of India's history and the history of Hinduism.

I took the task to heart since she had told me that Swamiji had asked for me to do it. For the next week and a half, I spent several hours each day on his 'opus', ignoring my own work responsibilities. Then Prabhakari called me to Swamiji's bedroom to discuss my edits.

I felt the usual mix of excitement and fear to be entering his private chambers, like Dorothy entering the room of the great and powerful Oz. I trembled as I kneeled down on the floor next to him and bowed.

He took one look at me and said, 'Oh, her? I thought it was the other Karen.'

My heart sank. He didn't want me, after all.

However, he reviewed my edits anyway as I sat there feeling dejected. Once he was finished, I was summarily dismissed with a nod.

Another brief interaction occurred out of the blue when I was alone in the kitchen one day. Swamiji padded in as I stirred a pot of soup. He wandered around looking at everything. All the drawers and cupboards had labels, and he was reading some of them aloud. He stopped at one drawer with a quizzical look. 'Micro dishes?'

'Those are dishes for the microwave, Swamiji,' I said, thrilled to have a reason to speak to him.

'Oh, I thought they were just really small dishes.'

We both laughed. Then he walked out of the kitchen, leaving me to revel in my good fortune to have spent a few precious moments of quality alone time with my guru.

Once I was passing through his sitting room on the way to the prasad room. There were only a few people sitting around him. This was always considered the greatest of times for devotees, to have him virtually to oneself without the usual crowd. I sat close to his feet, on his right. Someone brought him a peppery snack. He ate a couple of pieces, then glanced at me. He handed me a piece. I put it in my mouth. It was bitter and unpleasant. I coughed and struggled to swallow the food, knowing it was his offering to me.

'Do you like it?' he asked.

'It's a little bitter,' I admitted.

He laughed. Everyone giggled. Someone had left a box of high-quality chocolates on his seat. He opened the box and picked out a piece. 'Here, eat this,' he said, holding it to my mouth.

I opened my mouth and he put it on my tongue. It immediately melted into a puddle of succulent cocoa, drowning out the bitter flavour. 'Is that better?'

I smiled. 'Yes, Swamiji.'

'Good. Here, have another one.' He held another piece of the chocolate up to my mouth, followed by another and another. 'Is that enough? Is the bad taste gone?'

I laughed. 'Yes, thank you, Swamiji. It's much better now.'

'Great!' he exclaimed. Then he got up and walked out of the room. I felt like I was floating a few inches off the ground.

The other devotees glanced at me with envy – a look I was usually giving, not getting.

Misadventures in Photography

A Lesson in Humility

SWAMIJI'S FREQUENT ADVICE to his devotees was to be humble, a quality essential to reach God, according to him. I received a major lesson in humility when he asked me to learn photography shortly after I moved to the ashram.

Swamiji liked all events and celebrations to be documented on film and video. One morning in the prayer hall, he looked around the room and said, 'Who is good at photography?' Devotees began naming themselves or others. I sat quietly.

Swamiji listened to some of the names called out, then looked right at me: 'What about you?'

'I used to take photos for my college newspaper,' I replied nervously.

'Great,' he said. 'Study photography for the ashram.'

Those five simple words kicked off a stressful three months during which I tried to become the best photographer possible. However, bad karma or just bad luck worked against me.

It didn't help that many of the other devotees were jealous. Suddenly, everyone was a photographer, racing around with cameras, taking photos of Barsana Dham for Swamiji, hoping he would tell them instead of me to study photography. But for every package of prints brought to him, Swamiji would barely like one in the whole pack.

Greg, a resident devotee who ran Swamiji's infomercial business, came up to me one day and bludgeoned me with 'You know that Swamiji himself is the divine photographer, don't you?'

As if I needed more pressure.

My own role as photographer-in-training went from bad to worse, despite the fact that I actually had a good eye. I had taken dozens of photos for my college newspaper and for magazine articles I'd written after college and had a style that was both artistic and photojournalistic. But somehow my natural ability wilted under Swamiji's harsh scrutiny. He was hypercritical of everything – especially of his own images.

Prabhakari made a point to tell me, 'Swamiji is very picky. He doesn't like anyone's photos,' and added that he didn't even like the photos taken by a devotee who was a professional artist and photographer.

Then there was plain old bad luck. Once, the film got stuck in the camera and I missed every shot at a celebration. Another time, I accidentally opened the camera before rewinding the film.

The final blow to my future as a photographer came one afternoon when Vishi called me to take photos of him. Rushing to get ready, I changed into an acceptable outfit: a long skirt, frumpy blouse and a shawl. I was shaking as I hurriedly threaded the film through the camera – it would not be good to keep Swamiji waiting.

I ran to his bedroom door, then waited outside for ten nerve-shredding minutes. Finally, he walked out of his room. Vishi and I followed him wordlessly down the stairs. She was carrying his saffron shawl and a fresh flower garland. I was sweating as I sat on the back seat of his golf cart. He turned it on and hit the gas. I jerked forward and grabbed the railing, gripping it tightly for the entire bumpy two-minute drive to a field by the creek on the south side of the ashram. It was not an enjoyable ride on Swamiji's mythical golf cart.

Swamiji jumped off the cart and Vishi hurried after him. She handed him the shawl, which he whirled around his shoulders, then tucked one corner into the left side of his dhoti. She then lifted the flower garland to place around his neck. He leaned in slightly to accept the decoration. She adjusted it and fluffed his short, white, wavy hair.

As I watched him prepare for the shoot, I wanted to flee. I could barely see straight. Suddenly, he walked over to a tree and began posing. I lifted the camera and clicked. He held each position for only a few seconds. His movements were so quick that I kept capturing him in mid-pose.

'What's wrong?' he snapped after I'd taken a dozen poorly timed photos.

'I'm not used to this, Swamiji,' was all I could manage to say.

He said nothing, but looked displeased. He jumped into the cart and we climbed on after him. He hit the gas and drove to another location further down the river. Again he got out and began posing beside some flowering bushes. I looked through the camera's lens, praying that I would capture his image to his satisfaction. But my timing was still completely out of sync.

Finally, he jumped on the cart for the last time and raced back to the building. When we returned, he took the camera from me and disappeared up the stairs to his bedroom, Vishi scurrying after him.

I was stunned, unable to think. That night, I heard that Swamiji had sent another devotee into town to develop the film. When he got the photos, he flipped through the stack like a blackjack dealer in Vegas, glancing at each one for a nanosecond. When he was finished, he put the photos back in their paper packet and dropped the whole thing onto his couch with a thud.

Later, Vishi came up to me and handed me five photos. 'Swamiji wants you to have these.'

I cringed as I looked at them, each one worse than the last.

I had never seen him look so bad.

And that was the end of my brief, humiliating stint as photographer-in-training for Swamiji.

Escape Plans

Nowhere to Run

I HAD THOUGHT of leaving Barsana Dham many times.

Whenever problems became overwhelming, I would crave escape – a break from conflicts with devotees, exhausting service demands, the boring devotional schedule, and Swamiji's never-ending tendency to shower his attention on only a chosen few. These issues and my general lack of feeling any spiritual evolution often made me depressed, tired, sad and ready to run away.

At these times, I would daydream about escaping. I often envisioned myself packing up my few worldly possessions and driving out of there forever. In every daydream, I returned to someone or someplace from my past and successfully re-entered the real world, happier than I was before. But every daydream ended with the same fact: I had nowhere to go – no parents, no grandparents, no old friends, nobody.

My grandmother had been the only person who had ever unconditionally loved me, and I had relied on her love and support until she died when I was twenty-seven and she was eighty-four. In one of my elaborate schemes, she was still alive and living in an idyllic small town, north of my birthplace of Missoula, Montana, and I could move in with her into some darling small house with a flower-filled yard, living a life of gardening, taking long walks in the countryside, cosily reading books by the fireplace and dating local eligible bachelors.

In another one of my recurring daydreams, I returned to Olean, New York, my mom's hometown. Although Olean was a small, mostly blue-collar town and long past its prime, it was the only place where I had ever had any level of consistency in my life. We always stayed in my mother's childhood home on Seventh Street, which was an early-century two-storey duplex with an old-fashioned stone basement, a large cobweb-filled attic and a high-pitched roof. Even though I had lived there for only three years of my life, it was the one place where I felt truly at 'home'. In my Barsana Dham escape fantasy, I would return to my mother's home and remodel it into the ultimate bachelorette pad, complete with a supercool large attic hideaway.

In another fantasy, I returned to Seattle and was able to afford a hip condo on the top of Queen Anne Hill overlooking the city and Puget Sound. In my mind's eye, my home was on the second or third floor of an old school that had been converted into residences. The rooms were large and spacious, with large, multi-paned windows along one wall. There was a deck that provided me with plenty of space for a potted garden of flowers and herbs. One corner of my living room was my office, where I spent my days writing and looking out over the Puget Sound. I had two cuddly kitties and a boyfriend in the navy, who came home on the weekends.

I did leave Barsana Dham once, about two years after I moved in, but only for a long weekend. I wanted to get away and think about my life inside the claustrophobic devotional pressure cooker. On a Friday afternoon, I drove to a bed-and-breakfast in San Marcos, about forty-five minutes south of Austin, but a world away from the ashram. I revelled in being away from the group living environment and having a bedroom and bathroom all to myself.

On Sunday, after breakfast, I sat on a lounge chair in the establishment's backyard garden with a pad of paper and a pen and wrote down the pros and cons of staying or leaving the ashram. I was leaning strongly towards leaving when I wrote down one reason to stay: I wanted God more than anything else in the world.

I sat back in the sunshine and considered my dilemma. Should I escape the miserable life I was living in the ashram or grit my teeth and keep going on my quest to find God in this lifetime? I decided to stay on the path. I made up my mind that if it meant that I could achieve my primary goal in life, God realization, it would all be worth it in the end.

I drove back to the ashram, knowing I was going to dig in my heels and work harder than ever to be the best devotee I could possibly be.

Surrendering to the Guru

Mission Impossible?

ONE CONSTANT THEME of life under Swamiji's tutelage was total surrender to the guru.

He told us repeatedly that God's grace is easily attainable through selfless love and faithful surrender to a real saint and that we could not expect to enter the divine world until we had completely surrendered to him. In *The Science of Devotion and Grace*, Swamiji wrote that a person surrenders for his own good, for the saint remains unmoved by the followers surrendering to or abandoning him/her. It is part of his/her 'graciousness' and 'endless mercy' that the saint takes on a follower.

The concept of surrendering is a foreign one to most westerners. After all, we live in the land of the free, established by fiercely independent pioneers. I struggled daily with it myself. Despite Swamiji's explicit teachings on the subject, I could not grasp the concept. Did it mean that I would never have an independent thought again? Or that I had to give the guru every penny and survive just on my faith in him alone? Did it mean that I should lose all concern for my physical body, like a wandering yogi in India?

The best example of total surrender I could think of was from the

Bible. Luke 1:26–38 recounts the story of Mary, mother of Jesus, and how she said *yes* to an illogical request from the angel Gabriel with barely a moment's hesitation:

> In the sixth month, God sent the angel Gabriel to Nazareth, a town in Galilee, to a virgin pledged to be married to a man named Joseph, a descendant of David. The virgin's name was Mary. The angel went to her and said, 'Greetings, you who are highly favoured! The Lord is with you.
>
> Mary was greatly troubled at his words and wondered what kind of greeting this might be. But the angel said to her, 'Do not be afraid, Mary, you have found favour with God. You will be with child and give birth to a son, and you are to give him the name Jesus. He will be great and will be called the Son of the Most High. The Lord God will give him the throne of his father David, and he will reign over the house of Jacob forever; his kingdom will never end.
>
> 'How will this be,' Mary asked the angel, 'since I am a virgin?'
>
> The angel answered, 'The Holy Spirit will come upon you, and the power of the Most High will overshadow you. So the holy one to be born will be called the Son of God. Even Elizabeth your relative is going to have a child in her old age, and she who was said to be barren is in her sixth month. For nothing is impossible with God.'
>
> 'I am the Lord's servant,' Mary answered. 'May it be to me as you have said.' Then the angel left her.

Although I'm not a Christian, ironically, I held this story as an ideal of surrender while following my Hindu guru's teachings.

Uncomfortable Grace

The Women-Only Ritual

WHILE ALL OF Swamiji's devotees waited for him to grace them in multiple ways, behind closed doors he regularly imparted a secret 'grace'.

However, this blessing was bestowed only upon a select few. It was the grace of intimate touch. The first time I experienced this, it took me by surprise.

Before I moved into the ashram, I had entered his bedroom one evening after satsang to say goodbye after visiting the ashram for several days. Two of his women in orange were there with him when I walked in. He looked up from his bed where he was writing on a notepad, and growled a few words in Hindi. The two women bolted upright and scurried out of the room, shutting the door behind them.

I knelt down on the floor near him and bowed.

'I came to say goodbye, Swamiji,' I said.

He set his writing down beside him, reached out a hand and took mine in his. He held it without saying anything for a few moments, like a boyfriend. I was shaking a bit at finding myself all alone with the man I believed to be God. I had no idea what to do. I stared at him, hoping for a sign.

'Where are you going?' he said slowly, as if he were sleepy.

'Back home.'

'Okay,' he said softly.

Then he pulled me towards him and put his large arms around me. My face was buried in the orange cashmere sweater he often wore. The combination of the soft fabric and his wide, firm chest made me feel safe and comfortable. I wanted to stay in that embrace for a long time. But then he pulled away a little and with no warning, leaned in and began kissing me on the mouth, using his tongue. I was shocked – and repulsed. He tasted like sour grass. Then I felt a sharp pinch on my nipple. He had reached down and, through the fabric of my sari and blouse, pinched one of my nipples very hard. In fact, it was so hard that I reflexively said 'ouch' and pulled away abruptly.

I sat on my knees, looking at him in a daze. He gave me a casual look, tilted his head slightly and said, 'Okay, goodnight.' Then he leaned back on his pillows and went back to his writing.

Still stunned, but obviously dismissed, I said goodnight, bowed and fled the room.

My mind was reeling. I couldn't even think about what had just happened. I figured I had just been graced in some classified, special way, but didn't feel anything at all, except for a bit of disgust. But I forced myself not to think about it. I just returned to my room and packed for my journey home.

As it turned out, that was just the first of Swamiji's French kisses and nipple pinches I received over the next few years.

What's more, over my years in the ashram, snippets of comments from some of the other women clued me in to the fact that many of them had experienced their own moments of 'intimate grace' from Swamiji. Most of them seemed not only comfortable with it, but craved it. One woman in particular could not get enough of his sloppy kisses and body pinches. She would run out of satsang every morning in order to encounter him in the hallway of his sitting room. One time I walked in on them in an embrace. After that, I made sure to wait until they walked out of the hallway, usually hand in hand like lovers.

Another woman bragged to me about her 'private time' with Swamiji. She mentioned that she would lie beside him on his bed and cuddle with him. I didn't ask for any details, because I wanted to pretend that she hadn't told me that.

Once in Los Angeles, another female devotee and I went to his bedroom to say goodbye after a short trip over the holidays. She was clearly familiar with the intimacy and welcomed it. I was surprised by her exuberance and familiarity with him. She dived into his arms and he fell back on the bed. She was lying on top of his chest with her hips between his spread legs and French-kissing him, while making small moaning and smacking noises. When it was my turn, I just gave him a quick kiss and hug and was ready to leave.

I was simply unable to process these experiences and the short stories I heard, because I couldn't fit them into the image I had formed of this God–saint. I wanted him to be what I thought he was: divine, pure and above worldly cravings. In order to keep my dream alive, I buried these unsettling experiences in the dark recesses of my mind and did my best to forget all about them.

On the rare occasions when I thought about it at all, I assumed that there must have been something missing in me – some level of devotional capacity that I was lacking. Something was preventing me from appreciating the very special grace that Swamiji could impart only through his divine touch.

But no matter how much I told myself that the problem was within me, the 'special' encounters were always, to me, an unwelcome and unsolicited 'uncomfortable grace'.

Mad with Desire

Life without Sex

AT TIMES I thought I would go mad without sex.

Of all the rules Swamiji laid down, the most difficult one for me was celibacy. He taught us that abstinence was necessary to eliminate the distraction of the opposite sex and to help our devotional minds grow pure faster. But not having sex can make you think of it all of the time, which seems counterproductive. Especially considering that

I was in my thirties and forties – typically the most sexually charged years of a woman's life.

I was chronically tormented by desire. I concocted elaborate mental fantasies wherein I had part-time boyfriends and would sneak out on a regular basis to indulge my carnal needs. More than once, I seriously considered actually paying a man to satisfy me. However, the logistics of the situation would have been a nightmare, since I was locked inside the ashram from 11:00 p.m. until 6:00 a.m. every night. Plus, my days were bookended by morning and evening satsang. On top of that, I had my daily service and work responsibilities. No matter how I plotted out a possible plan for sex, it seemed that in every direction, I ran into an impenetrable roadblock.

One time, I worked for a man with whom I had an obvious physical attraction. I thought for sure if the opportunity ever presented itself, I would have sex with him right in his office, on his desk. He might have also had this on his mind when he asked me to meet him in his office one Saturday afternoon to work on a project. If it had been any other Saturday, I believe I would have gone. But on that particular Saturday, Barsana Dham was celebrating its annual Rath Yatra celebration; the parikrama of Radha in her chariot.

Since he didn't know about my life in the ashram, I gave Eric some lame excuse about why I could not meet him. I could tell he knew I was lying. He never asked me to meet him outside of normal work hours again, and I didn't have the nerve to be aggressive and bring up the idea. I had no choice but to take it as a sign that my purity was being preserved for God.

I met few potential lovers out in the world. After all, the only activities I engaged in outside the ashram gates were business meetings. Bars, social events and other multi-sex venues were out of the question for me.

And it's not like there were any desirable options inside the ashram, although a few of the men did come on to me over the years. But I had no interest in any of them. Perhaps the sight of grown men grovelling in front of another man put me off. I regarded the male devotees as either surrogate brothers, sycophantic guru worshippers or simply annoying people to be avoided.

My sexual desires were my own private matter, separate from my life in the ashram. I suffered in silence, never admitting my yearnings to anyone. It was a piece of me that I knew was alive and would not die, no matter how many hours I spent in satsang, no matter how much service I did while trying to think of Radha–Krishna, and no matter how many nights I slept alone in my twin bed in my small bedroom in a house filled with other single, sexless women.

Whenever I craved for a man's touch, I would talk myself out of it by reminding myself of the downside of sex: it was messy. Men could love you and leave you. I could catch a venereal disease.

Since everything worked against me, I kept my lust at a slow simmer in the back burner of my brain.

Thankfully, the ferocity of my lust finally waned and I entered a period of hormonal respite. I went into menopause in my early forties, about ten years sooner than most women. One side effect was that my yearnings abated and my fantasies retreated. It was a huge relief. I knew that much of my new calm was chemically induced, but I welcomed it as if it were a gift from God for all my years of heated torture.

Meanwhile, I knew that not every devotee in the ashram followed the celibacy rule to a tee. There were a few randy folks who skipped satsang and went out carousing. And then there were a few who actually had sex in the ashram.

To me, this was yet more proof of the impossible austere lifestyle we were expected to live to reach God.

Giving

How Much Is Enough?

SWAMIJI DID NOT hound his devotees for money through the 1990s, because he didn't have to. Several of his devotees owned businesses that were minting money in the infomercial trade. Some of these people had a considerable amount of luck and a shocking lack of morals. The net result was that Swamiji had a steady flow of serious money to spend on whatever he wanted, which at that time was creating Barsana Dham and building the 40,000-foot temple.

He spared no expense for the multimillion-dollar structure and surrounding features, which included a specially made 'sky' ceiling, a lotus-shaped pond with fountains and waterfalls (all inspired by trips to Vegas), and an elaborate 90-foot pink-and-grey temple steeple (which I later found was a near-exact replica of another Indian guru's building).

There was another reason that devotees living in the ashram were not really pressured to give money: Swamiji needed a workforce. In this area, we were expected to give until it hurt. He pushed us physically rather than monetarily. It took an incredible amount of effort to keep the ashram running. A minimum of seventy adults were needed to execute all the work – and still everything did not always get done.

But I moderated my volunteer labour, primarily because I needed energy to do my paid work, but also because I never saw any of the preachers work themselves to exhaustion. In fact, they were overall a pretty pampered and lazy bunch. I figured that if they were allowed to rest, then I should too. I learnt to say 'no' and draw clear limits for my time spent doing physical labour, which annoyed many people.

The largest sum I gave to the ashram in the early years was my monthly 'support payment', which was theoretically for rent and food.

They just didn't use the word 'rent' for tax purposes. This started out at about $450 in the early 1990s and had risen to $850 by 2008.

I also paid rent for my office space. First I rented space in the ashram warehouse, then I bought my own portable building. Though I purchased and remodelled my own building, which sat on a secluded spot in the woods on the ashram grounds, I paid rent for use of the land.

In addition to monetary support payments, devotees were asked to make annual pledges to help build ashrams in India. I usually gave $2,000 a year. However, a couple of years when my freelance writing business was slow and I couldn't make a pledge, I was never harangued about it.

The annual three-week-long intensive programme in the fall was another expense. Visitors paid $80 per day and residents $25. On Swamiji's birthday or for special events, many of us would write him a cheque or give him cash. Typically, I would give a couple of hundred-dollar bills.

Some people living in the ashram gave a lot more money than I did, a few virtually all their money.

But I made it a point to build up a savings account for myself. Despite being encouraged to 'surrender', my instincts told me to take care of myself financially. If I had been pressurized to pay, it would have easily been the straw that broke the camel's back.

However, once Swamiji's mysterious guru entered our lives in Barsana Dham, all low-ball money collection activities were history. Money collection went into high gear.

Epic Blast

The Guru's Wrath

NO ONE WHO was there ever forgot the day I was blasted by Swamiji.

'Blast' was the word devotees used when Swamiji scolded them. 'I got blasted today,' they would say. According to Webster's, one definition of blast is 'a violent gust of wind and an explosion or violent detonation'. It perfectly describes his infamous yelling, accusing and threatening tirades.

We were taught that even being yelled at or scolded by the guru imparted grace. But no one ever seemed very graced after a Swamiji blast. It was more often like a shell-shocked stupor. That was definitely my experience.

I didn't realize how truly epic my blast was until much later, when people brought it up to me on different occasions. One evening, after dinner, almost a year after the day in question, a visiting devotee said: 'So you still decided to stay here?'

'What?' I was taken aback by her question.

'I wondered what you would do after you got yelled at last year.'

It took me a minute to figure out what she was talking about. When I realized what she was referring to, I was surprised that she was even there on that day, let alone remembered the event. At the time, I had been so absorbed in my humiliation that I had completely forgotten the other people in the room.

'You remember that?' I asked.

'Of course. How could I forget it? It made a great impression on me. I decided that day that I would never move to the ashram. I was terrified by his outburst.'

I was stunned. 'What do you mean?'

'He screamed at you and told you to leave the ashram if you didn't like it. Everyone was talking about it afterwards.'

'Wow. It never occurred to me that people would remember that. I was pretty out of it that day.'

'You seemed quite defiant.'

'What do you mean?'

'You were sitting up straight and it looked like you were standing up to him, holding your ground.'

'Really? I don't remember it that way at all.'

Of course I remembered being screamed at. But I had not felt defiant. I had been devastated. I saw myself as slumped over, trying to withstand Swamiji's verbal pummelling.

It all started with a simple basketball hoop.

Some of the men and boys in the ashram liked to play basketball. But when I saw them putting up a hoop right outside my window, I lost it. The ashram was already noisy enough, and my bedroom was my only sanctuary. The hoop wasn't even up yet, but I could already hear the endless thudding of the ball outside my window. In desperation, I called Sureshwari, hoping she'd understand my problem.

'Don't be selfish, Karen,' she scolded when I asked if she could request the men to move the hoop somewhere else.

I didn't think the request was selfish. After all, wasn't this a spiritual community designed to promote meditation? How was the sound of a basketball dribbling like a broken metronome supposed to be conducive to God realization?

After satsang that evening, I told Vishi that I wanted to speak to Swamiji.

'What about?' she asked suspiciously.

Anger and frustration overwhelmed me. I broke down into a hysterical crying fit as I explained the situation.

'I'll go ask him,' she said, obviously wanting to get away from me. Ten minutes later, she returned and told me sheepishly, 'He said to ask him tomorrow morning at breakfast.'

I was crushed. I knew it wasn't a good sign that he didn't want to see me right away. He probably wanted to get the story from Sureshwari first. I slept poorly, contemplating the best way to tell Swamiji my problem and trying to guess the outcome. I dreamed about driving the backhoe and knocking down that stupid basketball hoop myself.

The next morning, satsang ticked by at a torturously slow pace. Afterwards, I couldn't eat. I went behind the temple and sat staring at Barsana Hill, wondering how I had arrived at this new agonizing place in my already difficult spiritual journey. Why did I have to suffer? Tears rolled down my face. I cried ferociously, all alone.

Finally, it was time for Swamiji's morning meal. I was the first person in the sitting room, and sat down in the space right next to his couch. I sat there morosely, slumped in unhappy anticipation and isolated misery. I could sense devotees arriving and sitting down around me, but I could not look at anyone.

He finally appeared, but said nothing. Vishi brought him his meal on his serving tray. He ate slowly and silently. When he was finished, he leaned back on his pillows and looked at me.

'You want to ask me something?'

I opened my mouth to speak, but the words caught in my throat. Now that it was time to speak, I was terrified.

'Tell me!' he commanded angrily.

I tried again. I could barely whisper. 'Swamiji, they have installed a basketball hoop near my bedroom.'

'So?' he growled. It was obvious he already knew what I was going to ask him.

'It's very loud and disturbing.'

'What do you want me to do about it?' Each time he spoke, his rage and volume escalated.

'Can they move it somewhere else?' I asked.

Swamiji went ballistic.

'What do you want? What would make you happy? Do you want to live all alone in the jungle? Do you think you'll be happy *there*? This is an ashram. You have to learn to live with other people.'

He went on and on for what seemed like an hour. Each comment was delivered with more venom than the last, and not a shred of compassion or concern or love softened the impact of his verbal punches.

I was shocked, but angry too. All I could think of was that I was being forced into an even worse living situation than I had already endured for the past few years. Finally, his rage abated and he switched from attacking me directly.

'No one appreciates what I've created here. If you don't like it here, leave.' He paused again. 'Barsana Dham isn't a prison. You are free to go. Go and see how happy you are in the world.' Then he added, 'I'm not saying this only to you. I mean everyone.'

He was silent for a couple of minutes. I could sense the anxiety of some of the other devotees. A couple of people were sobbing softly.

Then Swamiji glared at me again and delivered the final blow. 'Don't expect anyone to adjust to you. Adjust yourself!' With that, he stood up and left the room in a huff.

I rose from my sphinx position and left the room. I felt like a zombie as I prepared for a work luncheon with a group of writers. I was in a painful fog the entire time, and it was almost impossible to act normal in front of the other writers.

One of Swamiji's comments kept rattling around in my brain: 'If you don't like the ashram, then leave.'

After my business meeting, I drove around downtown Austin for three hours looking at apartments. I was hoping that something would magically jump out at me so I could instantly break out of my ashram prison cell. Despite what Swamiji had said, it did feel like a prison to me – with a particularly sadistic warden.

I was still depressed when I returned to the ashram, and my mood only blackened further when I heard the thump-thump-thump of the basketball on the pavement.

I sat in my room in paralytic misery, wondering what I should do. Then I remembered my new office space down at the warehouse, which was on the far north-eastern corner of the ashram property. I got into my car and drove the short distance to the building. I suddenly had a whole new appreciation for the tiny, dingy office.

I had been renting the space for about two months from the warehouse manager, a fellow devotee. Ironically, Sureshwari had arranged the relationship after I told her that I was working out of my bedroom. I had asked if there was any office space I could rent on the property. I had been hoping for a room in the brand new two-storey office building, which housed the growing media-buying company run by some of the devotees. There was a small apartment with two bedrooms on the second floor and I hoped that I could have one. Instead, she offered me space in the dingy old warehouse.

I hated the room. For starters, the warehouse was dark, dirty and full of cast-off junk. Every floor and wall was scuffed and stained. Wires and cobwebs hung from every corner and beam. The colour of the walls was unidentifiable under thick layers of dust and grime.

One wall of my office abutted the warehouse – a clanking, crashing, echoing cave of a room where they stored and shipped out the various products sold through the infomercials produced by a team of devotees. The room was filled with pallet after pallet of Ab Flex machines, miracle blades, blenders, supplements and other odds and ends sold through late-night thirty-second and half-hour commercial pitches.

My office was shaped like an L and was barely 150 square feet. It had a small clothes closet with wooden slat doors and a tiny window that looked out on a grassy patch next to the building. It also had one upholstered chair with wooden arms, a small bookcase and an end table, all recycled and shabby.

But at that moment, all I cared about was the noise – or rather, the lack of it. The muted hum of the activity in the warehouse didn't seem so bad compared to the hard smack of a basketball on pavement a few yards from my head.

As I sat in my tiny, forlorn office, I contemplated another one of Swamiji's comments during my epic blast: 'Adjust yourself.'

I looked around the room again, seeing it with new eyes. It was actually not as beat up as the rest of the building. The walls were clean and the carpet was in excellent condition. It was an appealing shade of dark mauve. Even the window had a pretty view of the sky from a certain angle. It was as if the room had been hermetically sealed off from the rest of the filthy, depressing wreck of a building.

I decided in that moment that I would adjust myself by fixing up my little office to be the sanctuary I needed.

I made a list. I would paint the walls, get a new corner desk, get a mini couch and cute pillows, hang pictures, get vases and dried flowers, hang curtains and buy a TV. I left the warehouse buoyant with new plans and a new outlook.

In less than a month, I had transformed my office into my version of Jeannie's bottle. It soon became my home away from home. I started spending more time there than in my bedroom. Even at night, after satsang I would drive down to the warehouse to spend a couple of hours reading and watching TV.

My little new world became a separation from ashram life that I grew to cherish.

More Bad Press

Royally Skewered

THE FIRST BAD press for Swamiji in 1992 was not the last.

In October 1995, three years after the unflattering article in the *Austin American-Statesman*, a new article was published in *Texas Monthly* magazine under the headline 'Swami Dearest'. The in-depth exposé uncovered much more of Swamiji's activities. It made public the amount of money donated to and earned by the ashram, the organization's damaging alterations to a once-historic Texas building, and the controversies involving Barsana Dham's handling of family grave sites on the property. It also contained many revelations about Swamiji's business practices and raised questions about the clandestine purchase of 200 acres of what had been part of the historic Friday Mountain Camp.

> Deed records show that the purchase was made on May 25 (1990) … Records also show that on the same day, in a separate transaction, (Dennis) Wagner optioned the land to the ISDL. Asked why he flipped the land so quickly, Wagner responds, 'I really can't remember that far back how the transaction all happened,' but he maintains that the ISDL's involvement was never covered up.

This was researched and reported by Jeannie Ralston, a freelance reporter hired by the magazine to write about the organization that had taken over land that had been home to the Friday Mountain Camp, a boys' summer camp which operated from 1947 through the 1970s.

I had been behind the scenes while the reporter was researching the article, because I worked for Jan and Dennis Wagner at the time. I knew that there was a lot of hubbub going on, with Barsana Dham trying to control who Jeannie had access to. Swamiji and his preachers handpicked several devotees for her to interview. But she was a seasoned reporter and clearly did not rely solely on the ashram for her sources.

Despite his efforts to control the story, Swamiji was his own worst enemy. He shot himself in the foot right from the start during a brief interview with her. Jeannie led off her story with an account of her attempt to interview the guru:

> He was agitated. His fingers twitched. His deep brown eyes seemed to grow even more impenetrable. Fifteen minutes into our interview, Swami Prakashanand Saraswati made it clear he did not like the questions I was asking about his writings and the spiritual philosophy that governs Barsana Dham, his ashram west of Austin. The 66-year-old leader of the International Society of Divine Love (ISDL) reached toward my tape recorder

> to turn it off. 'These questions are useless. I cannot explain. These are intellectual questions,' he said, shaking his head. His words came out in a breathy mumble, accentuated by the lilting accent of his native India. 'It takes years and years of study to understand these things.'
>
> Signalling an abrupt end to our interview, Swami Prakashanand, called Swamiji by his two thousand or more followers worldwide[1], slowly lifted his body – clothed in saffron robes, a saffron sweater, and saffron tube socks – from a chair shaped like a satellite dish. Then he walked toward the door of the room, past beatific photos of himself and paintings of the Hindu god Krishna. After telling me he did not want an article written about him, the small man with a bump of a stomach, flowing white hair, and a full beard paused and suddenly smacked the palm of his hand to his forehead, as if he had forgotten something important. He swooned slightly and collapsed in a controlled fall to the carpet, landing with his head near my feet. 'Krishn, Krishn,' he called out as he lay on the floor. Two female 'preachers', Western devotees who also wore saffron robes, rushed to his side. As they frantically administered to him, I was asked to wait downstairs.
>
> When I was called back upstairs a few minutes later, I found a groggy Prakashanand sitting in a rocking chair and was directed to join the two preachers kneeling at his feet. He told me with a sigh that his 'divine mood' had been 'upset unnecessarily'. Later, he explained what had happened in a written statement: 'I felt the situation was very negative so I turned my mind away from that side, and it, thus, went into total ecstasy. Because I was standing at the time, so, I think, my body fell on the ground.'

I would remember this article years later and be grateful that it existed.

---

1 This number was probably provided by Barsana Dham, but it is not accurate. At the most, he had maybe two or three hundred devotees.

PART THREE

In the Dark

Curiouser and Curiouser

'Acquire the transcendental knowledge from a self-realized
Master by humble reverence, by sincere inquiry, and by service.
The empowered ones, who have realized the truth, will teach you.'
– Bhagavadgita, 4:34

'You promise them heaven, they'll follow you to hell.'
– Harvey Washington, 'Imprisoned Pimp', *Newsweek*

Where Is Swamiji's Guru?

The Ten-Year Code of Silence

IN HINDU TRADITION, gurus have gurus – but Swamiji never talked about his guru throughout the entire decade of the 1990s.

In 1992 a visiting devotee mentioned another guru to me. I wasn't interested because I was hooked on Swamiji, but when I moved into the ashram I became more curious. I would hear snippets of conversations that made me wonder who this other mysterious guru was. Even more than that, I wondered why Swamiji didn't talk about him.

I later learnt that the people who knew about his guru, like the preachers and some long-time devotees, had been sworn to silence. It was like some fraternity initiation secret. It was all so hush-hush that Swamiji had even taken his book, *The Science of Devotion and Grace*, off the market in the 1990s. When I asked for a copy, I was told that none were available. But when I mentioned my disappointment to some others, a long-time devotee said, 'That's odd. I know for a fact that there are dozens of boxes of it in Ron's garage up in New York.'

On my next visit to the ashram, I begged one of the preachers for a copy. She told me she would check, but later abruptly informed me that the book was no longer available.

Luckily, a fellow devotee took pity on me and lent me his copy. I devoured the book from cover to cover – twice – and took copious notes before returning it to him. But it turned out to be a disappointment, since it only covered material that Swamiji had already revealed in his speeches. I wondered why it had been kept under wraps.

After seeing a mysterious photograph in one of the preachers' books, I became intensely curious about Swamiji's guru. The image was of one of the most beautiful men I have ever seen. He appeared to be about forty years old, with features that looked more American Indian than Indian. He had high cheekbones and a large nose, with light-brown skin. His hair was black, wavy and fell to his breastbone. His chest and shoulders were wide and muscular. He wasn't wearing a shirt, just a beaded necklace. He looked like he was leaning back in a chair, relaxing. His eyes were half-closed, kind of romantically, and he had the appearance of being deep in devotional thought.

The book was in Hindi, so I could not read it. But I assumed that the man was Swamiji's guru. The photo haunted me. I thought, 'Now this is a guru I could fall in love with.' Although I was devoted to Swamiji, I could never honestly say that I loved him; not like so many other devotees claimed they did. But I wanted to love my guru, since I believed that was fundamental to achieving God realization. Maybe I could love this guru instead, I thought, if only I got the chance to know him.

A few years later, in 1996, I saw an image of the man again when a long-time devotee named Kamani visited the ashram from Singapore. I went to her room to ask her to join me for lunch in town and noticed a cassette with a photograph of the man I'd seen in the book a few years ago.

'Is this Swamiji's guru?' I asked.

'Yes. But I'm not supposed to talk about him,' she said nervously, taking the tape from my hand and burying it under some clothing in her suitcase.

'Why not?'

'I'm not sure. When I arrived here, Sureshwari gave me a stern talk, telling me not to say a word about him to anyone.'

'Have you met him?'

'Yes,' she said with a girlish smile.

'Tell me something about him, anything,' I begged.

'Okay, but not here,' she said in a whisper.

Later, while we were walking on the path around Town Lake in downtown Austin, I asked her: 'What is Swamiji's guru like?'

She smiled like a schoolgirl with a crush. 'He's nothing like Swamiji. He's very vivacious and outgoing. He'll pull you into a big hug. He's a powerful speaker and gives the most amazing lectures.'

Her giddiness about this guru made me even more desirous of knowing him.

'He once told us that we can envision Krishna any way we want. For example, if Krishna were here on earth today, he would play cricket and baseball, just like any other little boy. So we can picture him out on the baseball field in his uniform throwing balls and swinging bats, instead of the traditional image of him wearing his dhoti and playing on his flute as he herds cows.'

It was obvious that her devotional heart strings were pulled by this guru, not by Swamiji. She soon left Barsana Dham and never returned.

Not too long after that, I was talking to a housemate, Ellen, in her bedroom. She had been a devotee of Swamiji since the late 1970s. I noticed a copy of his first book on her nightstand and mentioned that I had been trying to get hold of one. To my surprise, she told me that it had been taken off the market and hidden away.

'It was because it had his guru's bio and picture. Swamiji did not want his devotees to worship any other guru. At first, he had us tear out the photos of his guru. Then he just stopped selling the book.'

I couldn't believe what I was hearing.

'In those days, Swamiji talked about him occasionally. We even had his photo on our altars. Swamiji took twelve of his devotees from New Zealand to meet his guru in India in the mid-1980s. He said he would take more on a second trip. But when he returned, Swamiji announced that he wouldn't take any more devotees to India. It turned out that a few had left Swamiji for his guru.'

Now my curiosity was piqued. Who was this other guru who had the power to pull devotees away from Swamiji?

I wouldn't know for several more years.

Introducing Maharajji

The Guru of the Universe

SUDDENLY, AFTER YEARS of saying nothing at all about him, in the late summer of 1999, Swamiji began telling us about his guru, Kripalu Maharaj, whom everyone called 'Maharajji' (kripalu means 'gracious' and maharaj means 'king').

Swamiji started hanging photographs of Maharajji in the temple, playing taped recordings of him chanting and showing us videos of him from India. I was shocked when I saw his updated image. Gone was the stunning man I had seen in the photograph from years ago. Here was a skinny, wrinkled old man with greasy-looking skin and no muscle mass. The gorgeous guru who had haunted me ever since I first saw his photograph was apparently history and I felt no attraction whatsoever to this elderly Indian gent.

But when I saw the first video of Maharajji, I regained some of my original longing. In the video, recorded in India at one of his ashrams, he is walking back and forth on a decorated stage as the devotees in the audience chant and play music. Despite his much older appearance, he had a commanding presence and irresistible charisma as he walked back and forth, snapping his fingers, and occasionally singing a verse, seemingly absorbed in the chanting.

We finally learnt more about Maharajji when Swamiji delivered a thirty-part lecture series about him at the 1999 annual Fall Intensive (for life members) in Barsana Dham. The series, which was called 'The

Life History of Bhakti-Yog-Rasavatar Jagadguru Kripalu Mahaprabhu' revealed a multitude of fantastic insights about this other guru.

For example, Swamiji told us that Maharajji was a 'jagadguru', a 'supreme teacher of the universe'. What's more, he was the most important jagadguru to ever appear on earth. Further, Maharajji was an incarnation of Radha–Krishna. Even more astounding, he was also the reincarnation of one of the greatest saints of India, Chaitanya Mahaprabhu, who famously worshipped Radha–Krishna.

Other astonishing revelations included Maharajji's immaculate conception, his other-worldly academic and physical aptitude during his school years, and his profound arrival on the spiritual scene in his early twenties as a gifted orator and singer.

Swamiji started off the lecture series with a warning, delivered with great drama: 'You must know that Maharajji's life history is for your own personal devotional benefit. It is not for discussion or casual retelling. You must be very clear about this.'

Then he said: 'When Chaitanya left [earth], he disappeared into the deity, Jagannath.[1] When Chaitanya left the world, his life history was not written … when he left in the deity, people realized how great he was. Many devotees who had not fully surrendered felt very sorry.'

By now, Swamiji was so worked up that he couldn't get through a sentence without gasping. 'So this time the true devotees should not feel sorry …' he broke out into loud sobs before finishing his statement, '… when Maharajji is gone.' At this point, all of the preachers went into heaving sobs as well. As their wailing echoed through the prayer hall, a few other devotees joined in. I watched the scene, wondering about the over-the-top display of emotions.

After Swamiji's tears subsided, he continued in a staccato of heavy breathing, expelling a loud breath between every few words: 'That's why … I'm telling … the life history … so all the devotees who wish

[1] Chaitanya is believed to have left his earthly body by running towards a stone deity of Lord Jagannath and merging with it. It is said that he left an orange smudge on the stone.

... to realize divine love of Radha–Krishna ... in their life ... For that reason ... I'm restoring the divine secrets of his life.'

When Swamiji finally finished his lecture, he fell back in his decorated seat and sat in silence for nearly ten minutes. When he finally got up, he appeared woozy, like he'd had too much to drink, and wobbled out of the prayer hall on unsteady feet.

In the next day's lecture, we got to know about the immaculate conception of Maharajji, including how his mother had supposedly said, 'I felt no discomfort up until he was born. I felt very comfortable. I felt bathed in bliss all the time.' Apparently she was alone in her room, lying on her bed half asleep around midnight when Maharajji appeared. 'Only his mother knew the divine circumstances of his birth.'

Swamiji said that Maharajji's birth paralleled the birth of Krishna, who appeared at midnight, lying next to his mother Devaki. The resulting celebration of Krishna's birth marked the creation of Hinduism's annual Krishna Janmashtami celebration. Maharajji's parents were reported to have held a similar celebration.

Swamiji also told us that when Maharajji was sixteen, he went into the forest alone and came across an abandoned temple of Lord Shiva. Seeing a pond nearby, he entered the water until it was up to his chin, assumed Shiva's tandava nritya stance of ecstatic dance, and stayed there for four days.

'It's difficult to understand the actions of a divine personality if one has a material mind,' explained Swamiji. 'But I think he saw God Shiva in the temple and just felt like revealing a part of his personality. Shiva, Vishnu, Ram, Krishna are all one. So probably he revealed his form of God Shiva ... to show that God Shiva is part of his personality.'

Swamiji offered up many such curious explanations of Maharajji's 'divine' actions.

'When Chaitanya was on earth, he followed the strict doctrine of sanyasi,' Swamiji told us, 'which included not allowing anyone to touch his body and not allowing women into his satsang. But now in the form of Maharajji, Chaitanya decided to take a different approach. Maharajji thought, "If I, just in this time, give them the privilege to touch my body, it will be something that's good. It will reveal more of that love and people can feel more of my personality, closely.'"

'He was like Chaitanya,' Swamiji explained, 'but more liberally giving his association freely. He doesn't have a material body. He has a divine body, and divine body doesn't need any material thing. It has descended so any soul can see the personality. But the divine personality can't be seen except by a divine personality.'

As we were taught more and more about the greatest saint of modern times, one question nagged at me: If Maharajji was so great, why hadn't we heard about him sooner?

This must have been a common question, because there was already a pat answer circulating among devotees: We were all so devotionally barren when Swamiji found us that we were not ready to know about a saint as great as Maharajji.

Curiously, while Swamiji told us many fantastical stories about Maharajji, he never said a word about his mysterious decade of enforced silence about him.

Going to India

Suffering for God

TINY MANGARH VILLAGE is, as they say, 'in the middle of nowhere'. It's about 100 miles south-west of Delhi, India. On Google Earth, it's just a dot in the middle of vast nothingness. Like much of the countryside in India, there are only small villages and fields of crops for miles around. The cluster of buildings that comprise Maharajji's ashram are the most substantial group of structures in the area.

But Mangarh is holy ground for Maharajji's devotees, since it is where he was born and raised, and where he established the first of his three ashrams.

As soon as Barsana Dham's 1999 Intensive ended, Swamiji started taking groups of devotees to India to meet Maharajji in Mangarh. The first trip included a group of about two dozen of Swamiji's wealthiest devotees. These lucky souls returned home one month later with arrogance and breathless stories about Maharajji and his escapades. They were also loaded down with trinkets such as scarves, hats and jewellery – all received from Maharajji – along with the coveted red rakhi that he gave to all who visited him. Most of us didn't know at the time that each of these items came with a price tag. But once we got to India, we gained our own 'opportunities' to receive Maharajji's grace through material consumption.

The following spring, Swamiji took the next group of devotees for another month-long stay in Mangarh. This slightly larger group comprised primarily the second ring of the inner circle – people who regularly contributed large amounts of money to Swamiji and who were friends with the preachers. They too returned with stories, stuff and an air of superiority.

I was in the third and largest group of devotees to travel to India. We went in July 2000 and travelled not to Mangarh, but to another ashram in Barsana village to celebrate Guru Poornima in the huge new Vishwa Kaliandra Kendra temple, which Swamiji had been building for years. Neither the temple nor the dorm rooms were complete when we arrived. But Maharajji had insisted on holding the 2000 Guru Poornima there for the millennium. Devotees sacrificed comfort and health to live in what was essentially a construction site. It was hot, dirty, smelly, noisy and crowded.

While every trip to Maharajji's ashrams in India was a test of physical endurance – due to the weather, an unforgiving schedule, poor food, pollution and sleep deprivation – our trip went down in the history of Barsana Dham as the worst trip ever to India. The challenges began the moment we boarded the plane in Austin and continued over the two days it took us to travel halfway around the world. We flew coach from Austin to Atlanta to New York to London to Delhi. Then we spent over three hours on a cramped, hot and dusty bus in the dead of night from Delhi to Barsana. We arrived at the ashram at about 6:00 a.m. at the tail end of morning satsang and filed off the bus and into the building like a pack of disaster survivors.

I was exhausted and filthy when I first glimpsed Maharajji in the flesh. He was sitting on a decorated bed in the small prayer hall of the ashram's original building, called Rangeeli Mahal. We lined up in front of him and took turns bowing to him at the foot of his bed. He watched us intently, with amusement.

I sat on the floor with the other devotees who were singing the morning chant. I stared up at Maharajji, looking for clues to the divinity that Swamiji had told us he possessed. But all I saw was a sweaty, skinny, wrinkled old man.

I had imagined that I would feel some bolt of devotional bhao at my first sight of him. Instead I felt only a big emptiness. As I stared at him, panic started to rise up inside me and I wanted to stand up and run. I had come halfway around the world to a very different, very foreign world, all to see the man in front of me – and from the moment I laid eyes on him, he gave me the creeps.

Someone once told me that when Maharajji was young, he walked like he knew that all the women lusted after him. Now he was seventy-eight, and looked every bit his age. His other-worldly handsomeness and toned body were gone, as was the luminous black long hair. It was now thin, grey and greasy, and lay on his shoulders like strands of cooked noodles.

I later found a description of him in a book by psychiatrist Dr Gordon Warme, who had met Maharajji in Mangarh in 1992. The doctor's description seemed to find resonance with the image I remembered from the photos, but did not match the man before me: 'I was struck by his stature; he was the tallest man in the room, over 1.8 metres (6 feet), broad-shouldered and strongly muscled. Although he was over seventy, his thick shoulders were particularly noticeable, always shown off by sleeveless robes. Clean-shaven and handsome, his features were strong and bony.'

We had obviously missed Maharajji's glory days.

At last, the morning chant got over and Maharajji retired to his bedroom. Our trip manager immediately gathered us and led us to our rooms. We followed her in stupor. She led us down several dusty walkways and up a dangerously unfinished, narrow and uneven stairway with no railing. The rooms were filthy as well. Swamiji had rushed the construction crew to get the rooms habitable prior to our arrival but, in the rush, they had left behind a thick coat of drywall dust and dirt on everything. Each room had four wooden platforms with thin mattresses, crammed together with just about two feet between them. A thin pillow lay on each bed, but no sheets. There was a closet, but no rod or hooks. There was also a small kitchen, but no appliances or running water. The only running water was in the bathroom and it was cold.

But at least we had rooms. As thousands of people began streaming into the ashram for the three-day celebration, many set up camp on the walkways, sleeping side by side like logs in a lumber yard. It was shocking to find an endless sea of bodies lying on the cement just outside our doors. We literally had to step over people to get anywhere. It was the closest I've ever come to living in a slum.

The female devotees faced another unsettling challenge – peeping Toms. Most of the bedrooms had large windows facing the walkways, but there were no curtains. Bands of young Indian men brazenly stood staring in at us as we tried to get ready for bed. It was truly scary. Some women had brought extra sheets, which they converted into makeshift curtains by nailing them over the windows. But no one in my room had a piece of cloth to spare.

Nothing was easy to come by in this uber-austere Indian ashram – not an extra pillow, a pencil, or even a piece of tape, let alone a piece of fabric to drape over the window. But I was determined to cover the windows in my room. The next day I searched around for anything I could use and finally found a stack of newspapers, but had to beg our reluctant coordinator to lend me some duct tape.

Another challenge was the smoke from all the cooking and garbage fires that were constantly burning around the ashram. There was also a construction refuse pile right outside our back window. Within days, my throat was sore and I was coughing in ragged fits. By the time I left India, I was struggling for every breath, and when I later returned to the US, my doctor diagnosed me with 'situational asthma'.

As is usual in India, it was excruciatingly hot in the summer. The only air conditioning units in the ashram were in the bedrooms of Swamiji, Maharajji and his 'divine' family members. A few days after we arrived, Swamiji had swamp coolers installed in our bedrooms, but they just blew wet air into the room and made it more humid. But the humming helped drown out the constant banging from the construction, the chaos of the crowd and the non-stop chanting which was amplified all over the ashram over loudspeakers. This white noise at least helped me sleep a little better for the few hours we had each night to rest.

Sleep was a huge issue for me. Nothing was conducive to rest: not the schedule, not the sleeping conditions, nor the peer pressure from devotees to subsist on a few hours a night. It was a huge effort every day to get even the minimum amount of sleep I needed to function and not fall asleep during satsang, which was a huge no-no, as we soon understood. 'It's a sin to fall asleep while Maharajji is in the room,' a preacher scolded somebody who had dozed off during one of the sessions.

On the second morning, despite the scolding we had received, I passed out cold in a sitting position during Maharajji's two-hour Guru Poornima lecture. I had never fallen asleep in the prayer hall back home. But sitting amidst thousands of people, crammed in, with women's bodies touching me from all sides, sweating from the heat, blinded by the glare of the video lights, listening to Maharajji speak endlessly in Hindi (which I did not understand at the time), I could not force my fatigued body to stay awake. I remember waking up a few times, looking around, then passing out again. I came to know later that several other devotees had also fallen asleep during the marathon discourse.

I never could shake my feeling of jet lag or catch up on my sleep because the daily schedule – which started at 4:00 a.m. and ran until 10:00 p.m. – was brutal. Each day, there were four mandatory satsang sessions, each of which lasted two to three hours. Maharajji's satsangs are extremely noisy and raucous events, with people playing multiple instruments at once and devotees chanting and clapping loudly. I almost never took out my earplugs.

The food was horrible. Most days, breakfast was runny hot cereal and bland black beans. However, this soon became my favourite meal, only because everything else was worse. Lunch and dinner were flavourless yellow dals, gluey rice and stiff rotis. One day they gave us packaged dried bread that we discovered was infested with mould. For all meals, we sat outside in the dirt, men and women in separate rows. People walked up and down the aisles, serving us out of buckets from which they scooped portions of food onto our rectangular metal trays. At the suggestion of experienced devotees, I had brought some snack food, but not nearly enough. I carefully rationed my nuts and crackers over my thirty days in India. Yet, I was perennially hungry.

I quickly understood that Indians do not share westerners' need for a certain amount of space between bodies. They have no problem sitting right next to you in the prayer hall, bodies touching, or pushing into you in a line. It didn't help that the temperature was over 110 degrees Fahrenheit most days. With no AC and humanity literally breathing down my neck, I was constantly sweating. I got a severe heat rash – itchy, bumpy, red – all over my body, which took months to heal.

By my second week in the ashram, I started counting the days, then the hours, until I could finally leave that miserable place where I felt not the tiniest speck of divinity from anyone or anything. And it wasn't just me. Many devotees were having a difficult time. There were all manner of illnesses, from a nearly gangrened foot to intestinal problems. So many people were sick that a doctor was hired to visit the ashram daily and tend to the infirm.

When Swamiji was told how much the devotees were suffering, he said, 'It takes more than one trip to India to feel Maharajji's grace.'

When I heard that, I thought: I'll never know then, because I'm never coming back here.

The Maharajji Show

Show Me the Money

ALTHOUGH SWAMIJI HAD told us many stories about Maharajji, I realized that there were many things he had kept to himself. For starters, he failed to mention that Maharajji had an entire family – including a wife, three daughters, two sons and several grandchildren – and that they were all considered to be divine. They were even called 'the divine family'. Traditionally, most Hindu gurus live lives of renunciation, without families. They are fully dedicated to devotion to God, especially if they wear saffron, as Maharajji did most of the time.

Neither Swamiji nor anyone else ever offered an explanation as to why Maharajji chose to circumvent this long-standing tradition. The closest Swamiji ever came to explaining this inconsistency was a cryptic comment about saints often appearing with many of their 'divine associates'. Later he added some vague guidance for interacting with Maharajji's family members: 'We respect the members of his family but don't worship them.'

With no clear direction, devotees speculated wildly about Maharajji's family members. Some people thought his wife was actually Radha and that Maharajji was Krishna, despite being told that Maharajji was both forms of God in one body. Some thought his three daughters were incarnations of three of the eight personal associates (gopis) of Radha. Some thought that Maharajji's oldest son was the Hindu god Shiva.

But it didn't really matter who they were or were not, because life in the ashram revolved around Maharajji. He supported this obsession by instructing devotees to 'worship the guru as God with everything you have, including your mind, body and money'. In fact, his speech on Guru Poornima centred around this topic. He recited verse after verse from Hindu scriptures to support his point of view.

The vast majority of devotees seemed willing enough to buy into the non-stop 'Maharajji Show'. To me, the focus on him was maniacal and disturbing.

Maharajji had a large staff of people who did nothing but serve him all day, every day. He had two personal assistants who attended to him round the clock, several cooks to prepare meals for him alone, and laundresses to wash only his clothes in his personal laundry room. A few people tended to his cows, which provided milk just for him. There were also several people dedicated to capturing thousands of still images of him and hours of him on video. Still others sold his photos, tapes, posters and books in the ashram stores. On top of this, many visiting devotees were recruited for additional tasks, such as sewing his clothes and cleaning his rooms.

I found Dr Warme's description of Maharajji to be the most realistic perspective of any I've ever heard. He was not a devotee but a devotee's friend, when he went, out of curiosity, to the Mangarh ashram for the 1992 Intensive. This passage from his book, *Daggers of the Mind*, which explores people's search for spiritual healing, describes his experience upon arriving at the ashram:

> The ashram itself is made up of a cluster of buildings, dormitories or apartments, and a meeting hall, where a party was going on. The party celebrated the Maharaji. He sat on a platform – to me, it looked like a bed sprinkled with petals – and ate titbits, some of which he tossed to the devotees

> crowded around. In two corners of the room were thrones, really heaps of elevated pillows, colourful, gilded with banners and gold edging. I noticed spotlights and strategically placed video cameras pointed towards the thrones. Every eye was on the guru. The devotees cheerfully bounced him up and down. Although it was a party, only the guru was partying; the others cheered and applauded as *he* partied.
>
> I could see right away that the Maharaji's followers wished to make themselves – their souls – utterly subservient to him. Later, the devotees' thorough denial of their own interests – really a denial of their existence – became clearer … their self-cure was to have no soul at all, to shadow, ape and adapt themselves to the contrasting soul of the guru, which was alive, vivacious, throbbing.
>
> … [I]t [the ashram culture] saddened me; worshipful devotion to the guru left out fun and adventure for the devotees.

Despite all the craziness and hardships of living, even temporarily, in a third world country, 'going to India' became the Holy Grail for most Western devotees. They seemed to view trips to India as badges of honour, which they collected like scout badges. A competition seemed to have developed among some devotees regarding who went to India more often. The more trips they took, the more they acted like they were superior to others – the antithesis of a humble devotee. Many devotees claimed to be 'blissed out' when they were in Maharajji's presence, yet they did not seem to retain any of that bliss once they returned home.

I don't know what the devotees got out of their tours, but do know what Maharajji gained: cold hard cash. Before I went, I had no idea that his ashrams were basically set up only to collect money from visiting devotees – this was another titbit that Swamiji had failed to share. On my first trip, I paid $2,000 for room and board. At least that's what I was led to believe. I later gleaned that Maharajji didn't charge any room and board fees. You could stay in his minimalist ashrams for free.

However, what he did charge for was seva opportunities. Many devotees would spend even more, returning home from India owing anywhere from $1,000 to $15,000 in seva debt, sometimes more.

At Barsana Dham, we never paid to sit at Swamiji's meals, ride on his golf cart, offer pranam to him each day, or anything else. But we quickly understood that life surrounding Maharajji was very different. There was a fee attached to many things. The majority of fees were for personal interaction with him, including bowing to him every morning in the prayer hall ($2.50), bowing in his bedroom during special events ($100), having evening coffee with him in his bedroom ($250), receiving a cookie ($250), getting a rakhi string tied on your wrist ($100), 'washing' his feet ($250), painting his feet with mehndi paste ($250), pushing him on a swing for a minute ($250), getting slapped by him with a slipper ($100 per slap), riding in his car with him ($2,500), and watching him eat his afternoon meal ($2,500). He also sold personal items to devotees. Of course, these were things that other people had given him. One man paid $2,200 for a gold necklace, a woman purchased a bracelet for $700, and several people purchased discarded outfits and shoes for hundreds of dollars each. Maharajji was constantly selling his cast-off clothing and gifts.

Not knowing that my $2,000 was a pre-payment for seva opportunities, I assumed I had been freely invited to participate in a small variety of activities. One day, as instructed, I lined up with hundreds of other people outside his bedroom. The line slowly snaked up to his door and, after almost an hour, I made it to the threshold of his bedroom. A female preacher grabbed my arm and pushed me towards his bed. Like the devotees before me, I bowed with as much reverence as I could muster. Maharajji was lying back on a pile of pillows, talking in Hindi to a group crowded around the head of his bed. He didn't even look up at me as I gazed upon him. Then another preacher grabbed my arm and pushed me out through a door on the opposite wall. The total time I spent in his room was perhaps 45 seconds. It cost me $100.

The 'foot washing' ceremony was equally brief. When I arrived in Maharajji's room, he was sitting on the bed with one foot in an oversized metal bucket of water. Following the lead of the people before me, I stuck my hand in the water and briefly touched his foot. Then, as before, a preacher grabbed and pulled me out of the room, unburdening me of $250. These two interactions were so fleeting and stressful that I didn't feel anything but anxiety.

Coffee seva gave me my first substantial experience with him. About twelve of us were in his bedroom, sitting around his bed, while he watched the news on TV and ate a snack. At one point, he started laughing. I was sitting right in front of him, intently watching his every move, desperately trying to make the best of my confinement in his ashram. I tried to soak in the divine vibrations I wanted to believe he possessed. Glancing at me, he pointed to the TV. I turned around and looked at the image on the screen. It looked like the scene of some parade. I smiled at him and nodded.

One of his helpers entered the room with a cup in one hand and a spoon in the other. She walked to each of us one by one. We tilted our heads back and opened our mouths as she poured a spoonful of coffee into our mouths, like a mama bird feeding a baby. Presumably it was his leftover coffee, which meant it was prasad. Soon after that, Maharajji indicated that the coffee seva was over.

The spoonful of coffee had cost me $250.

No Titiksha for the Gurus

Gluttons for Creature Comforts

TITIKSHA IS A Hindu concept of tolerating sacrifices in personal comfort while on a spiritual path. Literally, it means 'bearing opposites with self-control'. In other words, in your quest for spiritual enlightenment, you should not become negatively or positively affected by conditions such as extreme weather, happiness or sadness, or being hungry or sated. India's original Shankacharya, Adi Shankacharya (AD 788 to 820), said that titiksha is an essential quality on the path to God realization.

Swamiji and Maharajji piggybacked on this Hindu tenet, telling us that we had to be devoted, no matter how uncomfortable the physical circumstances might be. They, however, appeared to be exempt from the rigours of bearing opposites as both were beneficiaries of many creature comforts.

Swamiji frequently instructed us to live more simply and scolded us for indulging in perceived luxuries such as having too many clothes or eating meals outside of the community kitchen. Once, he gave us an impassioned lecture on how people seeking God in the old days in India often lacked even the most basic comforts, including daily meals. He said, 'You all have everything taken care of here. You have rooms, electricity, AC, and not one of you has ever gone hungry, not even for a single day.' This talk was obviously meant to make us more humble and appreciative of what we had in his ashram.

However, as he was lecturing us, he was wearing a cashmere sweater, sitting on his luxurious custom-built bed with multi-hundred-count sheets and covering his legs with the highest-quality down comforter. A door to the right of his bed led to his private bathroom, which featured an extra-large jet-powered bathtub, a steam room and a sauna. His personal kitchen was custom built with high-end cabinetry and marble countertops. His cupboards were filled with top-of-the-line appliances, real silverware, fine china and delicious foods. His upstairs sitting room featured a balcony overlooking the most ornate part of the ashram, including a perfect view of a lotus-shaped pool with three fountains and two waterfalls.

His transportation always included a new-model, high-end Lexus. His front passenger seat was covered with a sheepskin throw and small pillows for his comfort. His golf carts were regularly upgraded to the newest models. He flew only first-class on his many trips to and from India.

In fact, no detail was too insignificant when it came to his comfort. A cadre of his followers was devoted to ensuring that his every whim was swiftly and unerringly catered to. Devotees bent over backwards to ensure that everything he sat on, wore, ate and experienced was to his liking. Any discrepancy would be considered a life-or-death crisis – from the shape of a particular pillow to an unwanted sliver of light peeking through his bedroom curtains.

I once observed a devotee nearly having a nervous breakdown because she couldn't get the shape of a small pillow sewn exactly the way he wanted it. She ran back and forth from his bedroom to her sewing machine, increasingly frantic to please him.

Swamiji's 'sanyasi' preachers followed his lead. They too wanted everything from cashmere sweaters to the latest cell phones to special food items. Devotees were happy to oblige and spoil them. They believed that by catering to the preachers' every whim, they would garner goodwill and gain Swamiji's grace.

Meanwhile, if Swamiji had his way, the devotees would have lived together in holes in the wall, eating tasteless food and driving beat-up old cars. He preferred people to live in one room and often complained, 'I don't know why anyone needs more than one room to live in.' He once came into my bedroom and said that I had too many pillows on my bed. (I had five, which was one less than what he had on his own bed.)

Swamiji expected the ashram kitchen to spend the minimum amount on groceries. We weren't allowed extras like salad dressing, pickles or crackers. This frugality, our vegetarian diets and a lack of creativity among the cooks resulted in a pretty boring diet centred around rice, dal, bread and overcooked vegetables. It wasn't surprising that many of the devotees would frequently cook their own meals or eat outside when they could.

Maharajji ran his ashrams in India with even greater austerity. He packed four to five people into each room, and fed them extremely bland food, including coagulated rice, watery dal, leathery rotis and an occasional vegetable such as waterlogged lauki. Even the daily tea became extremely watered down over time. He once said: 'If you don't like the conditions in my ashrams, leave.' His view was that devotees came to his ashram for devotional upliftment, not material comforts.

Meanwhile, he would retreat from the suffocating prayer hall to his air-conditioned, luxurious bedroom, where servants would ply him with the most sumptuous vegetarian Indian food imaginable. Whenever he travelled outside the ashrams, he was chauffeured in a custom-fitted Mercedes Benz. But after a while, even that was not good enough. In 2008, the organization purchased a helicopter so that Maharajji could travel more swiftly from city to city, swooping onto rooftops from Delhi to Nepal like some kind of army general.

Clearly, Swamiji and Maharajji taught from the gospel of 'Do what I say, not what I do.'

Returning to India

One Last Trip

WHILE THE MAJORITY of Swamiji's devotees clamoured for return trips to India, I shuddered at the thought after my nightmarish experience.

Even watching the home videos made during some of the other devotees' trips was too much for me to take. Every time I viewed scenes filmed in the ashrams, I would relive the feeling of being trapped. It depressed me almost as much as actually being in Maharajji's ashram had.

That's why I was blindsided by my decision to return to India in December 2003. This surprising turnabout was triggered by a particularly gruelling work experience that left me feeling, once again, that the world is merely the realm of pain and suffering and that I must improve my devotions to free myself of maya.

That evening, I learnt that a group of devotees was going to India for the new year. On the spur of the moment, I asked if there was room for one more, and the answer was yes. Without putting much more thought into it, I began the ritual of preparing to once again live in a remote village in a Third World country for a month – packing toilet paper, medicine, snacks and every other little thing that would be hard to come by.

There were at least a couple of positive aspects to this trip. One was that it was winter, so at least it would not be insufferably hot. The second was that the group was small: only about twelve people were going, and I considered them to be fairly relaxed and friendly. The actual trip to India was extremely pleasant. We flew Air France and the food was delicious. Also, because the plane was not full, we had room to stretch out and sleep. Plus, we watched the movies of our choice on the tiny screens on the back of each seat. This was a vast improvement over flying with seventy demanding adults in the middle of India's congested peak summer travel season.

We had a few days in the Barsana ashram before Maharajji arrived from Mangarh, which meant that we had time to catch up on our jet lag. We got our first glimpse of him in Vrindavan on New Year's Day. As is his tradition, he was sponsoring a feast for the new year. We all took the two-hour bus ride from Barsana to join him. Our first seva opportunity occurred immediately upon our arrival – a new year's hug and card from him, costing $250.

Now that I was here, I was determined to have a better experience than the first time. But when we got to his bedroom, he was yelling at three of his female preachers. I knew just enough Hindi by then to know that they were in trouble. He was saying basically, 'Why haven't you brought more people to see me?' They hung their heads and said nothing.

He was still chastising them when it was my turn to receive a hug and a card. While putting his arms around me for a few seconds, pulling away, and then handing me a large, stiff envelope, bestowing 'grace', he continued scolding the preachers, not missing a beat. I tried to understand the lesson I believed I was supposed to gain from this experience – perhaps it was a sign that I too must try harder to do the right thing for my guru.

Our next stop was a room where his three daughters stayed. It was a boisterous party in there. People were hugging the 'didis', as they are called, and purchasing the trinkets they were selling. His daughters had a parallel operation going in the ashram and sold photos as well as discarded saris, jewellery and other gifts people had given them. I bought a few wallet-sized calendars, which featured pictures of Maharajji on one side.

After this, we proceeded to the temple, which was filled with people chanting. Before long, Maharajji entered the hall and sat on his decorated seat at the front of the room. The chanting became more enthusiastic. I had trouble concentrating because I could smell the food for the davat (feast) being prepared by local food vendors outside, in the temple veranda, which ran around the entire building.

The feast began only after Maharajji circumnavigated the temple to examine and sample the offerings. Vendors from all over town were lined up, proudly serving their specialities. There was every kind of Indian food imaginable, as well as other cuisines. There was thick and rich pau bhaji, crispy dosas with spiced potato filling, barbequed paneer, tender rotis, Chinese noodles, home-made ice cream, succulent sweets of every variety, and much more. I paired off with another Austin devotee and walked round the circuit trying to decide what to eat. We knew better than to just eat anything and risk getting an intestinal illness. We finally chose a few delicacies and went to find a quiet place to savour them. The food was the most delicious I had ever eaten in India up to that point.

That evening we rode the bus in the dark back to the Barsana ashram. When we awoke the next day, Maharajji was in Barsana. Overnight, the ashram had turned from a ghost town into 'Maharajji World'. But even though the atmosphere was charged by his mere presence and the intensity of life was kicked up several notches, the environment was still more relaxed than what I experienced on my first trip.

The winter also helped my mood considerably. Even though we didn't have heaters and had to heat our bath water in a bucket with an electric coil, it was much better than the constant sweating and heat rashes of the stifling summer weather. The food was much better too, perhaps because they were cooking for fewer people.

Another plus was that we got to enjoy a second davat, thanks to a wedding celebration held in the ashram. In fact, if it had not been for the wedding, the trip might have been a complete bust, because Maharajji was itching to leave Barsana and go to Orissa almost as soon as he arrived. However, he felt obligated to stay, for the wedding was of the daughter of one of his oldest and wealthiest devotees.

On the night of the wedding, I had my best experience with Maharajji ever – and it didn't cost me a dime. That evening, I had tired of the raucous festivities and was wandering around the empty prayer hall with one of the other visiting devotees. Suddenly, Maharajji walked in, dressed in a turban and long flowing coat. He walked to his electric wheelchair, which he often used to get around quickly. We followed him as he rolled out of the building. Once outside, he hit a button on the chair and sailed off into the night towards the back of the ashram. We followed him on foot, running to keep up.

Soon, a few other devotees joined in. About eight of us ran beside or behind him, laughing as we chased our guru through the darkness. He drove towards a boisterous group of wedding revellers who were singing, playing instruments, dancing and setting off fireworks. Maharajji got up from his chair and dived into the middle of the melee. The people went crazy, dancing around him and kicking up the decibel level several notches. I hung back, watching the scene. When he was done, he got back into his wheelchair and raced away the way he'd come. The same small group ran after him again, laughing all the way. It was the most fun I'd had in India.

The day after the wedding, early in the morning, we were told that Maharajji was leaving in two hours. We stood outside his room waiting for our last glimpse of him. Some devotees were crying. Finally, he appeared. We followed him as he walked to his car, waved goodbye, and then he was gone. His entourage of servants and camp-following devotees crammed into other vehicles and took off after him.

I walked back into the temple. It was so empty and quiet that it felt like a tomb. I suddenly felt very lonely. There were four days left until we departed, and they passed like molasses through a sieve. Although this trip was not as miserable as my first, by the time I left India, I realized that I'd had enough of the hyperactive Maharajji show and that my second trip was the last I would be making to the country.

Where Is Sureshwari?

A Preacher's Mysterious Disappearance

A MONTH AFTER I returned from India in early 2004, Swamiji's main preacher, Sureshwari, disappeared without a word.

Her sudden departure was one of the most traumatic events in my spiritual life. A few other preachers had left Swamiji over the years for unknown reasons, but none of them had possessed Sureshwari's intensity and sincerity. She was the most admired person in the organization during her twenty or so years as preacher, then vice-president, and then president of the organization. She attracted many devotees to the path over the years, both in the US and in India.

Unlike most devotees, including the other preachers, she appeared to follow Swamiji's instructions to the letter. For many of us, she was the ideal pupil. I admired her greatly, and am convinced that I wouldn't have lasted as long as I did were it not for her example and support.

Swamiji himself always held her up as an example of the perfect devotee, and praised her publicly many times over the years. When he announced in the mid-1990s that she was going to take over his role as president, he told us that she has suffered more hardship than any other preacher and that 'she loves all of the souls'.

Sureshwari had met Swamiji in New Zealand in the mid-1970s when she was just nineteen. She was a pretty, spiritual and energetic young woman, and Swamiji showered her with his charismatic attention. She became his number one follower and secretary. He guided every step of her life from that point on, telling her where to live, when to do devotions, and instructing her to open a small flower and vegetable stand so she could make money to help support the small New Zealand centre he had established.

Shortly after that, Swamiji told her that it was her destiny to become a preacher. Sureshwari dived into her studies, learning the scriptures with total commitment. Swamiji sent her to India for several months to prepare for her new life as a Hindi-speaking, shloka-reciting, devotional-song-chanting Western woman dressed in saffron.

Then, without warning, in February 2004, Sureshwari disappeared on the day we were celebrating Swamiji's birthday.

I noticed her absence during the annual celebration. When Swamiji entered the party, Prabhakari was right behind him, but Sureshwari was nowhere in sight. Prabhakari looked particularly pleased with herself and, seating herself in front of Swamiji, she gazed up at him, smiling from ear to ear. I noted that she looked especially self-satisfied.

As soon as the party was over, I asked around, but no one had seen Sureshwari.

The next day I again enquired about her. No one knew anything.

The following day, I walked up to Lois, a resident devotee who managed the prayer hall and prasad. She was usually aware of what was going on.

When I asked her, Lois looked at me sheepishly and said, 'You know, we have to put all of our faith and love in the guru, not in anyone else.'

Her curious comment sent a chill down my spine.

'I can't tell you the details,' she continued, 'but Sureshwari might have left.'

I was stunned and scared, but Lois refused to divulge any specifics, saying she didn't know anything else. But I suspected she did.

That evening I sat through Swamiji's dinner, getting more and more distraught. After Swamiji left the sitting room, I went to the preacher Nikhileshwari's room, because I figured she would be privy to some information.

'I need to ask you something,' I said, my tone and demeanour edgy.

She immediately closed her door and told me to sit on her bed. She sat down next to me, staring at me with concern. 'What's wrong?'

I opened my mouth to speak and burst out crying. The tears quickly escalated into heaving sobs.

'What's wrong? Did someone hurt you? Tell me what happened.'

Finally, still sobbing, I blurted out, 'Where's Sureshwari?'

The question startled her. She took a deep breath and said, 'She's gone back to India for a while.'

I looked at her curiously. This made no sense. Why wouldn't they tell us this news? Why was Sureshwari's departure such a mystery?

Finally she explained further: 'She has gone to India because she has been in a negative state of mind and Swamiji wants to try to revive her devotion.'

She followed this perplexing news up with a curious story.

'Maharajji has said that while on the path, some devotees go almost all the way across the ocean of maya and reach so close to the divine shore that they believe they can walk the rest of the way by themselves. So they leave the guru's boat and drown immediately.'

One of the frequent teachings of the gurus was that people were floating through maya, adrift in their own little boats. Only a guru could steer a soul's boat to the divine world. Clearly, Nikhileshwari was trying to imply that Sureshwari had gone adrift because she had decided to try to steer her own boat.

In a few days, Nikhileshwari's story fell apart. People started to talk about how Sureshwari had left Swamiji and gone back to New Zealand. Another devotee tried to assure me that everything was fine. 'She just needs a break. She'll relax, walk on the beaches of New Zealand and return in a few months.'

A week later, Swamiji was preparing to return to India. The

followers were called to his sitting room for a meeting and I thought he was going to give us some information about Sureshwari. Instead, he just talked about the usual things: how important it was to go to satsang regularly, to not think anything negative about anyone, and to perform service with complete devotion. Then he stood up and walked out. I was sitting behind Lois and I put my hand on her arm and whispered: 'He didn't say anything about her.'

She looked at me with utmost compassion and said, 'No, he didn't.'

I burst into tears and fell into her arms. I cried for ten minutes. Now I knew for sure that something was very wrong. I was in misery, and being in the dark made it worse. Moreover, I was scared.

A few months later, I finally heard the details of Sureshwari's departure when I went out to lunch with another follower named Heather, who lived in the ashram and was especially close to Vishi. Heather knew the whole story because she had been pulled into the drama.

It all started when the preacher Divakari noticed Sureshwari's suitcase on the veranda by the front door. When Divakari walked by again later, the suitcase was gone. On a hunch, she went to Sureshwari's room. When she opened the door, she saw that her belongings were gone. She immediately went to tell Swamiji.

Swamiji called Heather at work and told her to get to the airport and find Sureshwari. Heather worked near the airport and had special security authorizations because of her job. She raced to the airport and began searching the terminals. A Western woman dressed head to toe in saffron is not difficult to find in any situation. Because the Austin airport is fairly small and has a simple floor plan, Heather was able to spot her quickly at one of the gates.

When she caught up with the departing preacher, she said, 'Swamiji wants to talk to you.'

Sureshwari just said, 'Leave me alone.'

Heather called Swamiji on her cell phone and held it out to Sureshwari, requesting her to talk to him.

According to Heather, Sureshwari got a crazed look in her eyes and walked away towards a coffee kiosk. When Heather followed her, Sureshwari turned to her and said, 'Get away from me or I'll tell airport security that you're bothering me.' Then she started walking towards a security officer. Heather left the airport rather than risk losing her security privileges and her job.

That evening, Heather endured a severe scolding from Swamiji, who screamed at her for not getting Sureshwari to do what he wanted. The experience traumatized Heather for several months and she was in tears as she recounted what happened: 'I failed Swamiji. I wish it had been someone else instead of me. She might have listened to someone else. I felt so bad that I couldn't do more.'

Later I heard an addendum to the story. When Swamiji realized that Sureshwari had left, he told someone to call the police to stop her from getting on the plane. When the police refused to intervene, Swamiji made a strange comment: 'Why won't they stop her? She's my property.'

I later heard that both Maharajji and Swamiji called Sureshwari in New Zealand dozens of times, but she didn't take their calls. A few months later, a surprising thing happened. Sureshwari sent a letter to Swamiji saying she had made a mistake and wanted to return. I was thrilled beyond belief. I think she wanted to come back to the US, but they sent her to India. But four months later she left again, this time for good.

Several months later, Peter S., who ran one of Swamiji's infomercial businesses and was an officer on the board, gathered us together for an announcement: 'Swamiji wants everyone to know that Sureshwari left because she is crazy. Not just now, she has been mad for years. Swamiji had been trying to help her regain her sanity for a long time.'

This story made no sense. If she was crazy, why was she the president of the organization? I had worked with her directly during the year before she left and knew that she was not insane. She was, however, becoming more honest about many of the chronic problems in Barsana Dham, including her constant power struggles with Prabhakari.

I eventually saw video footage of the devotees gathered for Guru

Poornima in India in the summer of 2004, when Sureshwari had briefly returned. She was sitting in the front row with the other preachers, and looked bloated, pale and miserable. She stood out, not because of the devotional glow that she had always had in the past, but because she appeared to be in intense pain. That was the last time any of us ever saw her.

Swamiji's Prescription

My Therapy Cure

AFTER SURESHWARI LEFT, I experienced what I would call a nervous breakdown – which lasted for a few months. I knew that something terrible happened to make her leave, and I had no way to find out what it was, because no one would talk about it. I started having panic attacks and nightmares. Frequently, I would wake up in the middle of the night in tears.

One night in satsang I started crying – softly at first, but I felt on the verge of losing control. I walked out of the prayer hall just in time. Lois was at the front desk. I ran over to her and knelt down, and started sobbing uncontrollably. She let me cry, all the while talking to me about how we can only trust in the guru, not in any other devotee, no matter who they are.

Her words did not soothe me at all. I still knew that something was terribly wrong.

My emotional disintegration was due partly to the loss of the only person I truly respected in the organization. However, there was another reason I was in that frame of mind. The person I disliked for her power-mongering and chronic poor treatment of others was now the sole person in charge of the whole ashram – Prabhakari. I was horrified at the thought of this woman having dictatorial power over the ashram and everyone living there.

Another devotee, Pam, knew about my depression and encouraged me to talk to Swamiji, but I resisted. 'How can I tell him that I'm frightened because his favourite preacher is in charge now?'

But she didn't give up. One day we were talking outside when another devotee named Jan came walking up the path. When Pam told her what we were talking about, Jan confessed that she too was frightened at the prospect of Prabhakari ruling the roost. Pam urged us to go talk to Swamiji together.

Jan agreed, but I was still reluctant, for I didn't want to run to Swamiji about every little problem. But Jan took charge and made the appointment for us to talk to him.

The next morning, I was shaking as we climbed the stairs to his bedroom, and still shaking as we sat on the floor of his bedroom and waited for him to finish some paperwork.

Still sitting on his bed, Swamiji finally set down his papers and turned towards us. 'What's the matter?'

'We're here to discuss our fears with you, Swamiji,' Jan said.

'What fears?' he asked gruffly.

'I'm worried about Prabhakari being in charge. I think she has a vendetta against our family,' Jan said.

Swamiji looked at her through his tiny black eyes with a bit of disgust. Then he turned and looked at me. 'What's *your* problem?'

I swallowed hard and opened my mouth. My throat was dry, my voice low. 'Swamiji, when Sureshwari was here, I felt like I had a friend. But Prabhakari and I don't get along that well.'

'What does she do?'

'Well, she continually criticizes and attacks me.'

'Give me an example.' His comments came quickly and in short bursts, like shots out of a rifle.

His line of questioning had thrown me off guard. My mind raced to recall a specific encounter to recount, one that would illustrate the severity of my problem, but I was so anxious that I couldn't think clearly. 'She once called me a *bully* during a kitchen meeting in front of everyone,' I blurted out.

It wasn't the worst example. However, the incident was much crueller than it sounded.

'So?' he said brusquely. I had no direct response, so I switched gears.

'I've been having panic attacks and nightmares ever since Sureshwari left.'

He stared down at us for several seconds, saying nothing. Then he turned to Jan and started talking to her about me as if I weren't present.

'When fears create nightmares, it's something deep in the person's head. She needs to see a psychiatrist. Help her find one.'

This was not the first time Swamiji had instructed a devotee to seek psychiatric help. At that time, a growing number of people in the ashram were on anti-depressants, most at his suggestion. It appeared to be his go-to solution for anyone suffering from any issues whatsoever.

Swamiji ended our encounter by telling us both to forget about Prabhakari. 'She has so many things to worry about: finances, construction, video ... she can't also worry about people's feelings.'

How could someone *not* have to worry about people's feelings?

The next thing I knew, I was in a psychiatrist's office. That day, I joined the growing population of devotees on anti-depressants. The low-dose Lexapro did seem to help. It smoothed out the raw edges of the emotional circuits in my brain, but what helped me even more was the therapist Jan also advised me to see. She had found the therapist for herself following a traumatic car accident.

Elise, the therapist, changed my life. Instead of talking about the ashram on my first visit, out of the blue I talked about my brother, Michael, and my chronic guilt over his suicide at the age of twenty-two. I'd had recurring grief ever since, and the cycles of despair had always followed the same pattern. They would hit me about once every two years and last for about three months. This had been going on for almost ten years. I had always believed that devotion to Swamiji would dissolve away the anguish, but it never did.

Within the first hour, Elise helped me see that I was just a child myself at the time of my brother's death, and was therefore not capable of truly helping him. He and I came from the same dysfunctional family, so it's not like I had the skills necessary to help him. After my first healing session with Elise, the cycles of depression stopped completely.

I felt more unburdened than I had in years – and the renewed surge of inner strength came just in the nick of time.

The Million-Dollar Trip

Maharajji Visits the West

BEGINNING IN 1999, Swamiji had been telling us that Maharajji was coming to the US. In May 2005 he finally arrived.

At the news of his impending visit, devotees were beside themselves with excitement, and leapt eagerly into the chaos of preparation. Delirious with anticipation, they were ready and willing to do whatever it took to get Maharajji to Barsana Dham – from construction projects to decorations to special purchases of food and personal items.

About three months before he was scheduled to arrive, we were all called to a meeting. Prabhakari told us, 'We need to collect one crore rupees (a little over $250,000) before Maharajji makes the trip.'

Despite the excitement, there was a collective pause in the room. However, everyone rallied quickly, accepting that this was the price to pay for the embodiment of God to grace our lives in our own country.

Once the money issue was dealt with, devotees resumed the seemingly endless preparations that had to be made for the arrival of Maharajji and his 'divine family' members. Preparing for his arrival was not a simple matter. For one thing, he travelled with a minimum of four servants and his three daughters (all in their fifties), who shared three or four servants between them. On that trip, he also brought his two sons and three of his grandsons.

The accommodation requirements were exacting. No detail was too small for consideration – from a particular brand of hard-to-find toothpaste to the type of food stocked in their personal kitchens to the size of their big-screen TVs. It took a small army, a large bank account and a considerable number of man-hours to ensure that they were properly hosted.

Then there were the preparations for the hundreds of people who would come to see Maharajji. Although the accommodations and food preparation for devotees and visitors were far more spartan than they were for the 'divine family', it still required extensive manpower to house, feed and tend to a constantly revolving crowd of 200 to 500 guests.

Once he and his entourage arrived, we quickly realized that the down payment of $250,000 was just a drop in the 'collection bucket' for Maharajji's trip abroad. In fact, by the time he left Barsana Dham after a four-week stay, he had raised over one million dollars. This was accomplished through a well-orchestrated seva operation that rivalled nothing I had ever seen or heard about in India.

'Seva opportunities' in Barsana Dham USA included: attending a daily 'picnic' ($100), inviting him to your room ($600), going on a boat ride with him ($200), receiving a bite of his snack ($100), receiving a cookie from him ($250) and sitting in his room while he ate dinner ($2,500). He would even visit someone's house outside the ashram for the 'paltry' fee of anything between $5,000 to $10,000.

Seva opportunities began immediately upon his arrival in the ashram – a welcome with all the pomp and circumstance befitting a conquering king. Devotees dressed in authentic Indian garb welcomed his Mercedes at the main gates, and walked and danced beside his car in a slow-moving procession, chanting, playing drums and cymbals, and waving colourful flags and a banner all the way to the temple doors.

When he arrived at the temple entryway, someone opened the car door and he emerged to the traditional shouts of joy in India: 'Jay ho!' and 'Jay Shree Maharajji ki Jay!' Devotees parted like the Red Sea as he strode confidently into the prayer hall and straight to the throne at the front of the room, which was bedecked with a huge headboard, multicoloured flowers, golden embroidery, plush pillows and other decorations. As soon as he lay down, he instructed the devotees to begin the ritual of bowing to his feet – for $100 cash.

After collecting about $5,000, Maharajji retreated to his bedroom. Many of us followed him. He lay down on his perfectly adorned bed in his lavishly decorated bedroom and announced in Hindi that it was time for coffee. One of the preachers announced in English: 'Maharajji has graciously invited everyone to stay for coffee seva. Those who don't want to do the seva, please leave his room immediately.'

Someone asked: 'How much is the seva?'

'$250.'

I stayed in his bedroom, relishing the chance to sit in his presence during his first-ever trip to America, watch him eat toast and hear him tell jokes in Hindi. The seva lasted less than fifteen minutes.

The word 'coffee' is a misnomer that goes back to this particular seva's initial meaning of drinking a few drops of Maharajji's leftover coffee. Now that he no longer drank coffee, the seva had changed. He had toast and water instead, and we each received half a cup of soda and a handful of popcorn as we sat with him.

I attended the coffee seva again the next afternoon, sitting as close to the foot of his bed as possible. I went again and again, becoming so addicted to this semi-private time with Maharajji that I ended up attending nine coffee sevas in a row – for a grand total of $2,250. That was more than I'd spent on each of my two trips to India.

But that wasn't my only seva expenditure this time around. By the time he left, I had logged over $13,000 in seva debt. The group mentality that believed one should do whatever one possibly could for and with Maharajji was infectious. Clearly, I had been swept up in the mass hysteria.

Almost immediately, life in our westernized ashram began to emulate life in the ashrams in India. In fact, from the minute he stepped foot on the property, Barsana Dham USA seemed to morph into 'Maharajji World' – and it was difficult to remember we were still in America. One morning I even witnessed one of his preachers burning wood in a small stove outside his kitchen. Now our air had the same throat-tickling tinge of smoke that I had tried in vain to escape in India. Prior to Maharajji's visit, one devotee had rented a couple of cows in order to supply fresh milk for him. Seeing his attendants enter the kitchen twice a day with fresh buckets of milk became a common sight.

Our schedule was just as crazy as it had been in India, with the day beginning at 4:00 a.m. and crammed with satsangs and sevas. Just like in India, I felt like I was always trying to catch up.

With the frenzy surrounding nearly every minute of his visit, calculating the money owed for seva was a challenge. Most devotees kept little notebooks handy to jot down a running list of their expenditures. Often, the sevas happened so fast that it was easy to forget how quickly the debts were adding up. However, those expenditures never slipped through the cracks of the people in charge of money collection. Each of us was assigned to a money manager, who carefully tracked all our seva activity. The five or six seva managers fed our seva debts to one primary devotee accountant, who then tracked the rapidly escalating debts on a central spreadsheet.

While I was racking up thousands of dollars in seva debt, others were spending more than I was. One time when I checked my records, I noticed that the devotee listed directly under me had a tab of $90,000.

At least that woman was wealthy. Some of the poorer devotees were also going into significant seva debt. I asked one woman, who was a secretary and single mother, why she was spending so much money – money I knew she didn't have.

'I have very little fun in my life,' she said sheepishly, 'and this is my only opportunity for it. So what if I have to get an extra part-time job to pay off my seva?'

Other devotees had other reasons for giving way more money than they could afford. Perhaps it was one of Maharajji's repeated themes: Give your entire tan-man-dhan to the guru, meaning your body, mind and personal wealth. He stated that if we failed to do this, we likely would not make it into the divine world.

Prakashanand planned many special events to give the devotees plenty of reasons to give Maharajji more money. One of them was a Mother's Day celebration in his honour, since he had arrived in May. For the occasion, Maharajji visited a person's room or home for $600. The person would 'host' him for a few minutes, doing arti to him and offering him a snack. The 'fund raiser' was such a success that, later that day, he bragged about the number of room visits he'd done in one morning – over eighty. Inspired, Maharajji added several made-up holidays to the schedule: Maharajji Day, Sister's Day, Brother's Day and Lover's Day – all of which provided opportunities to *buy* time with him, even if it was just a minute or two.

He also added boat rides, swims in the pond and other unique activities to the seva schedule. After a while, when the preachers could not gather enough volunteers for some of the sevas because people were running out of money, they began asking devotees directly to do a particular seva.

One day Divakari asked me to attend one of his dinners for $2,500. When I told her that I couldn't afford it, she seemed frustrated and cited Maharajji's oft-spoken advice: 'You should give him all your money – it's all his anyway.'

Maharajji Returns

And Chaos Ensues

IN 2007, JUST two years after his million-dollar trip to Barsana Dham, Maharajji decided to leave India once again. This time for a grand, four-month 'world tour'.

This trip originally included stops in Singapore, Fiji, New Zealand, San Diego, Austin, Trinidad and Canada. We were expecting him in Austin on 9 May. But just days before he left India, we got the first of three calls regarding last-minute trip changes. He was not going to Fiji after all, and he would be arriving in Austin two weeks earlier than expected. Within a week, we received the second call: Maharajji was not going to New Zealand, and would arrive at Barsana Dham on 9 April. Then, the final itinerary change came: Maharajji would not be going to San Diego and would be arriving in Barsana Dham on 1 April.

We were not given any explanation for these mysterious schedule changes.

We had originally assumed that we had more than four months to get ready. With each update, preparations become increasingly frantic. On this trip, apart from his three daughters, he was also bringing his wife, Amma, who was his age, frail, and always dressed like an Indian-style China doll, with a decorative sari and lots of jewellery. Like her daughters, she was always accompanied by a servant or two to tend to her every need.

Due to his changed arrival date, we had to squeeze several months of work into two weeks. Just two days before his arrival, the place was still in a shambles and the new video camera had not yet arrived. This was a critical problem, because it was expected that nearly every waking moment of Maharajji's public life would be filmed.

After many days and nights of non-stop preparation, the devotees greeted Maharajji's arrival with a frenzy of chanting, drumming and cymbal playing. When he was helped out of the Mercedes in the temple's porte cochère, he threw his hands in the air, waving to the crowd, and did a little bouncing dance. Devotees quickly placed flower garlands around his neck. Then he bounded up the steps and walked rapidly into the prayer hall. A crowd of devotees stood on either side of a plush saffron cloth that had been laid on the floor for him to follow, like the Yellow Brick Road. The path led him through the centre of the prayer hall and directly to a bed with an oversized headboard that was ostentatiously decorated in fancy fabrics, beads, lights and other bric-a-brac.

Closely following on the wheels of Maharajji's Mercedes were the luxury cars carrying his wife and three daughters. Behind them were several ordinary cars and vans containing the family's many servants and devotees who were tagging along on the 'world tour', like groupies following rock stars.

A sea of ecstatic faces beamed at Maharajji as he entered the prayer hall. The crowd of devotees smiled widely, eyes focused squarely on him, as they shouted 'Maharajji ki Jay ho!' over and over again.

As he sat on his bed, the devotees danced and chanted around him. With his encouragement, the chanting grew louder and louder, which incited the drummers and cymbal players into a frenzy of booming percussion and ringing metal. Singing turned into screaming. People crowded as close to him as they could, pushing and shoving to get a better look at him. As always, he loved the attention.

As Maharajji's wife entered the prayer hall, she was directed towards her own smaller and more simply decorated bed. His wife slept in her own bedroom, and they did not eat meals together. They did not spend much private time together. The devotees had been intimated that sex had not been required to produce their five children.

His daughters sat on the floor on carpets placed around their mother's bed. The prayer hall seating arrangement in Austin replicated almost exactly the seating arrangements in their India ashrams.

For the next six weeks, Maharajji ruled the world inside the ashram gates. In Maharajji World, his every command was followed, every word gobbled up and every desire catered to.

I was not at all happy about his second visit. I couldn't understand why everyone seemed so ecstatic to have him there again, since our lives had been turned upside down in a test of endurance that seemed lost before he even arrived. But seeing the devotees go crazy around him, I felt all alone in my irritation.

My solitary displeasure did not go unnoticed – by Prabhakari.

One day she stopped me in the hall and told me, 'You have to be happier when you are around Maharajji, because you are ruining the videos.'

'What are you talking about?' I asked, mystified.

'Go see Allison, she'll show you what I mean.'

I knocked on the video room door. Allison, Prabhakari's right-hand woman, sat me down and proceeded to show me an already cued-up video. The camera panned across a sea of smiling faces in the prayer hall. Then, in the middle of the blissful crowd, one clearly unhappy face stood out – mine. I wasn't just not smiling, but was actually grimacing. It was shocking to see video evidence of how badly I hid my feelings.

I lied to her that I'd had a headache – it would not do me any good to admit my feelings about Maharajji's intrusive presence. After assuring Allison that I would try not to ruin any more of the videos, I fell into a routine that included a very unique seva: baking birthday cakes. One of the seva opportunities that devotees could purchase from Maharajji was to celebrate their birthday with him, whether or not it was actually their real birth date. A surprising number of people wanted to participate, even though it cost $2,500. So many, in fact, that a cake was needed every evening for the occasion. Maharajji would cut it and blow out the candles on behalf of the 'birthday' person. The cakes had to be large to look good on video. Before he left six weeks later, I had baked, decorated and served over fifty giant birthday cakes, which netted him more than $125,000.

Maharajji had many desires, some of which were well known. He wanted people to attend the multiple hours of satsang and chant loudly and not fall asleep in the prayer hall. He wanted devotees to get by on simple (often tasteless) food and austere (often crowded) living conditions. He wanted devotees to do as much monetary seva as possible, even if it meant going into debt. Above all, he wanted them to reduce their worldly relationships and increase their 'relationship' with him – a bond which which he claimed was eternal.

However, some of Maharajji's wishes were known only to a few of the devotee women. Among his private desires were what kind of sheets he liked on his bed, what kind of perfumes and oils he used, and what kind of girls and women he preferred to spend 'private time' with.

These desires were not known to devotees in the general population until the summer of 2007. Until then, he and his inner circle had somehow managed to keep these a secret from the majority of his followers for nearly six decades.

But three weeks after he left Barsana Dham for Trinidad, his bedroom doors were opened wide for the whole world to have a look – and what we saw was not pretty, wholesome or divine.

Charan Seva

My Initiation into a Secret Ritual

THERE WAS A shortage of women when Maharajji arrived five weeks early in Barsana Dham in 2007. That's how I ended up in his bedroom one afternoon doing the secretive 'charan seva'. The euphemism means, 'worshipping the guru's lotus feet', but in Maharajji's case, the activity had very little to do with his feet.

I was leaving the prayer hall early in the morning the day after Maharajji arrived when Carla stopped me. It was 5:30 a.m. Most of the devotees were still in the prayer hall, chanting. I was going back to bed to get some more sleep.

She approached me purposefully and asked, 'Would you like to press Maharajji today?'

Of all the questions Carla could have asked me, this is the last one I would have imagined. I'd never been asked to press him before. I didn't know exactly what it meant, or that it was an option.

I was astonished. After all, spending time in Maharajji's room was considered a great honour among the devotees. Up until then, I'd only spent time in his bedroom when I was spending money on seva. I felt a rush of happiness – maybe this was my chance to actually feel his divinity.

'Yes, I would. I'd love to. Thank you so much for asking me.'

I was gushing, partly because I could not believe my luck to be in the right place at the right time, and partly out of concern that she would take back the offer if I didn't show the proper level of interest and appreciation.

Carla studied a small notebook she was carrying. Using a pen as a pointer, she said, 'You can either press him at six this morning after his walk or at five this afternoon, right after arti.'

Since I had planned to go back to sleep that morning, I told her I'd take the 5:00 p.m. slot. Then I instantly thought better of not taking the first opportunity available. 'Well, maybe this morning instead.' I was overly excited by the enormity of the event and probably wouldn't be able to sleep anyway.

'I've got four women already, and have a couple more to ask.' I could see the page she was studying. It contained lists with times and women's names. There were five or six separate lists.

The last thing I wanted to do was create a problem for Carla, and possibly lose my chance. 'Five this afternoon is fine then,' I said. She seemed satisfied with my decision.

'Meet me in the hallway outside his bedroom fifteen minutes early,' she said. 'Take a shower, cut your nails really short, don't wear any jewellery and don't tell anyone.'

'Okay,' I said without hesitation.

She looked up to see if I comprehended her directions. Then her eyes squinted slightly, as if second-guessing her decision to invite me to do the precious charan seva. 'Do you have a firm grip?'

'Yes,' I blurted out, not sure if I actually did and fearing that I didn't.

She put her arm out. 'Here. Press my arm.'

I gripped the muscle of her forearm and pressed as hard as I could.

'That's good,' she declared. 'Press him really hard. The harder the better. That's how he likes it.' Then she pivoted and walked away.

In the bhakti tradition, pressing (or massaging) a guru is a sacred honour for a devotee. Typically, it is the charan or the feet of the guru that is massaged. However, few followers actually get to press their gurus' feet, because the guru has such a large following that it's impossible for the majority of his followers to get physically close to him or her. Often it's because the guru is no longer living. As a result, the idea of pressing the lotus feet of the guru is more a concept than a reality for the average devotee.

My guru was very much alive and had a relatively modest congregation compared to other gurus. However, some devotees had much more access to Maharajji than me. So after fifteen years on this spiritual path, to be asked to 'press my guru' made me feel like I'd reached the pinnacle of my spiritual journey. I must have finally reached a significantly high stage of devotion to be included in such an intimate activity. In that moment, I felt that every hardship I had endured along the way was now paying off. I couldn't wait until evening to experience such an exquisite blessing.

All five of the women selected for the 5:00 p.m. pressing session showed up fifteen minutes early. The other women in my group were Indian, ranging in age from late twenties to mid-fifties. Carla directed us into a small hallway with two doors, one of which led into Maharajji's bedroom via his bathroom. The space was about six feet by three feet.

'Wait here for his assistant to open the door,' Carla instructed authoritatively. 'Maharajji is still walking, but he'll be in his room soon. Keep quiet. We don't want anyone to know you are here, especially the men.' Then she disappeared.

As we waited silently for several minutes, I tried to savour the moment, but as the seconds ticked by, I grew increasingly nervous about what was about to happen. The hallway was stuffy, and with five bodies crowded together, the space was growing warmer and more uncomfortable by the minute. I began to sweat. Finally, I broke the silence to distract my mind from my nerves and physical discomfort.

'Have you ever done this before?' I asked one of the women in a low tone.

'No,' she said softly, shaking her head.

I looked at the other women.

'No,' said two others.

'I've done it many times,' said the fifth and the oldest. 'I press him all the time. I travel with him a lot.'

I was relieved to have at least one experienced person among us. All four of us looked to her.

'What do we do?' I asked.

'Each of us has to take a position on his leg or foot, but only his right foot, because the left one hurts from an old injury. You have to be very careful while massaging his other foot. It is very delicate. And use the palms of your hands, not your fingertips, so you don't hurt him.'

'I don't want his foot,' I said, fearful of causing him pain.

'I'll do it,' she offered. 'Who wants to do his thighs?' None of us answered. Then I said, 'I will.'

Another woman said, 'I will too.'

'Okay, you two take a thigh and you two take a calf. If you have any jewellery on, take it off.' Clearly, this woman knew the routine. Two women took off rings and put them in their bags.

The door finally opened and Neelu, Maharajji's main assistant, waved us in briskly, 'Come on, come on. Maharajji is waiting.'

We hurried through the bathroom into his bedroom. The air-conditioned coolness was a relief after the stifling hallway, but was laced with the strong smell of foreign perfume.

Maharajji was lying on his bed in his orange short-sleeved shirt and dhoti against a neatly positioned pile of pillows. His legs were spread open in a diamond shape. His arms were open too, resting on pillows positioned on both sides of his body.

Each of us hurried to our predetermined spot, climbed onto his bed and kneeled on the mattress. I placed my hands on his thigh and started to grab the muscle. It was difficult to massage him since he was very thin and there was very little meat on his bones.

Within a minute, Maharajji said something in Hindi and Neelu barked at us, 'Maharajji wants you to press harder.' Then she flipped the switch, dimming the lights, and left the room through another door. Maharajji continued to lie in the same position, saying nothing.

I was shaking, but concentrating on massaging him as firmly as possible, without digging my nails or fingertips into his flesh. I moved my hands up and down his thigh, gripping whatever muscle I could find. The fabric of his thin dhoti kept bunching up under my fingers, threatening to spread open at his groin. I paused a few times to quickly straighten the fabric to preserve his modesty.

After I'd been massaging him for about five minutes, he touched my hand with two of his long, bony fingers and nudged it towards his groin. I assumed he was indicating for me to massage higher on his thigh. But I was already massaging as high as I possibly could. I moved my hands a few millimetres higher, taking great pains not to come into contact with his private parts.

Then he touched my hand again, pushing it still closer to his crotch, but with a little more force. I couldn't imagine what he was actually suggesting, and kept my hands just short of the top of his thigh. He didn't try again, and, lost in the thrill of being so up close and personal with my guru, I pushed the strange incident into the back of my mind.

After another ten minutes of massaging him, my legs were shaking from squatting in a kneeling position. I was starting to sweat despite the room's frigid temperature. Fearing that a drop of sweat would fall on him, I quickly wiped my face with the edge of my sari.

Finally, after almost fifteen minutes of massage, he abruptly indicated that the charan seva was over with a curt 'Jao!' As we scrambled off his bed, he repositioned himself and reached for a buzzer on his night table. As we scurried out through the bathroom door, Neelu entered from another.

I walked around the ashram for the rest of the day in a daze, which I assumed was devotional euphoria. It was intoxicating to be in on this secret seva. Now I understood why female devotees kept such things hush-hush. It was like some kind of initiation into a super-secret club – the kind where people say, 'I could tell you, but then I'd have to kill you.'

That's how secretive charan seva was.

More Charan Seva

Seeing and Not Believing

DESPITE MY MYSTERIOUS first experience, I craved the intimacy of pressing Maharajji. As it turned out, there was plenty of opportunity. Since he had arrived ahead of schedule, very few devotees from outside Austin had been able to rearrange their plans fast enough to be there during the first week of his visit. I gleaned that Swamiji had told the women organizing charan seva to include all the female devotees in Barsana Dham. I also realized the service was typically the domain of young, pretty or wealthy women. But at a pinch, any female would do, after all, there were at least five time slots each day to fill up with five to six women each. And that was just for charan seva.

My second time in his bedroom followed the same routine as the first, but with one difference. As I approached his bed, intending to take the same position on his left thigh, he grumbled a few words in Hindi. I had no idea what he said, but I felt that he was indicating that he did not want me in that spot again. I instinctively turned to see who was behind me. It was a nubile Indian woman in her mid-twenties. I indicated for her to take the position. Maharajji didn't say anything, but he did smile, and I sensed that he was pleased with the arrangement. I climbed up on the bed and kneeled next to his left calf. We all started pressing our assigned sections of his body.

Maharajji was downright skeletal. His calves had even less meat on them than his thighs, and it was a real challenge to find anywhere to grip. I struggled to find a muscle and press him with the required degree of pressure, without merely pinching his skin. I was concentrating so fully on the task at hand that I barely noticed what the other women were doing.

In about fifteen minutes, he began to shift his body upright. This was the signal that he'd had enough. We all scrambled off the bed and hurried out of his bedroom. At least, I assumed we had all left. Later, after learning more about Maharajji's private habits, I cannot honestly say that every woman came out at the same time that I did.

A few days later, I approached Carla. 'When can I press Maharajji again?'

She glanced down at her daily lists. A slot in the afternoon session was open. She wrote my name down and reminded me to show up fifteen minutes early. 'Some women aren't showing up on time and I have to run and find a replacement at the last minute,' she said with irritation. I was surprised to hear that any woman would miss the chance of a lifetime.

This time I planned to take position on his calf again. But I was the last one to enter his room, and as I walked towards his bed, all the positions except his left thigh had been taken. So I climbed on the bed and started pressing his thigh again. At one point, when I tried to straighten his slipping dhoti, I noticed something strange. The woman massaging his right thigh had both of her hands under the fabric of his dhoti, over his groin, and was moving them up and down. I couldn't believe what I was seeing.

As I concentrated on my thigh-pressing duties, I couldn't help but keep glancing over, trying to understand what I was seeing. After determining that she was, in fact, massaging his private parts, one thought entered my mind: *I'm so glad that is not me doing that to him.*

The woman was a long-time devotee, whom I'd known my entire time in the organization. I would have been mortified to have someone see me engaging in such an activity – even on the 'divine master'. I left the room, handling this shocking experience the same way I'd handled other uncomfortable experiences over the years – I buried it in the dark recesses of my brain.

After this experience, my enthusiasm for charan seva began to falter. I didn't ask to go into Maharajji's bedroom again for a while. But then the euphoria of being part of the inner circle overrode my common sense. I asked Carla for another chance to massage him.

As I waited for my fourth charan seva, the group of women discussed which positions we wanted to take. Right away, I said, 'I want a calf.' At least that way I would not be in the dangerous thigh area. I was soon thankful for planning ahead. As I massaged his left calf, I saw some movement out of the corner of my right eye. I glanced over and saw that Maharajji's left hand was under the sari of the woman next to me, and he was squeezing her breasts. Again, I kept trying to verify I was not imagining things. Again, I thought instinctively: *Thank God that's not me he's doing that to.*

When I walked out of the room, I knew that was the last time I was performing charan seva, for I knew more than I wanted to about the ritual.

However, what I didn't know was that there was another secret seva, also available only to female devotees, and it was called 'private time'.

Maharajji Leaves

The Beginning of the End

FINALLY, AFTER SIX weeks in Barsana Dham, Maharajji left for the next leg of his 'World Tour' – Trinidad and Tobago.

As soon as he was gone, the ashram became deathly quiet. But I felt a collective sigh of relief from the devotees after a month and a half of non-stop cooking, cleaning, chanting and chasing after Maharajji. Everyone was exhausted.

But our relief was short-lived. A few days later, Swamiji called a meeting of all the ashram residents and we gathered in his bedroom. There, he told us that while most of us had done a lot of physical seva during Maharajji's stay, the majority of us had not done our service with 'the right devotional feelings'. He then informed us that we might get a second chance to serve Maharajji the correct way. 'He might return to Barsana Dham for a couple of weeks before he returns to India. If he does, you will all have to work harder to get closer to him.'

One devotee asked: 'Do you mean internally or externally closer to him?'

He shot her a dirty look. 'Internally,' he barked.

Swamiji ended his talk with a curious statement: 'Some of you have had personal experiences with Maharajji that are very private. Very, very private. And you must keep them private.'

I left his room miserable. He can't be serious, I thought. Everyone is beyond exhausted. How can we whip the 'Maharajji Show' back into action with no energy, no time and no more money? And it wasn't just me feeling negative this time. I looked around at my companions' faces as we filed out of Swamiji's bedroom. They did not look happy.

In fact, no one was smiling this time.

PART FOUR

In the Cult

Losing My Religion

'Filled with insatiable desires, full of hypocrisy,
Pride and arrogance, holding unwholesome views
Through delusion, they work with unholy resolve.'
– Lord Krishna, Bhagavadgita, 16:10

'I heard many things in hell.'
– Edgar Allan Poe, *The Tell-Tale Heart*

Maharajji Is Arrested

Bad News Rising

I HATE TO receive news and then have to wait to hear the whole story.

On 25 May 2007, all Barsana Dham and Austin devotees received an email from the administration asking us to attend an important meeting that night after satsang. There was some 'sensitive news' about Maharajji that had to be shared. My gut told me something was very wrong. We were rarely told anything at all, so why now? But even my instincts did not foretell how bad this news would be.

In the hours leading up to the meeting, I desperately wanted to know what was going on. The minutes ticked by slowly. That evening when I went to the dining hall for dinner, Raj, an Indian devotee who lived in the ashram, was preparing the evening meal. He might know something, I thought.

'Raj, what is tonight's meeting about?' I asked.

'You'll find out soon,' he responded cryptically.

'Just give me a hint. I've been waiting all day. I'm a nervous wreck.'

He sighed.

'Please,' I implored.

'Something happened in Trinidad. A person accused Maharajji of something he didn't do.'

'What happened?'

'Let Prabhakari tell you tonight. She'll explain the whole story.'

Naturally, this titbit only fanned my curiosity. The rest of the evening passed at a crawl. Finally it was 9:00 p.m. As was the custom in Barsana Dham for group meetings, we gathered in Swamiji's sitting room.

It took about ten minutes for the devotees to gather. I sat on the floor, against the back wall, impatiently watching everyone meander in. When all of us were finally seated, Prabhakari strutted into the room with the usual self-important look, casually holding a piece of paper. She sat on the floor near Swamiji's couch in front of a microphone stand and adjusted it with pomp and circumstance.

She began by prepping us and setting the stage, explaining how 'when a great spiritual power appears on earth, evil powers also appear to oppose him'. Then she gave us an abbreviated history lesson about the ongoing culture clash in Trinidad and Tobago. She told us how the country is roughly split between Indian and Black citizens, how there's tension between the two groups, and how, when she was there with Swamiji in the early 1990s, she'd been told that one of the newspapers basically printed only sensational stories and was always on the hunt for 'yellow journalism'.

Then she told us that this lowly newspaper had reported an incident that had occurred in Trinidad involving Maharajji and a young woman. Without saying the word 'black', she made it clear that this particular woman was from the country's non-Hindu population. Prabhakari stressed that the woman 'was not even a devotee or a potential devotee' but had accused Maharajji of 'assault' and that he had been arrested six days ago. That was the only word she used to describe the incident – assault. No further details of the accusation were given.

'The woman went to the home where Maharajji was staying for satsang, but was never alone with him,' explained Prabhakari. 'Everyone knows that Neelu is always with Maharajji. Many devotees were with him and know that nothing took place. We believe that her story is a set-up by a rival spiritual organization, which has been doing everything it can to sway public opinion against Hindus prior to an upcoming election.'

For one thing, I knew that Neelu was not always with Maharajji, so the story was not all that foolproof.

Then she told us how Barsana Dham was going to respond to the situation. She referenced a recent event about an Amish community in Pennsylvania, where a man had walked into a classroom full of children, taken them hostage and killed several of them. It was widely reported that the Amish community's reaction in the midst of their grief was to show compassion for the shooter.

Prabhakari said: 'We're going to take the high road like the Amish did when their children were killed. We are going to show compassion for the person who tried to slander Maharajji. We're going to ignore the accuser and feel sympathy for her.'

I found this reference curious because, usually, Swamiji would never let anyone compare his organization to any other, let alone admit to following in its footsteps for any reason. This was completely out of character.

Prabhakari added: 'In response to the incident, we have prepared a statement from Jagadguru Kripalu Parishat (JKP), Barsana Dham, and it has been signed by the members of our management committee. This is going to be our formal reply to the accusation.'

Then she read from the paper she'd carried into the room. As she read the note, I could hear JKP, Barsana Dham's public relations minds at work. Part of the page-long statement said: 'For the people responsible for fabricating this unfortunate and defamatory scenario, we can only feel pity that personal greed and political ambitions have driven them to such a terrible and hurtful act of trying to defame a great spiritual leader and to shake the faith of Hindus in their divine religion and greatest saints.'

Then she said, 'The good news is that, so far, this story has not been picked up by the Western press. As far as I know, it is only being covered in the Trinidad papers and in a few of India's news outlets.'

Prabhakari concluded saying, 'I asked Swamiji what I should tell you, and he said: "Don't think about it." Maharajji told me to tell everyone: "Don't talk about it."'

She then added her own opinion: 'I feel that no devotees should go on the Internet to read anything about this. That would be a transgression.'

Instinctively, I did not believe her evasive explanation to this shocking and upsetting turn of events. I sensed there was something more to this story. Perhaps it was because of what I had seen during the charan seva sessions. Anyhow, Prabhakari's instructions had the opposite effect on me. I was not going to blindly accept this organization's party line. I was going to find out for myself exactly what was going on around there.

Con Realization

A Crack in the Façade

AFTER PRABHAKARI'S DISCLOSURE about Maharajji's arrest, I returned to my office and typed three words into Google – Kripalu, Maharaj and Trinidad. Within minutes, my world was shattered beyond imagination.

The search result was filled with news articles from Trinidad and India. The headlines were generally the same: 'Visiting 85-year-old Indian Swami Charged with Rape in Trinidad' and 'Indian Swami in Trinidad Rape Row Gets Bail'. The word 'rape' jumped out at me like a flashing red light. Prabhakari had clearly said 'assault', which could have meant anything, but rape meant only one thing.

I continued to read, and realized that Maharajji had been arrested on 20 May. It bothered me that we were hearing about it only five days later. We were his dedicated followers but the rest of the world knew about this event before we did. They were treating us like children while acting like all-knowing parents once again.

I was in shock over the news. But still, a new emotion began to bubble up inside me, like molten lava just waiting to erupt. I was angry. This emotion replaced my normal apathetic acceptance of the organization's line.

The news reports revealed the real story. A twenty-two-year-old Guyanese girl had gone to see him at the home of the wealthy family with which Maharajji was staying. She had gone for spiritual benefit but was invited into his bedroom instead. First with a group of ladies to press his legs, and later to spend time alone with him. During her private time with him, in which she thought she would be given private spiritual guidance, Maharajji told her to take off her clothes. He then sprayed her with perfume and told her to put his penis in her mouth. He then pulled her into his bed and penetrated her.

While this news was shocking in itself, the comments on many of the articles sent my nervous system over the edge. There were dozens of comments written by people from around the world – the US, India, Australia, Fiji, Ireland, and more – many of which seemed to refer to long-held secrets about the man I called my guru. As I read them, I felt panicky, suffocated.

On 24 May, someone using the moniker 'Satya' wrote a comment on Guruphiliac.com:

> You don't know this guy, it seems. He was already charged with rape a couple of decades ago in India, where the newspapers were headlined 'Bhakta Bhalaat Ka'. I have the old news clipping and I know a bunch of people whom he's made sex advances to over the years, which is why I'd like to see him pay for his crimes. One woman told me he tried to rape her just last year. How does anyone know how old he actually is? Seen his birth certificate? The guy's a fraud through and through, he'll tell any lie to get his ends. He fakes language difficulties, he may be faking his 'aged frailty' too. And ask any woman in India

> which men you have to watch out for with roving hands and eyes, the old or the young?

The next day, Satya added the following comment:

> I have an article from 1991 in Hindi, which I am not good at reading. It has a picture of this Ram Tripathi Kripalu surrounded by police and is headed 'Bhakta Bhalaat Ka' which in my limited understanding means something like 'Holy Rapist' – Bhalaat means rape and Bhakta means devotee saint. I forwarded a copy of that article to journalists covering the court case. Other than that, an American woman I know went to this 'Jagadguru' Kripalu's ashram in India last year, lured there by an Indian woman who is a close devotee of the 'Swami'. After some days of prepping, she was led into Kripalu's bedroom, where he grabbed her in 'inappropriate places', but she was able to struggle free and get out of there. Outside, the disciples told her the Swami's molesting was the pinnacle of his 'mercy' and tried to make her pay a *biwentll* for the privilege of his inappropriate services...! 15 years ago I knew some women who went to Kripalu from the west to become disciples, but he told them they would have to sleep with him.

I could barely comprehend what I was reading. But there was more. I learnt that this was not Maharajji's first arrest. He had been arrested before in 1991 in India for allegedly raping three underage girls. Along with being freaked out by this news, I also realized one curious coincidence: this was the same time that Swamiji had stopped talking about Maharajji.

I couldn't help but search for more information. I stayed up researching and reading comments until late in the morning. By 3:00 a.m., I had read all the news and commentary that I could find. I shut off my computer and went to bed.

I felt dizzy and disoriented with the avalanche of new information.

In the past few hours, the world I had known had cracked, turned to dust and had been blown away by the wind. My mind was overloaded, racing with the news and revelations. And I had no one to talk to about it with – because to do that would be a serious transgression.

Where in the Hell Am I?

The Guru's Secrets are Spilled

FOR THE WHOLE of the next month, more and more news and comments kept spilling out online. I fell asleep each night only after I had read everything that was discussed about him that day. When I woke up each morning, I only wanted to know what new information had been revealed while I'd slept.

Every morning I got dressed, ate breakfast, went to office and logged on to find new comments posted by people from around the world. Clearly, many ex-devotees and informed third parties had been holding in much pain and torment, and many skeletons. Now, they finally had an outlet; it was as if someone had lanced a wound and all the disturbing secrets came pouring out. The dam that had held Maharajji's secrets for so long had been breached, and people were unleashing decades of pent-up knowledge, experiences and frustration.

My world had shrunk to the space of my fifteen-inch computer screen. Within days, I came to the conclusion that Maharajji was the diametric opposite of the kind of person we thought he was. I was determined to get to the bottom of this organization.

The most revealing commentary was posted on 22 June by someone using the name 'Insider' on Guruphiliac.com. S/he opened up the doors to Maharajji's bedroom in a way that no one else had to date:

I was an insider (I mean a real insider) in Kripalu Maharajji's organization. I was extremely devoted to him and to his organization and had many spiritual experiences and great spiritual insights. I later found out that spiritual experiences arise out of your own sincerity and efforts and have nothing to do with the so-called guru or teacher. After all, God or Krishna (call him what you will) is still there, and He responds to sincere seekers regardless of how big a fraud the teacher is.

My heart was broken when, slowly but surely, the fraudulent nature of Kripalu Maharajji's mission became known to me. There were many, many examples of corruption of the mission that came before me, before I took the extremely difficult step of renouncing this teacher and organization. I could write a book on this, but I'll simply sum up some key points for those of you that have an open mind on such things. Trust me (actually trust yourself), without willingness to stand up for the truth, you will never get anywhere spiritually.

1. Kripalu Maharaj definitely has an obsession with sex, although he teaches others that there is no 'anand' in this world. There have been many instances of very creditable reports and charges against him. Most of these are from very good and sincere people that are bastions of the community and really sincere to God. However, modesty, embarrassment and the fear of a powerful organization that could hurt them makes them hesitate to speak out. The father of the girls from Nagpur that took the case against him all the way to the Indian Supreme Court was a rare and very brave exception. This father could have settled easily for large amounts of money that Kripalu's organization would have been too willing to pay to end this case. That he and his daughters fought and are still fighting for justice shows that they are not motivated by money or fame. They just want justice!

2. This is how it works today. To sit in Maharajji's presence, to touch his feet, to have coffee with him, to drink charanamrit

and even to be hit by his slippers means that there is a charge. They call it 'seva', but basically nothing is free. Have a chappal hit you and enjoy the 'grace' of 'chappal seva', then pay $100 for the privilege!

3. However, there is one special 'seva' open only to women. A secret 'seva' called 'charan seva' that is free. For this, Maharajji's preachers take all the unknowing women into the room where Maharajji is lying on his bed. The lights are dimmed and the women surround him and press his body. The most attractive women are positioned around his pillow and within reach of his hands. The lights are then turned out completely, giving Maharajji the chance to grope the pretty women close to him. If they do not pull back, they are invited to stay back!

4. Maharajji's children and grandchildren often travel with him at the cost of devotees' donations. Their slightest wishes, no matter how materialistic, are again fulfilled at devotees' expense. Huge sums of money are raised through 'sevas' with little, if any, accounting of where it goes, while no expense is spared for the 'divine family'. Any spiritual person can tell that this family is quite materialistic and has no spiritual virtues. Maharajji himself is driven around India in a Mercedes.

5. Brainwashing is accomplished by telling 'devotees' to not read or listen to any other teachings and to limit their association with only 'devotees'. Maharajji wears special scents to create the impression that his body exudes divine fragrances and the entire field of senses is used to create the aura of divinity. His publicity department is the most professional and his preachers claim that he is the most divine descension ever, greater even than Krishna or Rama!

6. In Trinidad, Maharajji's organization is called Radha Madhav Society. Its head in Trinidad is called Didiji. She is yet another fraud whose last organization in Oklahoma had to be shut down because of many sexual allegations against her and

> her relationship with Kripalu Maharaj. Even her website was erased so that nothing embarrassing about her would come out.

Along with Insider, there were hundreds of other people sharing information. Each revelation provided another brushstroke to the new picture I was formulating about the strange and scary world in which I suddenly found myself.

> He (Kripalu) makes his disciples believe that he is no less than the Lord Krishna; and this sleeping with his female disciples is as similar as Lord Krishna's flirtations with thousands of Gopis! How do I say this? Because I was a part of this organization for a long time (5 yrs) and know quite a lot of the insides that remain hidden from the common eyes. The atmosphere there within is full of secrets that most people do not know about. I repeatedly used to see women go into his room during the resting period in the afternoon and at night; but it was justified as for massaging the master's feet!! It was when he tried to sexually exploit my OWN mother on one instance, that his past history was confirmed. I no longer believe in his path nor his organization. It is nothing more than mockery of true spiritualism … he is nothing more than a perverted sex-machine.
>
> – Anonymous, Guruphiliac.com, 30 May 2007

> Witnessing his ashrams similar to brothel(s) … Most of the men may not know the secret sexual encounters happening as it is seen from outside that these girls are simply doing their kitchen seva or domestic chores. But his personal female aides regularly arrange appointments for the 'intimate seva of the guru' … behind the closed doors of their guru.
>
> – JSR, Monsters & Critics, 7 June 2007

One young woman shared the steps to her own abuse by Kripalu. It started with being taken into charan seva for 'approval'. Next, the didis (preachers) took her into his room and closed the door behind them. Then, trapped, he took full advantage of her, including putting his tongue down her mouth and touching her body anywhere he pleased, all the while telling her that what he was doing was divine. She indicated that she could not even tell exactly what inappropriate acts he forced her to engage in, perhaps due to modesty or embarrassment.

> He sexually abused me!! … You think of him as God … You question he is 85, why can't you just leave? … The reason being: shock. As he does what he pleases ...
>
> – Anonymous, Big News Network, 22 June 2007

As I read comments like these for days on end, I felt like I was living in an altered universe. I was so overcome with shock and terror that, most days, my world felt as if it had tilted off its axis. Some days I wasn't even sure that if I lifted one foot off the ground, the world would still be underneath me when I set it back down.

The more I read, the more I wondered: where in the hell am I?

Reading Between Their Lies

Grasping at Excuses

AS PEOPLE REVEALED more disturbing facts and exposed Maharajji's criminal behaviour, his supporters wrote in to defend him. With comments ranging from the uber-pious to the absurd, these people seemed to have an answer for everything. Some said he didn't do it. Some made excuses for his behaviour. Some said it was a 'smear campaign' against Hindus in general or him in particular. Some said the 'worldly' people could not understand his 'divine actions'. Some claimed that all great saints who appeared on earth have had to endure the slings and arrows of heathens.

On 8 June, 'Crusader' accused those bringing Maharajji's misdeeds to light as having ulterior motives on the website Topix:

> You dirty minds, plotting stories & trying to defame the 5th Original Jagadguru ... I'm sure you were associated with him for your own personal (materialistic) gain not for spiritual gain.

'Ramjee' wrote the following regarding the plight of all saints on earth on Topix on June 9:

> History bears evidence that Godly saints have always been misunderstood .... Their divine reality was recognized only after they left the world. The Truth will be revealed in course.

Another commenter insisted on Guruphiliac on 12 June that, because Maharajji is divine, the entire incident is one big leela:

> It surely is nothing but a leela of shree Maharaj Ji and he will be declared innocent pretty soon but this will happen as and when shree Maharajji wishes so because he only knows his leela. We cannot reach to his level in hundreds of our life to understand what his leela is.

When all else failed, 'Anonymous' pleaded with devotees on Guruphiliac.com on 25 July to stop reading the revelations:

> We all know who our Maharaj Ji is and by reading these mean things about him we are only hurting ourselves. We must think

what would make our Maharaj Ji happy and it wouldn't be reading and corresponding with these people and this blog.

What his supporters failed to realize was this simple fact: Kripalu's secretive dark world had now been exposed to the bright light of day – and that could never be undone.

Thank God for the Internet

A Chink in the Guru's Armour

WHILE I WAS rapidly learning who Maharajji really was, I could not figure out how Swamiji fit into his secretive history.

I wondered what Swamiji knew about this man's secret life; what role he played, if any, in it; and why he brought us to this man and claim he was God incarnate, when he clearly was not.

Since he declared himself to be Maharajji's 'foremost devotee', Swamiji should have been aware of these goings-on and could not be completely innocent. Yet I wasn't ready to accept that he too was not who he claimed to be.

But among the revelations about Maharajji, we got some surprises about Swamiji as well. And slowly, with the help of anonymous comments and my own independent sleuthing, I gathered that Swamiji could only be one thing: Maharajji's foremost co-conspirator.

I read the following comments (and others) with growing concern about the man I had left the world to follow:

> Barsana Dham swami Prakashanand also has so much anger and egoistic personality. He preaches to leave your family and ruined many good families we know.
>
> – Anonymous, Guruphiliac.com, 20 May 2007

> One day a mother with a baby was sitting next to him (Prakashanand) as he ate. The child fussed and cried, which irritated the Swami. After his meals, the Swami gargled with water, and spat the water out on the baby's face (the Swami is a very angry man with little self-control)! This is the level and status of this organization. The devotees just thought that he is 'gracing' the child!
>
> – Anonymous, Guruphiliac.com, 26 June 2007

> Swami Prakashanand also claims to have been offered the seat of Shankaracharya! Another spurious claim! My God, but the lies and distortions are mind blowing!
>
> – Unregistered, Big News Network, 4 August 2007

As I learned more about these two men, I remembered a curious event from the past. In the mid-1990s, a devotee described the then emerging Internet phenomenon to Swamiji. He seemed upset by the idea of a worldwide communication system. The more he heard, the more upset he got. He kept shaking his head and said that it was just a passing fad.

Had Swamiji's irritation masked a worry that some day his ugly secrets would leak out? In the past, they could be pretty sure that what happened in India would stay there. Clearly, the Internet had proved to be a chink in their decades-old armour.

Down the Rabbit Hole

Wonderland Implodes

I DIDN'T KNOW what 'cognitive dissonance' meant until I realized I was suffering from it.

According to Wikipedia, cognitive dissonance is 'the uncomfortable tension that may result from having two conflicting thoughts at the same time or engaging in behaviour that conflicts with one's beliefs'. Coincidentally, the concept was first proposed by social psychologist Leon Festinger in 1957 in his book – titled *When Prophesy Fails* – about a cult. In it, he described the counter-intuitive beliefs that members of a UFO doomsday cult had when aliens did not destroy earth on the prophesied day.

Despite the failed prophecy, the members continued to proselytize their faith. According to Festinger, the disconfirmed expectancy increased dissonance between the members' conflicting cognitions. Most members lessened their discomfort by accepting a new prophecy – that the aliens had spared the planet for the sake of the cult members.

Similarly, many Barsana Dham devotees who heard about Maharajji's bedroom activities assimilated this new information into their existing belief system. One of the new, openly spoken beliefs was this: Just as Krishna 'makes love' to the gopis in the divine world, Maharajji behaves lustily with women on earth.

However, this new concept clashed with our original teaching that Krishna was pure and divine, and above worldly lust. Swamiji even got angry once when a devotee enquired about Krishna's divine intimate activities with gopis. 'Divine love is nothing like worldly lust,' he had growled.

Clearly, that view was no longer convenient. People knew that Maharajji was getting it on with women, many of whom apparently consented. Comparing him to the amorous Lord Krishna seemed to be the best solution.

It wasn't that I didn't want to believe the new spiritual fantasy. In fact, nobody could have wanted to believe it more than I did, for I had given up my life (some would say the best years of my life) for this spiritual path. However, unlike so many other devotees, I could not pretend away the facts.

In an attempt to process my pain and try to make sense of the changed realities, I started writing in a journal one month after learning the truth. The act of writing everything down turned out to be an important step, for it helped me deal with the insanity around me and to gain clarity, and also gave me the idea that I should write a book.

My first journal entry on 20 June 2007 speaks to my discordant pain.

> All I've wanted my whole life was to find God. Now I think I've found the Devil. If my spiritual teacher is right, he has guided me to the living form of the highest possible manifestation of God. If the world is right, I've been following the teachings of one of the wickedest men on earth. Sixteen years and one month ago today, I was sure that I had finally found the one true spiritual path that would lead me, finally, to God. Now I don't know what the hell I've actually found.

My next entry on 3 July continues to show the utter shock and horror that I was living in during the weeks following my realization of the truth about Maharajji.

> Oh God! I feel so sick, so heartsick. Please wake me up from this nightmare. What am I to believe? On the one hand, people say Maharajji is your very form on earth, here to lead us to your highest, most intimate abode – with Radha–Krishna. But on the other hand, he spends many hours each day alone with women,

> doing the most intimate worldly sexual acts. Can this really be your leelas being performed on earth, as they say?
>
> I feel you deep inside of me, in the furthest reaches of my mind, telling me to continue remembering you. No matter what the external circumstances of my life are, perhaps you will still lift me out of this world some time soon and take me into your arms and finally, finally, let me drown in my one true eternal love. Please give me inner strength and guidance, for I fear that there is no pure guidance for me here on the Earth in the form or shape of any man.

On 12 July, my pain and confusion had reached their pinnacle. I implored God to give me answers and guide me.

> Oh Lord! Where am I? What in the world have I done to deserve this life? I am facing two very different, but equally unbelievable situations. And I can't make sense of either one. I can't find the answer. I don't know the truth. Either you have guided me to the most amazing incarnation of your highest form ever to grace this planet. Or I have landed in the centre of one of the many Hindu cults operating in the world today. You yourself must admit that this is a very precarious dilemma, to which I can only apply my head, because my heart is broken – no matter which situation is true. In the first situation, others (but not me) have supposedly been intimately embraced by you in the form of this guru. In the second situation, I've been duped by an organization devoted, not to God as they claim, but to ego, money, and very worldly sex. Have I completely wasted my life?

For months, I could only feel despair at the thought that my devotional dreamworld was destroyed. So acute was my pain that I wondered how I could keep living. When I tried to envision a new life for myself beyond the ashram, I felt fearful of the world I had left behind – the one that we had been told repeatedly was dark, ugly and full of pain.

But I could not imagine a darker, uglier or more painful existence than the one I was living then.

Follow the Money

A Mysterious Trip to Trinidad

I READ SOMEWHERE that in most corrupt countries, court cases are decided before anyone even steps into the courtroom. The circumstances surrounding the Trinidad incident certainly made me wonder if something underhand had saved Maharajji from prosecution. Among other things, Swamiji took a mysterious trip to Trinidad the week before Maharajji got off on his rape charge. The timetable of the entire incident went like this:

On 4 July, Maharajji left Austin in the middle of the night for Dallas, from where he left for Trinidad. (He had been allowed to return to the US from Trinidad while waiting for his trial.)

On 5 July, Swamiji called a meeting of his well-off devotees and told them that Maharajji was too old to withstand a trial. He requested cash. The purpose of the funds was implied rather than stated.

On 6 July, Swamiji quietly flew to Trinidad (very few devotees even knew that he had gone).

On 13 July, Swamiji returned to Barsana Dham, and seemed smug and chipper, even though Maharajji's trial was only forty-eight hours away. He even disparaged Trinidad as a 'backward' country, laughing at the fact that a dog had been running around on the tarmac as his plane departed.

On 16 July, at 9 a.m., Maharajji appeared in a Trinidad courtroom and, before noon, he walked out a free man.

The *Trinidad and Tobago Express* published an article under the headline '... Evidence Weak; State Drops Case against Guru'. Here are excerpts:

> The State yesterday abandoned its attempt to prosecute an 85-year-old Hindu holyman on charges of rape and molestation ... after Assistant Director of Public Prosecutions Roger Gaspard made the surprising decision to offer no evidence ... 'the alleged rape victim's lack of consent is particularly tenuous ... the State will not be able to make out a prima facie case.'

What had happened behind closed doors? Was there really no evidence? Was there a pay-off? I didn't have the answers. But, like many others, I felt there could have been a 'financial negotiation'. Jody, the blog administrator for Guruphiliac.com, posted his opinion on 16 July under the headline, 'Kreepalu Exonerated, But Still Way Creepy'.

> It was the expected outcome, and one that may have had a lot less to do with innocence and likely *a lot* more to do with influence. Kripalu Maharaj has been cleared of the rape charges in Trinidad-Tobago. It all came down to a 'he said, she said'. And since she's a poor black girl of 22 and he's an alleged God-on-Earth with tons of cash, with it all coming down in a part of the world where it's sometimes just a bit easier to get what you pay for, you *know* how the math was going to add up.
>
> Interestingly enough, some of Kreepalu's Kool-Aid brigade weren't so sure, one going so far as to attempt to post a comment containing a Wikipedia entry about the 'persecution of Hindus' in Trinidad-Tobago. But for those stunningly duped devotees who believe the randy guru is Krishna, God has decided to smile on you today.
>
> Our thanks and our heart goes out to those many abused devotees who came forward in the comments of the Kreepalu posts. The scoundrel got away with it again, we're afraid. It all

> proves one of our general findings about life so far: God is one kinky Bitch with a very strange sense of humor.

Maharajji supporters continued to lash out with their vindictive fury, such as in this account:

> Lot many people got carried with false allegations against the biggest divine personality on earth Jagadguru Shree Kripalu Ji Maharaj.

Jody posted this comment later that day:

> Give us a break! He's playing God for name, fame and financial gain! Not to mention all the special attention he seems to 'command' from the ladies. A lack of evidence can mean he got away with it just as much as you believe it indicates his innocence. Many people have come forward with stories of abuse of all kinds, mostly sexual, but also financial. He's not scot-free. Many folks understand what's really going on, but an amazing fact of life is that there are always adults looking for space-parents to believe in, and Kripalu can use these children to project his 'innocence' regardless of what crime he commits.

Jody's last sentence was sad, but all too true.

Maharajji Returns

Without a Hero's Welcome

AFTER HIS ARREST, Maharajji's much diminished 'world tour' shrank even more. Originally, he had planned to go to Canada for a couple of weeks after visiting Trinidad, but it was shelved. It's not like he had been welcomed there in the first place. The Canadian consulate in India would not give him or his crew visas because of his other outstanding rape charges. Someone reported that they called his followers 'Kripalu Kookoos'. However, before the Trinidad incident, one of Swamiji's Poland-based devotees who had government connections somehow worked the system while Maharajji was in Barsana Dham, and secured Canadian visas for Maharajji, his family and his servants.

I was sitting in Swamiji's sitting room when the Polish devotee told Maharajji what he was going to do, with someone trying to translate his English into Hindi. Maharajji could not understand the explanation of the process involved and finally said, 'Okay, okay, do whatever you need to do.'

Three days later, the man returned to a hero's welcome. When he walked into the sitting room, Maharajji was all smiles. He said to us all: 'He has done a very great seva.' Everyone cheered. But when Maharajji was arrested, all bets were off.

Barsana Dham was the one place in the Western world that he was always ensured admittance into – and that's where he returned for two-and-a-half weeks before heading home to India. We were left guessing about the reason for the change. Either Canada had rescinded his visas or he was too afraid to enter another country, especially one that hadn't wanted him in the first place.

Maharajji's re-entry into Austin in late June was a cloak-and-dagger operation – very different from when he arrived in early April. His family split up into two groups – one flew out of Trinidad to Dallas and the other to Houston. They both landed in the middle of the night and were driven into Austin by devotees.

Just before he returned, several hurried changes were made in the ashram: the closet full of his special sheets was reduced by half and the perfume and lotion bottles were removed; a small room between the side doors of the ashram and Maharajji's bedroom was converted into a makeshift bedroom for Swamiji; and the Mercedes that transported Maharajji from Dallas to Austin was fitted with curtains.

Immediately upon his arrival, Maharajji kicked the seva machine into high gear through aggressive debt collection and by offering enticing new and expensive seva opportunities, such as speedboat rides and photos with him in the shrine (a place rarely photographed). Before he'd left for Trinidad, we had been told that we could pay off our seva debt in a year. But when he returned, a preacher announced in the prayer hall every day that devotees had to pay whatever seva they could right away – at least one-half of what they owed and preferably in cash.

Devotees were reminded that there was an ATM right outside the temple doors. One day when the machine broke, it was fixed at lightning speed and the news was broadcast by the preacher at the very next satsang session.

Other curiosities took place upon Maharajji's inglorious return to Barsana Dham. The ashram security guard started sleeping on the floor outside Maharajji's bedroom door every night; and men were brought into his room every day to do the charan seva, while women were excluded.

But that modification to the schedule was short-lived. By the end of the first week, women were once again being secreted into Maharajji's bedroom several times a day.

Confronting the Guru

An Invitation to 'Private Time'

AFTER MAHARAJJI'S RETURN to Barsana Dham, I stayed far away from him. I didn't go anywhere near the temple, not even to satsang. I refused to do any seva, including baking birthday cakes for the $2,500 'birthday seva'. I told everyone that I had to get back to work and had no more free time or money. That did not go down well. However, I wasn't the only one staying away.

Many devotees were either too tired or had to return to their jobs. As a result, the prayer hall was almost empty during Maharajji's daytime satsang sessions. I heard that Swamiji asked Prabhakari for a list of the names of ashram devotees not attending Maharajji's satsang.

One day, I was in the kitchen of The Girls' House, making a snack, when Madeline called out to me. 'Swamiji was just here, looking for you,' she said.

'What?' I asked incredulously. My heart started pounding. I still hadn't figured out Swamiji's role in Maharajji's secret world.

'I told him you were in your office. He went there.'

I ran back to my office. Swamiji was sitting outside my rented office building in his golf cart and Vishi was up knocking on my door. I called out: 'I'm right here.'

As I approached them, Swamiji said, 'We came to see your office.' He had never visited my office during the entire time I lived in the ashram, so I knew that he was there for some other reason.

I unlocked the door and let them in. Swamiji made a beeline for my couch. I walked behind him, then knelt down on the floor, next to him. Vishi sat off to the side, leaning on a bookcase.

Despite my obsequious behaviour, I was not happy to see him. My mind was racing. What could he possibly want?

He looked around my office and commented on my framed prints of trees. 'I like that picture,' he said.

'It's one of my favourites,' I replied. I knew this was just small talk, and braced for whatever it was that he was there for.

He sat quietly for a minute. As the seconds ticked by, I sat rigidly in anticipation, scared to death over what it was all about.

Finally, he spoke matter-of-factly: 'You're not going to Maharajji's satsang.'

I stuck to my story. 'Swamiji, I can't take any more time off from work. I already took more than I could afford during Maharajji's first six weeks here.'

'You have to go to see him. This is a rare opportunity.' He was talking in a normal tone, but I knew from experience that his mood could change any moment.

'Is there something wrong?' he asked.

I was not prepared for this question. I was still in shock about everything I'd learnt in the past few weeks but still believed in Swamiji's divinity to some extent. I decided to use the opportunity to try to understand what the hell was going on.

'Well … I … I'm not sure …' I struggled to find the words to voice my convoluted thoughts, and to figure out how to answer without getting blasted by Swamiji.

'What?' he said, with only a hint of impatience.

'I was wondering …' I could not say the words.

Vishi piped up. 'You can tell Swamiji anything. Just tell him,' she insisted.

I finally squeaked out one sentence. 'I don't understand who Maharajji is.'

'What?' Now he was irritated. 'What don't you understand? I told you his whole life history.'

'I know Swamiji, but I don't understand about private time.'

'What do you mean?' he said, his voice a controlled growl.

Vishi spoke to him in Hindi, obviously explaining to him what I had just said.

He looked at me with a mixture of puzzlement and disgust and said, 'What does Maharajji need from a woman's body?'

'I don't know,' I answered in a tone that said: *You tell me.*

He snapped back: 'He doesn't need anything. He doesn't do it for his benefit. He does it for *their* benefit.'

I was stunned. He had not denied it. In fact, he had just admitted that Maharajji did spend private time with women – and there was no mistaking that it was a euphemism for sex.

He sat silently fuming for a few seconds, then said, 'Do you want private time with Maharajji?'

I realized this was a trap. If I said no, Swamiji would immediately know I wasn't a true believer. So I gave the only answer I could under the circumstances: 'Yes, Swamiji.'

'Then you have to be in satsang, sit close to him, and long for him in your heart. At least go once a day, in the morning. That is very important.'

'Okay, Swamiji, I will.'

Apparently satisfied with my answer, he got up and walked out of my office.

Vishi trailed after him and looked up at me. 'Come talk to me sometime,' she whispered conspiratorially.

'Okay,' I nodded, realizing I'd just been invited to be prepped by her for private time with Maharajji.

Prepping Me for 'Private Time'

Decoding the Secret Language

I HAD NO intention of ever participating in 'private time' with Maharajji. However, Vishi's invitation to talk was my opportunity to learn exactly how women were prepped before going into Maharajji's bedroom alone. This was the one fortuitous result of Swamiji's surprise visit to my office.

The next morning, as promised, I attended satsang in the morning. But after sitting in the prayer hall watching the fraud Maharajji perform his usual shtick, I decided I couldn't stand the sight of him any more. I stopped going as much as possible.

A few days later, I met Vishi in her bedroom to discuss private time with Maharajji. 'What does Maharajji do during private time?' I asked innocently.

'I don't know myself,' she said, acting demure – unconvincingly.

'I don't see Maharajji in that way, because I serve Swamiji. But what I tell women is: "Be prepared for anything."'

'What does that mean?'

'Anything could happen with Maharajji. He's our divine lover.'

How many times had she told women this same thing, I wondered.

'So, you mean *anything*, like *sex*?' I was trying not to alarm her, but I needed to get to the bottom of it while I had the chance.

She sighed and looked down at her bed. Then she looked up at me. 'You see, Maharajji was Chaitanya Mahaprabhu when he appeared on earth 500 years ago. And Chaitanya was a strict sanyasi, so no one could touch him. Women could not even go to his satsang. This is our chance to love Krishna physically in the form of Maharajji.'

This is not the first time I had heard that Maharajji was the reincarnation of Lord Chaitanya. Swamiji had spelt this out in his series of speeches on Maharajji's life history. But I now finally understood what he had meant when he told us that we had the rare opportunity to have a 'physical relationship' with Chaitanya in this lifetime. I realized that Prakash had to know exactly what was going on in Kripalu's bedroom. After all, his own personal assistant was one of the people prepping women and girls for sexual interactions with Kripalu. At last, I was starting to decode some of their secret language.

Under the Radar

My Year of Living Dangerously

AFTER LEARNING THAT I was living in a cult, rather than a pure spiritual organization, I had to carefully plan how and when to leave. On the one hand, I was petrified to leave what I had been conditioned to believe was the safe confines of Barsana Dham's 200 acres. For a decade and a half, I had felt protected inside the ashram's gates and had believed I was going to live in this ashram until the day I died. Now I had to leave and re-enter that world all alone.

I started having horrible nightmares. During the day, whenever I thought about my future, I was often gripped by rolling panic attacks.

But, in spite of my fears, I started the process of preparing to leave. The first thing I did was return to therapy sessions with Elise. One day in late December of 2007, I explained my fears and my plans to leave the two-faced organization.

At my next session, she took me by surprise. 'I've been thinking about you. And I think you should not leave the ashram right away. You should sit tight, relax, and make a solid plan for yourself before you go. Leave only when you feel more confident.'

'But how can I stay in such a place, where the leaders are so wicked?'

'You've been there fifteen years; what difference will a few months make?' Elise asked me. 'Why not just stay and live your life under the radar? Leave on your terms when you are ready. It will give you time to make a plan, and also give you the opportunity to continue gathering information about what is really going on.'

I thought about it over the next couple of days, and it slowly began to make sense. If I could slow down, take my time, and carefully create a Plan B, I could leave with a bit more self-confidence. Plus, I liked the idea of unearthing more secrets before I left so I could help others avoid the two conmen.

The pressure was off and I relaxed for the first time in months. I lived with a new sense of purpose. The switch had flipped. To the casual observer, I was the same mild-mannered devotee going about her life of work and seva. But undercover, I was engaging in casual conversations with as many people as possible, so that I could dig for information that would reveal more about these men and their decades-long spiritual con game.

Most days, I wrote in my journal to record what I was learning and all the roller-coaster emotions I was feeling. I began to piece together the puzzle, and a picture emerged – of two men who had duped thousands of people with promises of divine guidance when all they really cared about was collecting millions of dollars and having sexual conquests with female devotees and children.

Over the next few months, I learnt so many things that I wished I had never known. For example, I got to know how many female devotees willingly engaged in sexual acts with the gurus and how the preachers were part of a network of people bringing Kripalu a steady supply of women. I learnt how young girls were offered to Kripalu by the preachers, and even by their parents and grandparents. I unearthed how much money the organization was collecting and possibly taking to India by illegal means. I also realized the lengths they could go to in order to keep their secrets – intimidation, pay-offs, nothing was off limits.

But no matter how many new and offensive things I dug up, I never stopped being shocked by the newest disgrace that came to light. Privately, I could no longer call them Maharajji and Swamiji, since these were terms of endearment. Instead, I would refer to them in my journal notes (and whenever I was talking to ex-devotees) by their names: Kripalu and Prakashanand ('Prakash' for short).

One day, while chatting with Lois, I casually mentioned Kripalu's arrest. She looked at me with disgust. 'That girl and her family were trying to blackmail Maharajji. She knew just enough to make up those lies.' Clearly, his arrest had hardened her resolve that this man was still God.

I did not ask Lois the obvious question: how could she have found out anything, let alone 'just enough' to make such detailed accusations? I knew Lois knew more than she was willing to tell me.

Another person I talked to in my search for truth was Jack. He and his wife had become devotees about a year after I moved to the ashram. They eventually moved to Barsana Dham, along with their two young children. Jack had a rough exterior and was overly flirty with many of the women. I avoided him for years, but we found common ground years later as we analysed the secretive activities within the organization. But even though Jack had strong opinions about the preachers and others in positions of power, he would never criticize the gurus. He held fast to his belief that they were saints.

I tried to help him understand that this 'sainthood' was false by sharing the information I had got online. He was curious to hear everything, but nothing seemed to make him relinquish his faith in the gurus. He himself already knew many things I did not, which he shared with me. The most unsettling story involved his own daughter. It happened in 2005, during Kripalu's first trip to Barsana Dham.

One day, Kripalu saw Jack's beautiful blonde sixteen-year-old daughter and told one of the preachers, Janeshwari, to go get her for him. Janeshwari found the girl walking behind the temple and told the girl that she had the opportunity to gain a divine experience with Kripalu. She could be alone with him in his bedroom and enjoy his company like the gopis enjoyed Krishna, the preacher said. She instructed the young girl exactly how to prepare for the encounter: she should take a bath, remove her jewellery and unbutton her shirt before she went into Kripalu's bedroom. The girl started crying and fell down to the ground, screaming. Janeshwari looked around, embarrassed, and walked away.

Another female devotee saw the girl sobbing and ran up to her. 'What's wrong?' she said, kneeling beside her.

The young girl looked up through her tears and screamed: 'They want me to have sex with Maharajji.'

The woman picked her up and took her home to her parents. Jack's wife was deeply upset and wanted to leave the ashram, but he thought differently. As he told me: 'I think she should have gone to see him and been graced.'

I was so disgusted that I almost stopped talking to him. But I realized I could learn more by hiding my true feelings.

Jack also told me that, during Kripalu's 2005 trip, the temple priest Gopal Das and David had driven bags of cash to New York. If this really happened, I wondered where they had taken the money. Was there a network of devotees involved? Jack also said that he'd heard that Prakash had collected a large sum during his clandestine trip to Trinidad following Kripalu's arrest. If this was true, what was the purpose of all that cash?

Jane was another person I talked to at great length during my year of living dangerously. We had become friends as a result of our shared estrangement from the organization in light of the criminal revelations. Our awakening of the true nature of the cult followed a similar timetable.

One day, she told me a horror story about one of her charan seva experiences, stating that no one would ever believe that a person could rape someone in a room when four others were present. I could not imagine what she meant – but she provided more details later.

During one of her charan sevas, she was positioned on Kripalu's left calf. Neelu had turned the lights so low that the room was nearly completely dark. As Jane massaged his thigh, she felt his hand caressing her butt from outside her clothing. Before she knew it, his hand had moved between her legs. She continued pressing his leg as he began shoving his finger inside her vagina through her clothes, which included three layers of cloth: her panties, her slip and her sari. He proceeded to push his finger in and out for several minutes.

'The pain was so excruciating that I thought I was going to faint,' she said. When he finally stopped, she had trouble getting off the bed and walking home. And she was bleeding.

When she told the woman who arranged the charan seva about Kripalu's digital rape, she was shut up with 'Keep your private experiences with Maharajji to yourself. Don't tell anyone anything, including me.'

I also talked to Peter M., who was in charge of ashram security. He also knew many things others did not. After the news broke about Kripalu, he went through a period of disillusionment himself. Somehow he sought me out and we had a few heart-to-heart conversations in the privacy of my office. At one point, he was going to leave on a two-week vacation in the mountains of Colorado to try and make sense of everything. 'I can get clarity when I'm 14,000 feet up,' he said.

But during a layover in Phoenix, before he turned off his cell phone for his two weeks of escape, Prabhakari called him. 'Swamiji wants you back in Barsana Dham right now.'

Peter M. did as he was told. He cancelled his trip and returned to Barsana Dham. Soon after that, he disappeared. I asked where he was and was told that he had been sent to India. I heard that Prakash sent him there 'because he knew too much'. Peter M. would not return to the US for three years.

Behind Closed Doors

The Guru's Sex Factory

KRIPALU'S LIFE BEHIND bedroom doors can best be summed up in two words: sex factory. From my research with victims and other sources, I discovered that Kripalu was engaging in a wide range of sexual activities with women and underage girls, several times a day, on a scale incomprehensible to the average person. Strangely, the sheer volume of activity helped keep his underground sexual lifestyle a secret, simply because no normal person could imagine such a massive sex operation, complete with every detail executed like clockwork, down to changing and washing his bed sheets several times a day. But, piece by piece, I put together an outline of this part of his life.

Kripalu had the perfect smokescreen. From the outside, he seemed to live an orderly life that included regular appearances in the prayer hall, daily walks around the ashram, watching TV, reading the newspaper, eating and taking naps. The population of devotees not involved in sex acts with him, which included many female devotees and all the male devotees, believed that when he was not engaging in his public activities, he was resting in his bedroom.

People like this anonymous commenter defended Kripalu: 'Maharajji has a *very* strict schedule … and *no* one enters the master's room without permission, and Neelu his assistant is always there!'

It's true. He did indeed follow a strict schedule in the public eye. However, he spent a lot of time out of the public eye, and that part was unknown to most people. One thing is for sure: he was rarely 'resting', as most people assumed. In fact, Kripalu lived a life that would put most certified hedonists to shame.

Kripalu's bedroom activities started in the early morning hours, when most people were still sleeping, with the first of five daily rounds of charan seva and its requisite pressing and groping. Following each charan seva session, one of the women would stay behind or, if none of them were good candidates, another woman would be brought to him for 'private time' to do whatever his heart desired. Just as there were definite time slots for charan seva, there were specific times for the one-on-one private time sessions, and women could request a slot in the schedule.

A resident devotee who spent a lot of 'private time' with Kripalu said the following about his 2007 trip: 'If we wanted to go see him alone, we'd ask Carla what times were available and she'd put our name on the list.'

New female recruits were given precise instructions and prepped for their first experiences by the guru's helpers and female preachers. Women and young girls were told things like 'expect anything to happen' and 'consider him Krishna and yourself a gopi'. He would engage in anything from kissing to petting to getting or giving oral sex to intercourse. One of his favourites for a while was a young woman from Ireland. She told someone that once, as she walked into his bedroom, Kripalu told her in English: 'I'm going to fuck you.'

Another time, he made a move to perform oral sex on her and she pulled him away. 'No Maharajji, not that.'

She later told a friend: 'I just didn't want God to do that to me again.'

His bath was also a time for more sexual activity – this was called bath seva. This is one of the only sex-related sevas that women paid for. The fee was one lakh rupees. It consisted of getting the bathroom ready for him, including the precise placement of the rugs, towels and soap. Then Kripalu would walk into the bathroom naked and sit down on his bath stool. The woman would wash and dry his whole body, including his private parts. Once clean, he would indicate that it was time for her to perform fellatio.

Apparently, it was sometimes a challenge to find enough women to fulfil Kripalu's needs every day, in which case, his helpers would scramble to find women and girls. One afternoon, the woman from Ireland received a call from Neelu, telling her to come over for private time. 'I just didn't go; I was too tired and didn't feel like it,' she told another woman.

One day Neelu said to a woman who washed Kripalu's multiple sets of sheets each day: 'Bring a woman or girl for Maharajji. Get anyone.'

Right after the Trinidad incident, I found the following post on a blog: 'All the women in JKP know about Kripalu having sex with women devotees and young girls.'

That was not true. Kripalu, Prakash, the preachers and the helpers repeatedly told the women and girls to 'keep quiet' about what happened inside his bedroom. And they did, because they either believed they were being graced or they were ashamed and embarrassed. Since no one spoke out, the rest of us remained in the dark.

On 21 June 2007, an anonymous person who had been sent for private time wrote the following on Guruphiliac.com: 'Then they (yes, he Kripalu) tried to lay their hands on my self-respect. I had not given them permission for this, I was not expecting this, I was not told this is "leela". I was just considered so brain-washed that I would be easy picking.'

Of course, the children were complete victims at the hands of the fake guru and his cadre of accomplices. One of the underage women involved in the 1991 arrest of Kripalu reported that he had told her he'd give her 'a curse' if she didn't take off her clothes, have sex with him and keep quiet about it.

It's possible that threats kept many people quiet, along with the fear of opposing a spiritual organization which had a reputation, real or manufactured, for harming people who spoke out. Victims must also have had to deal with their own feelings of public humiliation and shame, which kept most of them silent for years. This was true especially in India, where the stigma attached to victims is much more.

Although I had never participated in any of the sexual activities, I was an insider now. And was not one to keep mum about the depravity of the gurus.

Clueless

Omniscience Debunked

DEVOTEES ALWAYS SAID, 'Swamiji knows everything,' yet he didn't have a clue when I looked him in the eye and lied to him three times in early 2008.

I was away from the ashram, running errands when I received a call from Prabhakari. 'Swamiji wants to see you right now,' she announced sternly.

'I'm at the drugstore.'

'How soon can you be home?'

'In about thirty minutes.'

'Well, come straight to Swamiji's sitting room.'

It was always nerve-wracking to be called to see Prakash. You never knew what he wanted, or if you were going to get screamed at for some mistake, known or unknown. But getting summoned when you are half an hour away from the ashram is a kind of hell.

I was shaking as I pulled out of the drugstore parking lot, and almost collided with another car. I drove home in a hurry, barely seeing the road in front of me as my mind raced with possible scenarios that would demand my appearance before the guru. Had someone complained to Prakash about something I'd said? Had I done something unknowingly that he deemed wrong? Or worse, did they go into my room and find my journals? I was worried about my journals and computer, because they contained so many of the activities I was documenting.

My mind finally settled on the most likely scenario: I hadn't been going to satsang. Although I had a clear purpose for staying in the ashram for a little longer, I could barely stand to live the ashram lifestyle any longer, including attending satsang every day.

I mentally prepared my response for Prakash, which was my recurring fallback position: migraine headaches. I had started suffering from migraines a couple of years earlier. They were painful episodes that drove me into my bed for a day or two at time. To survive, I used my disability as a reason to stay away from everyone.

Despite having an excuse ready, I was troubled by one thought: what if Prakash really could read my thoughts and know exactly what was on my mind, how I really felt about him and his slimy organization, and what I'd been up to the past few months? It was always understood among devotees that he was omniscient, clairvoyant and all-knowing. If this were true, I was in real trouble.

I finally pulled into the ashram and parked outside my room. With pins and needles tap-dancing across my nervous system, I entered my room and immediately checked to see if my journals and laptop were where I'd left them – under the pillows on my bed. I was relieved to find them lying there undisturbed.

I quickly changed from pants into a skirt, grabbed a shawl, and ran across the lawn to the temple. On the way, I was concentrating on blanking out my negative thoughts and thinking of Radha. 'Oh Radha, help me get through this.'

I found him resting on his puffy brown recliner in the preacher's sitting room with three women sitting on the floor around him: Prabhakari, Karen L. and Allison. I sat down in the empty space on the floor to his left side. I looked up at him and waited.

He was dictating something to Karen L. I was surprised to hear that it was an email he wanted her to send to Jane, a follower who had moved out of the ashram a couple of months prior. I couldn't believe they were discussing it in my presence.

The email said: 'All the time you were criticizing everyone in Barsana Dham, criticizing Maharajji and committing grave transgressions hundreds of times every day. Swamiji, out of his care and kindness, gave you a chance to come and talk to him personally if you have problems, while he was here before the twenty-third. As you haven't responded yet, it seems you are neglecting Swamiji and, as such, stay wherever you feel happy in the world. We are sending your stuff to your address by post.'

When Prakash was finished, he said, 'Okay, email it to her.' Karen L. got up and scurried out of the room.

Prakash looked at Prabhakari and said, 'Is anyone talking to Jane these days?'

'I don't know, Swamiji.' Then she looked at me and said, 'Are you talking to her?'

'Only a couple of times,' I said. This was my first lie. In truth, I had been talking to her or emailing her every day about things happening in the ashram.

Prakash looked at me and growled, 'Don't talk to her again.'

'Okay, Swamiji,' I said with all the fake humbleness I could muster.

'Why are you here?' he said, looking at me.

'I don't know,' I answered.

'You wanted to talk to her, Swamiji,' Prabhakari quickly interjected.

'Oh yes,' he said and pulled a square yellow post-it note out of his shirt pocket. I could see a list of names on it, with several crossed out. He found my name written on the list and scratched through it with a pen.

As he looked at me, I forced my thoughts to be as still as possible, hoping he could not read my mind. 'How are you feeling about Maharajji these days?'

'I feel good.'

'But you had some doubts last time I was here.'

'Oh yeah, that was before. I'm doing fine now.' This was my second lie.

'That's great,' he chirped, seeming to accept my statement. He paused for a minute as he stared at me through his watery black slits for eyes. Then he said, 'I heard you aren't going to satsang.'

'I haven't been feeling well and I'm very busy with work, Swamiji.'

He growled, 'You need to make satsang a priority, otherwise you'll just keep wasting your life.'

'I'm trying my hardest,' I said, acting as humble as I could. 'But I'm having trouble sleeping and can't wake up in the mornings.'

He started yelling at me. 'Try? Try? You have to try harder. I'm trying to save you from hell. And by that I mean the world.'

All of a sudden, I started bawling. Prabhakhari and Allison sat looking smug, enjoying the sight of me being tortured by the guru. Of course, they thought I was crying because I was being scolded by Prakash. In reality, I was crying because of my pent-up anger at discovering the truth about the cult. I continued sobbing for a couple of minutes. When I stopped, he indicated that I could leave.

I walked back to my office and wrote an email to Jane with the headline: 'Do not reply to Karen L.'s email!' I told her: 'I just overheard Prakash dictate it to her. Whatever you do, do not respond to them.'

I hit the send button and sat back with satisfaction.

A Forgotten Secret

The Depths of My Denial

IN A STORY full of exposed secrets, I had my own secret that pained me greatly to remember years later. This story illustrates how people can deny and make excuses for some level of untoward behaviour on the part of their mentors, no matter how much certain moments conflict with their moral fibre. I too had been in denial for years about a particular incident. But my memory of it was buried so far down that I had not thought about it for years. It came back to me as I began learning about the dark side of the organization.

One day, Kate and I were returning to the ashram after one of our many outings into downtown Austin. We had hung out many times during the years when she was fifteen to eighteen. Although much younger than me, she was mature for her age, and appeared to me to be the most sensible person in the ashram. In fact, we shared a common distaste of the more illogical and unfair aspects of ashram life. However, we lost touch when she moved out at eighteen.

On our return to the ashram that day Kate (who was seventeen) and I were talking about an unsettling experience that happened to her two years earlier. The temple priest, a man my age, molested Kate one night at her home when her parents were away. I was mortified and told Prabhakari, who seemed concerned at the time. She told me that she would tell Prakash and that he would 'take care of it'. She even insisted that she believed Gopal Das would be asked to leave.

Kate and I waited for months for Gopal Das to disappear, but nothing ever happened to the man, and I finally gave up waiting for Swamiji to do the right thing.

A year or two later, I was telling Kate how disgusted I was that nothing had ever happened to him. Prakash had clearly let him get away with his crime. This had been a major blow to me.

She said, 'Well, I'm not surprised, considering what else has happened to me.'

I looked at her with distress. 'What else happened?'

'I can't tell you.'

'Did Gopal Das touch you again?'

'No, not him.' She was silent for a few minutes. Then she said words that made me sick to my stomach: 'It was Swamiji.'

My heart beat faster. This was not what I expected to hear. Not only did I not want anything else to have happened to her, but I didn't want to believe my guru would do anything to harm a child.

'What did he do?'

'I don't want to tell you.' She seemed to shrink back into the passenger seat.

My mouth was dry and my head ached. I felt dizzy. 'What happened?' I pleaded.

'I'm afraid if I tell you it could hurt your devotion.'

I was dying inside as I struggled to drive safely as I approached the L-shaped curve of the new Highway 45.

'Where did he touch you?' I asked. Kate was silent.

'Was it sex?'

'No. Kissing and touching.' She wouldn't tell me anything more.

I stared at the road, my hands gripping the wheel. This couldn't be happening. What was I going to do with this information?

I struggled for words to make sense of the awful situation. My mind went to the only solution that gave me any relief – I thought that Swamiji had bestowed his grace on Kate. I said: 'You know, I've heard of things from other women whom he's touched and kissed. They like it and call it grace. He has touched and kissed me that way too.'

She glared at me. 'You mean you know about this?'

I flinched. 'I know a little bit.'

She glanced at me in disgust, then turned and stared at the window.

In fact, two women had told me part of what happened to them when I was a fairly new devotee. But I didn't want to know the details from either of them. On a flight back to Seattle, Karen L. started to tell me about her 'private time' with Prakash when she would lie with him in his bed. She mentioned that they 'cuddled' before I changed the subject. Another time, she mentioned off the cuff that she and her husband no longer had sex, 'because I would be cheating on Swamiji'.

When we were out for coffee one day, Suzy started to tell me about some intimate experience she'd had with Prakash in his bedroom. But I had cut her off and changed the subject.

Of course, I had experienced Prakash kissing me and pinching my nipples – his signature move. But it was easy to push these experiences out of my mind. I was not going to let anyone else tell me stories that would demolish my dreamworld. I had joined the group and moved to the ashram believing it to be a pure spiritual path to God. And that is what I wanted to continue to think.

At that time, I had no idea what to say to Kate. We were silent for a few minutes, and then I started talking about something else.

That was the last time Kate and I talked about the incident, until we reconnected after the Trinidad incident. Somehow, for all of those years, I had pushed the memory back into my subconscious, where I chose to not examine it.

After we reconnected, Kate and I talked about it and I cried. I was distraught that I had not done anything for her back then.

'What could you have done?' she said, trying to comfort me. 'Nothing would have changed, except that you probably would have been told to leave.'

I knew she was right. But I still cringed with disgust, wondering how my morals could have been compromised so. I had always been horrified by stories of child sex abuse. Yet, when an underage girl told me about untoward advances from an older man, I had failed her. Like so many brainwashed men and women, I allowed what I wanted to believe about my guru to override the cold, hard truth.

The Girls Speak Out

Breaking Their Silence

IN AUGUST, AN innocent email to Kate from AR, the son of one of the devotees, kick-started a whole new problem for Prakash.

'Isn't that stuff with Maharajji in Trinidad bizarre?' AR wrote to her.

Kate had no idea what he was talking about. So she did a Google search and started learning Kripalu's secrets, just as I had a few months earlier. Although her parents, sister and brother still lived in the ashram, they had never said a word to her about Kripalu's arrest. She immediately shared the news with her younger sister, Vesla, and another woman, Shyama, who had also grown up in the ashram.

Hearing about Kripalu's arrest, the girls became angry. Years ago, Kate and Shyama had tried to tell their parents about their own abuse at the hands of Prakash. He had kissed them on the mouth and breasts, and fondled them dozens of times over several years when they were children. But no one would listen to them, and a few adults told them that if Prakash was touching them, he was simply giving them grace.

Since their parents did not take action, the girls processed their molestation in their own way as children do and went on with their lives. Now they realized that by keeping silent for so long about their own abuse, they had potentially put other girls in danger. Kate told me: 'By not speaking out sooner and trying to stop Swamiji, we allowed him to continue abusing other children. We cannot stay silent any longer about our own abuse.'

The powers-that-be had got wind of the girls' discussions about speaking out and people in the ashram were saying that Kate was causing trouble. Though I supported the girls fully and was in fact in touch with them, I panicked a little. I still had not completely shaken off the years of cult conditioning. Since I was still living in the ashram, I had to stay under the radar.

Kate and I arranged to speak on the phone. Our first conversation lasted three hours. It was like two lost souls reuniting and understanding each other's pain and turmoil without having to provide any back story. We were both in shock and outraged about the details that were tumbling out.

Kate shared her experience about growing up as a child in the ashram with me in greater detail. It was far from the idealized childhood the adults wanted to believe. She told me that some kids at school made fun of her and the other ashram children, even calling them 'devil worshipers'. She said there were always dozens of adults sticking their noses in her business, telling her how to dress and how to behave. Plus, her parents pressured her to go to satsang and to spend time with Prakash. With all the criticism directed at her, she felt like she was never good enough.

Then Kate told me more about the abuse at the hands of Prakash, including the many times he got her alone in his bedroom, and how he rubbed her breasts and tried to French-kiss her. 'I always kept my teeth clamped tightly closed, so he would just rub his tongue over my teeth,' she explained.

Once when she resisted, he asked her: 'Don't you like it when boys in school do this to you?' It was a bizarre question for an adult male – and a so-called saint at that – to ask a child.

After the first time it happened, she stayed in her bedroom for three days. Her mother, Sondra, grew suspicious and read her diary in which Kate had written about her experience. Sondra took the diary straight to Prakash – not to confront him, but to warn him. Then she called Kate and asked her to talk to Swamiji and work it out between them. Kate didn't have much to say, while Swamiji insisted that he won't do it again. But he did.

There was also a harrowing incident where she was made to sleep in his bedroom one night. Her mother and Prabhakari helped arrange the sleepover. They placed a mattress on the floor next to his bed. Kate said she lay on it while he worked. When he was finished working, he told her to go brush her teeth and then get into his bed. He proceeded with his usual ritual of touching her breasts and trying to kiss her. 'I thought, if he tries anything else, like touching me below my waist, I will know for sure that this is wrong.' After more kissing and breast touching, he told her to go back to her mattress. In the middle of the night, he woke up once and made her get him a glass of water.

Later, the preacher named Divakari handed her diary back to her – with all the pages that mentioned Prakash torn out.

After learning about Kripalu's arrest, Kate had reached out to other women and children who she believed had been touched by Prakash as children. A few spoke to her, but most refused. Kate's abuse was already over the ten-year statute of limitations for child molestation in the state of Texas. However, the abuse of her sister and Shyama had not yet reached the statute of limitations. They had decided independent of each other that they were going to report the molestations to the Hays County sheriff's department.

Kate and I continued our correspondence. She knew so much that one day, during a heated exchange with her father on the phone, she told him something that I had told her. 'I know they are calling us demons,' Kate said.

He responded with exasperation: 'Where are you getting your information, Kate?' But she did not reveal her source.

One day, the girls' parents, Sondra and Adolph, and their half-sister Prabhakari, appeared at Kate's door in Seattle and tried to talk the girls into staying quiet. But they had decided to do what was right. In November, Vesla and Shyama flew to Austin to give Hays detectives their testimony about their sex abuse at Prakash's hands.

The Demon Speech Trilogy

The Fear of God

AFTER KRIPALU'S ARREST in Trinidad, we began to hear about demons for the first time. Never before had I heard that there were demons among us. Now, out of the blue, Prakash and his people were telling us about how saints on earth faced 'opposition from demons'. In fact, there were three 'demon speeches' within a five-month period.

Prakash gave the first speech in Los Angeles on 5 June 2007, about three weeks after Kripalu's arrest. At that time, Kripalu was stuck in Trinidad, because the court there had taken his passport. Meanwhile,

Prakash was in the US, trying to raise support to get him off. The second demon speech was given at Barsana Dham by Divakari on 26 August. Prakash gave the third speech on 15 October.

These speeches were the organization's new way to explain why some people – including a handful of ex-devotees and the girls – had become openly negative about the gurus. I was not surprised by their reactive behaviour. It was typical. But I was amazed at how low they had sunk in their treatment of former, once faithful, generous devotees and children who had grown up there.

Prakash's first discourse on demons was recorded on a CD entitled: 'Divine Descension and Material Opposition'. He began his twenty-five-minute-long diatribe with the usual devotional spiel.

About eleven minutes into the speech, he described how, when Bhagwan Ram appeared on earth in about 5000 BC, a demon named Ravan appeared to oppose him. When Krishna appeared 500 years ago, Kans and other demons emerged. Prakash said that demons appeared with the incarnations of God, because 'that is the nature of maya; when a big power comes, another power tries to oppose'. He said if a smaller divine power appears, it gets a weaker opposition. 'Big divine power, big opposition.'

Then Prakash segued into a discussion about Lord Chaitanya Mahaprabhu who, when he appeared on earth 500 years ago, did not encounter demons like Kans. But there were 'lots of demons in human form' who revolted against him and opposed him. 'Demonic powers (appeared) through those people who have evil hearts. Through them, those evil powers of maya, they revolt against the supreme power. That is natural to happen. It has to happen with every great power.' He added, 'Descended supreme divine personality, great opposition.'

He said that thousands of devotees were longing to love and serve Chaitanya directly, but couldn't go near him because he was a sanyasi. Chaitanya thought to himself as he was leaving this world, 'I'll come again. All the souls who love me, I'll liberally give them my association then – in my speech, physically, (and) in my writings.'

According to Prakash, Chaitanya returned to earth in AD 1922 in the form of Kripalu.

Next, Prakash talked about Kripalu in hushed tones and somewhat breathlessly. He said that he was innocent, 'like a child. That's a very great thing. He's giving his love by all means. By speech, by physical association, by talking to people. Sometimes he sits among us and does some chanting. He's so great'.

Then he returned to the topic of demons. 'Those evil powers, they do their work opposing Maharajji. They do their work. Let them do their work.' He chuckled and the audience laughed. 'We have no concern with that. They are doing their work, we are doing our work. *Good people* do our work. Let them do their work.'

Then he put the fear of God into his audience: 'He's here. And that chance is extremely rare. In billions and billions of years, it has come once.'

Just before concluding his speech, Prakash added another titbit about the alleged demons among us: 'In the world, the other evil powers, they keep on playing. This is the mayic world. Don't even look to those people; what are they doing or what they will do.'

For demon speech number two, we were summoned to a meeting in Prakash's sitting room. Divakari, the ashram's president, told us that the Hindu scriptures lay out the guidelines for the behaviour of a true devotee. She listed five or six guidelines, emphasizing one in particular: that followers should never think, speak or listen to anything negative about their gurus – a concept that had been shoved down our throats since day one. She added that some former devotees had been actively opposing Kripalu and that it was 'our duty as good devotees' not to talk to them. She said that these people were actually demons.

Then, in October 2007, on his first night back in the ashram from India, Prakash delivered the third demon speech. Just as in his June speech, he started off explaining that there are no demons like Kans on earth these days, who were divine entities in demon form. Instead, 'there are demons in human form' now. He said that many of the demons among us started out as sattvic (pure) devotees, but had turned into tamasic (impure) demons. According to Prakash, any devotee can flip from being a good devotee to an evil one in a nanosecond.

Prakash added that there were people in India as well as in the US who were once Kripalu's devotees and some who 'used to be children in this organization', but who now opposed him. He said that he knew one of these girls in her childhood, and that she used to have visions of Krishna. But the last time he saw her, she was 'married and completely worldly'. He added that no one should communicate with any of these demons in any way. Then he stated his main point: 'If any of these evil-hearted people are members of your family, you should consider them *dead*.'

The next day, I talked to a naïve devotee while cooking with her in the kitchen. She was genuinely afraid that her family members, who were not devotees, including her grown son, could be demons. She said that they openly opposed her activities in the organization. 'I wonder if Prakash is talking about them. I might need to get them out of my life.'

Clearly, she didn't know what was going on behind the scenes. But, at that time, I could not share the facts or reveal my true feelings, because I was still living undercover. I realized that her terror, like so many, was part of the collateral damage of the gurus' behaviour and cover-up activities.

In the end, the great irony of the demon speech trilogy was this: who were the real demons in this story?

Pre-emptive Strike

Creating Their Defence

ON LABOUR DAY 2007, I spent a rare day away from the ashram from sunrise until after sunset.

Alice and I had gone to the Schlitterbahn water park in nearby New Braunfels to relax and enjoy water rides all day. As we were unloading my car back at the ashram, Katie W., an ashram board member, appeared out of nowhere.

'I was looking for you earlier,' she said to me pointedly, taking me by surprise.

'What did I do?' I said. It was never a good thing to have Katie looking for you.

'Nothing. I've been talking to devotees in the ashram about a situation and I need to talk with you too.'

Just then Alice came back outside. 'I need to talk to you as well, Alice,' Katie said to her. I felt a little better knowing I was not the only person she needed to talk to.

We all went into The Girls' House and sat in the living room. Katie read from a notepad clipped to a brown clipboard – basically reading from a script that had been provided to her. She started by telling us that she and three others on the Barsana Dham board were instructed by Prakash to talk to all the devotees and tell us about a situation that had developed. The reason they were sharing this information was that any of us could be contacted by some troublemakers, and they wanted to warn us in advance.

She turned to me and said, 'Especially you, Karen.'

'What do you mean *especially* me?' I was alarmed. Nothing good could come out of being singled out of the pack during this crazy time.

'Well, you used to be friends with the girls.'

'That was *years* ago,' I said, hoping to throw her off my scent.

Katie went on to tell us that Kate had grown extremely negative about Barsana Dham, because Prakash had once 'hugged and kissed her'. She said this young woman was now accusing Prakash of assault. She added, sounding quite insincere, 'Of course we love her and wish her the best. In fact, I wish I could just take her in my arms and hug her until she feels better.' She added that her (Kate's) younger sister had joined Kate in her insinuations.

'Vesla?' I said, faking surprise.

Katie gazed at me. 'Yeah, I know,' she said, as if she were shocked too.

Later, a recurring theme I heard was how taken aback some devotees were that the mild-mannered Vesla was speaking out. Almost no one was surprised that Kate was involved, as she was viewed as outspoken and considered a bit of a rebel.

Katie had also said that Kate was engaging in a wide variety of destructive actions, including contacting people and talking negatively about Prakash, filing a complaint with the Hays County sheriff's office, starting a private Yahoo! group for ex-devotees, and filing a warning with Child Protective Services (CPS) about a thirteen-year-old girl who stayed in the ashram on a regular basis.

Katie said that someone had shared with her some of what people were writing on Kate's Yahoo! group. 'I've seen it myself. It's not good,' she stated.

Katie went into some detail about the CPS situation. The girl's parents did not believe the allegations and were angry with Kate for lodging the complaint. She said that it had torn their family apart for several weeks while they were under investigation. The father apparently said, 'I trust my mother-in-law and daughter. And if they say nothing has happened, then nothing has happened.'

Katie also told us about the parents and Prabhakari travelling to Seattle to try and sway the girls, which I had already heard from Kate. In Barsana Dham's version, Kate had told her parents: 'Choose us or choose Barsana Dham.'

One of the parents had said, 'We cannot choose. We love you and we love Barsana Dham.'

So Kate allegedly said: 'Then our family is over.'

But Kate told me quite a different story. It was her parents who had indicated that their relationship would be over if the girls didn't roll back their plans to speak out.

During the course of the discussion, Katie called Kate a 'troubled narcissist' and that Barsana Dham was considering suing Kate for libel. They never did follow through on that threat.

One of the many interesting things about Katie's disclosure was that in all my years in the organization, the powers-that-be had almost never shared anything with the devotees who were outside the inner circle. For them to have revealed this much of the situation to us was a big deal.

Why were they sharing now?

Gaining Shakti

My First Radha–Krishna Experiences

IN THE MONTHS after Kripalu's arrest, I felt like I was living in a modern-day Mahabharata war – with the two opposing sides squaring off to do battle.

The heart of the Mahabharata is the Bhagavadgita, when Krishna has a conversation on the battlefield with Arjuna. In the scene, all of the kings, princes, gurus and soldiers are gathered on the battlefield, with opposing sides facing off. Arjuna looks around and sees family members and friends on both sides, and tells Krishna: 'I cannot fight these people; they are my family, friends and spiritual guides.'

Krishna explains to Arjuna why he must fight – for it's his dharma.

A few months after I discovered the truth, I watched a documentary called *I'm Your Man* about Leonard Cohen, a well-known Canadian writer of songs and stories. He was very spiritual, and had even lived for several years in a monastery in California. During the film, he shared some of his spiritual insights. I was particularly intrigued by a comment he made about the Bhagavadgita. Cohen describes a scene from the Bhagavadgita, where Arjuna is standing on his chariot, ready for battle. When, upon seeing his family members and friends on the other side, Arjuna wants to stop the war. Cohen says, 'Krishna ... says to him: "You will never untangle the circumstances that brought you to this moment. You are a warrior. Arise now mighty warrior ... This is my will. You are caught up in the circumstances that I determined for you. That you did not determine for yourself ... Embrace your destiny ... Stand up and do your duty.'"

Later that day, I went for a walk around the ashram property. I was angry with God for bringing me to this place. As I walked down a narrow dirt road through the trees, I said out loud: 'Okay, Krishna, you brought me to this ashram and had me live this renounced life. I came here to find you and instead found two wicked conmen, performing the vilest of acts on innocent spiritual seekers and children. This is all your doing. Now tell me what you want me to do next. Tell me my destiny and I will do my duty to you.'

For the first time in all my years there, I felt Krishna right in front of me. He was taller than the trees, standing straight and strong, and dressed in full warrior regalia. He was dazzlingly beautiful: a very pale blue, with thick black wavy hair down to his shoulders. He had human features, but he wasn't human. His ornaments shined despite the lack of sunlight. I lost the sense of my surroundings, and only felt the fullness of his presence.

Leonard Cohen's words reverberated in my brain: 'Embrace your destiny, your fate. And stand up and do your duty.' I felt as if Krishna were imparting this message to me directly. Then he was gone. But a new feeling of strength, of shakti, settled in my mind.

That evening I sat for satsang and looked up at the life-sized deity of Radha in the shrine, sitting regally on her thrown. I'd seen her thousands of times as a pretty stone statue, always dressed in the most beautiful saris and ornaments. But when I looked up at her this time, she seemed to be glowing from every side. The more I stared at her, the more she shimmered. I felt as if she was actually looking at me. At one point, I thought I saw her smile. A feeling of peace and contentment washed over me.

Just before arti, Prakash entered the hall and took his seat on the stage. I knew I was going to have to offer him prasad at the end of the ceremony, and I braced myself for the moment of proximity with him – an experience that repelled me now.

As I offered the bowl of nuts and fruit to Radha, I felt deeply connected to her. As I offered the bowl to Prakash, he picked up a nut and reached to put it in my mouth as he'd done dozens of times before. I opened my mouth, but the nut fell to his couch. I picked it up and walked away. The experience felt like a metaphor for my broken link with him.

My connection and duty now was to God alone – with no guru middleman.

Escaping the Cult

Break on Through to the Other Side

BY EARLY 2008, I was wondering when exactly I should move out of the ashram. I knew that it was just a matter of time before Prakash was arrested, and I wondered which would be better: stay and witness the aftermath or get out before all hell broke loose.

Jane gave me the perfect answer. She had come to Austin in February for business. I picked her up at the airport and we spent the day together. On the way home, we stopped for dinner in a small cafe in Dripping Springs.

'When do you think I should leave the ashram? Before or after his arrest?' I asked her.

She didn't hesitate. 'You should get out of there before his arrest. There is no telling what will happen. Law enforcement might raid the place. Maybe the media will be camped outside. People might retaliate. It could become dangerous and even difficult to leave.'

That was all I needed to hear. I knew she was right. I would definitely clear out before he was arrested. Our best guess for his arrest was the next time he visited the US. Jane had been informed by someone in the Hays County sheriff's office that he would not be arrested in Austin. We knew it would occur in whichever city he flew into on his return to the US. Prakash had too many faithful followers in Austin, and the authorities could not predict how they might react.

Finally, his return date was announced – 24 April. I put my plans into high gear and put my plan into place without anyone in the ashram getting a whiff of it.

After viewing several apartments, I found a lovely place in a safe neighbourhood, which was to be available from 16 April. I started moving carloads of my possessions from the ashram to my new home on that day. I marvelled at the fact that, after so many years, I finally had my own bathroom, kitchen and living room. The apartment felt downright luxurious after life in the ashram.

However, I worried about selling the portable office building that I had purchased two years earlier. After all, how does a person sell such an odd item? But I advertised it on Craigslist and found a buyer who lived only about five miles away. It was truly a miracle.

A few days before the building movers were scheduled, I realized that I needed to make sure that the ashram service gates were open. That would be the only way to get the portable building off from the property. I decided to announce my move to Prabhakari. In a simple, direct and humble half-page letter, I told her that I was moving and asked for permission for the gates to remain open on Saturday. I made up the excuse that I could no longer abide by the rules of Barsana Dham, and so was moving into town. It was my last act of pretending like she had any authority over my life.

I ran into her later that day and she feigned niceness, but I could tell she was happy I was leaving. She said, 'Of course, we'll open the service gates for you.' Then she added insincerely, 'I'm sorry you are leaving. You should really talk to Swamiji before you go.'

Faking humility, I said, 'I have already spoken to him,' referring to the time when I had broken down crying.

She faked concern and said, 'I know,' nodding her head.

'I have one request,' she added. 'Will you tell the devotees you are leaving at the Saturday morning meeting?'

My first thought was, 'Hell, no!' But instead I just gave her the first excuse that popped into my mind: 'Well, I'm afraid I'll burst out crying.'

'Think about it and if you feel up to it, I think it would be very nice.'

Of course, she thought it would be nice – she viewed it as a public relations move for her. No one who had ever left the ashram during the entire fifteen years that I'd lived there had ever announced in a public forum that they were leaving, including former preachers. Typically, most people just disappeared in the middle of the night, and that was the last we saw of them. I didn't want to be the first to make a public announcement because I didn't want anyone to know my true feelings.

But when I woke up the next day, the perfect words for a short departure speech were fully formed in my mind. I quickly wrote them down. I realized that I could say the truth – but with a double meaning. This was apt, I thought, considering that for years I'd listened to the fake gurus talk in secret code, telling us one thing while meaning another.

As we did every Saturday morning after satsang, we all congregated in Prakash's sitting room for the weekly meeting where we discussed ashram issues. Every person who had an announcement put his or her name on the meeting manager's list. Jaresha called me first.

I cleared my throat and began reading my short message. But before I got through the first sentence, I burst into tears – not of sorrow at leaving but of frustration and anger that I'd been conned by such wicked men.

Lois came over and put her arm around me. Then Pam sat on my other side and held my hand. I could hear others in the room crying as well. Several devotees were in tears as I spoke the following words, which could be interpreted in another way if one wished to:

> As many of you have probably already heard, I am moving out this weekend after having lived in Barsana Dham for over one-and-a-half decades. While I am physically leaving the ashram,

> I am in no way leaving the path of Radha–Krishna devotion. Everything I've gained devotionally is staying with me forever – and hopefully continuing to grow. But Barsana Dham has grown and changed since I moved here in April 1993, and, for me personally, things recently reached a tipping point in my ability to participate as required. You'll still see me, as I plan to continue in my devotions and seva to Radha–Krishna for the rest of my life.

In the end, saying one thing and meaning another was about the only thing I had actually learned from the two fake gurus.

After all the planning and worrying over the past few months, my move was executed with military-style precision. The furniture movers came on the day before I made the speech, the building movers came on Saturday, and I finished cleaning up the last of my stuff from my bedroom on Sunday. I was finally done at 8:45 p.m. – just before everyone got out of satsang. I drove off the property for the last time, waving goodbye to Jack, who was on guard duty near the front gate that night.

As I drove out of Barsana Dham for the last time and into the real world, I felt the most profound sense of freedom. I rolled down the windows, turned up the music and sang all the way to my new home.

Exactly four days later, when he landed in Washington DC, on his way back from India to Austin, my former guru was arrested by US Marshals on twenty counts of 'indecency with children by sexual contact'.

PART FIVE

In the World

Divine Intervention

'All that is necessary for the triumph of Evil is for good men to do nothing.'
– Edmund Burke, British statesman

'You must fight. It's your dharma.'
– Lord Krishna, Bhagavadgita, 18:59

The Guru's Arrest

All Hell Breaks Loose

ON 24 APRIL 2008, just four days after I moved out of the ashram, all hell broke loose in Barsana Dham. That Thursday afternoon, US marshals arrested Prakash as he debarked from an international flight in Washington DC, while en route to Austin from India. After the arrest, the US Department of Justice issued the following press release:

Hindu Leader Charged with Groping Underage Girls

Austin, TX – Swami Prakashanand Saraswati, 79, known to his followers as Shree Swamiji, was arrested Thursday afternoon at Washington Dulles International Airport by the Capital Area Regional Fugitive Task Force as he arrived aboard a flight from Europe.

Saraswati was indicted by a Hays County, Texas Grand Jury in April 2008 after a criminal investigation conducted by the Hays County Sheriff's Office resulted in a 20 count indictment alleging Saraswati committed indecent acts with two children from 1993 thru 1996.

Saraswati was remanded to the custody of the Alexandria

> Sheriff's Office in Alexandria, Virginia, pending extradition to Hays County, San Marcos, Texas.
>
> LaFayette Collins, United States Marshal for the Western District of Texas, states, 'The Lone Star Fugitive Task Force is committed to pursuing criminals who victimize our children and we will not stop in our effort to make our communities safer.'
>
> Members of the Lone Star Fugitive Task Force in Austin are the Austin Police Department – Intelligence Unit, Hays County Sheriff's Office, Texas Rangers, and the U.S. Marshals Service.

I heard about the arrest that evening in a two-word email from Jane. 'It's done.'

After the thousands of words we had exchanged wondering if, when, where and how he would be arrested, her message was simple and perfect. I was excited, relaxed and happy knowing that Prakash was finally going to be held accountable for some of the crimes he had committed over several decades. The next forty-eight hours were among the most satisfying in my life, knowing he was behind bars.

The same cannot be said for the residents of Barsana Dham. On that day, they were deep into preparations for that year's annual mela, the Indian-style fair. Prakash was supposed to preside over the mela and give a speech. From what I heard from various sources, I pieced together the following chain of events.

On Thursday, Prakash was supposed to arrive in Barsana Dham at about 9:00 p.m. After the evening satsang, it was announced that he would not be returning that night because he was 'held up in customs'. The line hadn't changed till the next morning.

However, by this time, the local media had received the US justice department's press release and five television stations sent their broadcast trucks with media towers to the ashram. They had been planning to park on the street, but Prabhakari, who was worried about people seeing the media vehicles, invited them inside the ashram gates. They began filming immediately, conducting interviews with random people and with her, since she was the ashram spokesperson and vice-president.

A couple of devotees were even recruited to get snacks and beverages for the media. For several hours, the followers were not given any information as they continued to prepare for the next day's mela. In fact, a few assumed that the media was there to cover the mela.

By late afternoon, word spread that Prabhakari would be holding a meeting at 4:30 p.m. in Prakash's sitting room. My informers told me that she walked in with a big fake grin on her face, acting like everything was under control. Someone even said she was laughing. Yet, they made the children leave the room. Then she rambled on about how Prakash was innocent, without ever saying what exactly it was that he was supposedly innocent of. She then ended the meeting with a surprise announcement: 'If you want to see me on TV, watch the news tonight.'

One of the residents of the ashram and a person who had revealed many secrets to me, Jack, called me right after the meeting. The first thing he said was, 'It's a shit storm from hell here. Five news trucks and their towers have been here all day.'

Just before 5:00 p.m., I gathered my four small portable televisions into my new living room and tuned them all to different channels. Prakash's arrest was the lead news story on every local station. In her interviews, Prabhakari looked suspicious and insincere. Her most ridiculous statement was: 'No one who knows him would ever believe he could have done this.'

The truth was that quite a few of us believed that he had committed these crimes – and many others that he had not been arrested for yet.

Extradited

Free on $1 Million Cash Bail

ON SATURDAY, PRAKASH was extradited from Washington DC, to Texas under armed guard. US marshals escorted him to the Hays County sheriff's office, where he was booked on twenty counts of indecency with children by sexual contact, fingerprinted and photographed. His bail was set at 1 million dollars. They also confiscated his passport and limited his access to Barsana Dham, the scene of his alleged crimes.

That afternoon, a few of his wealthier followers coughed up the cash for his release. Someone wired the whole 1 million to Hays County. Within hours, Prakash was released. He even made it back to the ashram in time to make a grand appearance at the temple and give a short speech.

A reporter from Channel 7 was given exclusive access to film Prakash's return at the doors of the temple, where he was greeted by adoring devotees, a few of whom placed fresh flower garlands around his neck. I learnt later that Barsana Dham thought it would get special treatment from Channel 7 because the station employed an Indian reporter.

Although Prakash made an appearance at the ashram, one of the terms of his bail was that he could not live on the Barsana Dham property since it was a public place frequented by children, and he was an accused paedophile.

The ashram launched a full-scale media battle to simultaneously bury the bad press that was already out about Prakash, and to try and spin any new stories that were developing. They hired two public relations firms – a local agency called Hahn, Texas, and a high-priced firm in California.

Multiple websites began popping up, spouting the organization's propaganda. In just a few hours of searching, I found several small, cookie-cutter websites with the same launch date. There were also blogs for the preachers, and pages on multiple online forums. At one point, I counted over three dozen websites, pages and blogs. The ashram was clearly hoping to bury the bad news – a common PR strategy in the Internet age. What it never imagined was a bigger PR disaster – a former devotee becoming an informant for a tenacious investigative newspaper reporter.

Becoming an Informer

The $10 Million Article

ON 19 MAY 2008, almost a month after Prakash's arrest, three opportune bits of information came my way.

First, I received an email from Madeline, one of the devotees living in the ashram, asking me to call the Barsana Dham office to let them know the address to which to forward my mail. When I called, I was told that Prakash was due to leave Austin for India the next day.

'You should come and see him tonight,' Mary said in an upbeat tone.

'I will, thanks,' I lied.

Then Kate called me about Prakash's recent hearing, which we assumed was going to be a pre-trial hearing. But instead, Prakash's lawyers had requested a hearing so they could ask for his passport to be returned and to get the terms of his bond changed so that he could freely enter Barsana Dham.

'Do you want to know what happened at the hearing last Wednesday?' she asked.

'Of course,' I replied, excited to get the inside scoop.

Someone who was at the hearing had told Kate that it was basically nothing more than a dog-and-pony show. Prakash's lawyers trotted out some professor of religion from St Edward's University to say that Barsana Dham professed 'a real religion'. They also presented several letters from government and religious personalities, mostly from India, who wrote glowing recommendations of Prakash. Then Peter S., Prakash's main man and the owner of several infomercial businesses, took the stand to testify to Prakash's sincerity and spirituality.

While Peter S. was on the stand, the defence lawyer asked him how much he had in personal wealth.

'About 10 million,' Peter S. said.

The defence lawyer then asked: 'Do you have such high regard for Swamiji that you would stake your personal wealth on his return for the trial?'

'Of course,' was Peter's confident response.

With this pronouncement, Cathy Compton, the assistant district attorney (DA), saw her opportunity and took it. 'Your Honour, I think that the defence has just made a motion to raise the bail.'

District Judge Charles Ramsay called her and the defence lawyers into his chambers. By the time the private powwow was over, the defence had agreed to a $10 million bond assurance from Peter S. in exchange for Prakash's passport. The terms of the agreement stated that if Prakash missed any of the pre-trial hearings or did not show up for his trial, then Peter S. would have to pay the court $10 million. Further, the DA had requested that Prakash's restrictions with regard to Barsana Dham be upheld, that is, he was still barred from entering Barsana Dham.

When the judge returned to the bench, he specifically asked Prakash's lawyers: 'Do you agree to these conditions?'

They all agreed. Peter S. and Prakash signed the agreement.

Once Prakash had his passport in hand, I could sense that he would high-tail back to India very soon.

Kate then told me about a newspaper reporter from the *Austin American-Statesman*, who had tried to contact Shyama. She refused to speak with him, but agreed to take his name and number in case she changed her mind.

After we got off the phone, Kate emailed me his name and contact information. At first, I thought I might contact him sometime in the future, when I was not so afraid to speak out publicly against the ashram. Just the thought of speaking directly to the media made me a nervous wreck. I'd heard too many stories of threats and worse that other former devotees had suffered at the hands of the gurus. I figured that anything was possible in an organization with so much money, and so many people willing to believe anything and everything the gurus said.

After a brief mental tug of war, I realized that I had to contact the reporter right away and share what I had just learnt from Kate, especially since I knew that Prakash would be leaving the country the next day. I was, however, determined to stay anonymous.

At 12:48 p.m., using an email address with a fake name, I sent an anonymous message to the reporter, Eric Dexheimer: 'Hello Eric, I've been told you are doing research on an article about Barsana Dham and the recent arrest of its founding guru. I can supply you with insider information anonymously, but no interviews. I have information today that is particularly timely. Let me know if you wish to pursue this. Best, OT'.

At 12:53 p.m., I received a two-word response: 'I do.'

At 1:12 p.m., I wrote: 'Will you keep me anonymous?'

At 1:16 p.m., Eric wrote: 'Yes, of course. But we'll have to figure out a way I can confirm what you tell me. If I don't interview you, how will we communicate?'

At 1:21 p.m., I wrote: 'Email is the best way for now. Let's see how it goes.'

Eric sent me some questions about the ashram and its leaders. He also told me that he had been assigned to write an investigative report about Prakash. His editor wanted him to dig up whatever he could find about the girls' allegations of abuse.

At 1:44 p.m., I wrote: 'Do you want timely information right now for an immediate article, or just as part of a longer future report?'

At 1:50 p.m., Eric responded: 'If the information was newsworthy enough to the general public, and I could confirm it, I'd write about it soon. But I'm primarily gathering information for a longer, more comprehensive article to be published later, whenever it's ready.'

At 2:13 p.m., I wrote to him: 'He was given his India passport. The terms of the bail were raised to $11 million. One devotee had to personally guarantee that he would pay the $10 million if Prakash doesn't return for all court dates.'

At 2:21 p.m., Eric wrote: 'Hmmm. This comes pretty close to meeting the criteria to write something soon (although my main project continues to be the longer, more detailed article later). Is there any way you can tell me who guaranteed the $10 million bail? I'm going to speak to my editor to see what he wants to do.'

At 2:58 p.m., I wrote: 'It was a long-time devotee named Peter Spiegel.'

At 3:15 p.m., Eric wrote: 'Ha! I would've guessed Peter Spiegel. I've traced a few of his businesses by searching for addresses on Barsana Road. I think he's also the registered agent for the temple. You've proven very reliable and accurate, for which I am grateful.'

Within the hour, Eric wrote back to say that he wanted to write something for the next day. Over the next few hours, he emailed me several questions to help him prepare his article.

At 6:39 p.m., he sent me a final question about one of the women he was planning to mention in the article: 'Is there any way to confirm, through some public document or other, that she has been involved at Barsana Dham?'

After searching through my files for some kind of tie linking her with the ashram, I hit pay dirt online when I entered her name on WhitePages.com. Her listed address was on Kalindi Lane – one of the roads on the ashram property.

At 7:14 p.m., I sent Eric the link: 'Just found this.'

At 7:26 p.m., I received his last comment for the day: 'Thanks for the link! Got it just in time. The story is running on the front page tomorrow.'

I immediately called Kate. We were thrilled that the news was going to reach the public.

I was so excited that I could barely sleep that night. In the morning, I hurried to get the newspaper, and was smiling when I saw the story on the front page, satisfied in the knowledge that I helped get the word out to the public.

Eric was an intelligent, well-balanced investigative reporter and an excellent writer. I felt that I could trust him for the longer, more in-depth article he was researching. Thus began my four-month, wild ride as the 'Deep Throat' of Barsana Dham.

Barsana Dham Calls

Fear and Loathing

TWO WEEKS AFTER I moved out of the ashram, I received a phone call from them that freaked me out.

My new apartment was in a gated community in a safe neighbourhood, where security guards regularly patrolled the streets. I felt protected surrounded by wealthy people who could afford extra security.

I believed that with Barsana Dham anything could happen. Prakash and Prabhakari had shown up at the doorstep of several ex-devotees in the past, including the home of a girl raped by Kripalu, the son of an ex-devotee, and the apartment of a girl whom both Prakash and Kripalu had molested. There were also stories of JKP hurting former devotees who had dared to speak out. One of Prakash's own preachers who left him said that she was afraid of them. Now, with me out of the organization and on the girls' side, there was no telling what they might do to me. For all I knew, they might send some thug to threaten me – or a rogue devotee might decide to take matters into his or her own hands in an attempt to become a vigilante hero.

Now I got an unwelcome phone call from an ashram phone.

It was Pam, who left a chirpy message: 'Hi, Karen. I just wanted to see how you are doing. I miss you and want to be sure you are okay.'

Pam was one of the sweetest people in the ashram. We had taken Hindi classes together for years and had been study partners. She had always been supportive of me, but I couldn't help wonder if she had been put up to the phone call by the powers-that-be. I had no intention of calling her back to find out.

Much to my chagrin, Pam called again the next morning. This time she sounded anxious. 'I really want to talk to you. Please call me as soon as you can.'

When she called a third time later that evening, I finally picked up the phone. I needed to put an end to this invasion into my new life.

'Hi, Karen. It's nice to hear your voice. How are you?'

'I'm doing great,' I said truthfully.

'I just wanted you to know that I miss you and want to stay in touch with you. We should have lunch some day.'

'Are you sure you want to have a friend in the world?' This was a pointed question, because she had once said of another devotee: 'Why would anyone need friends in the world?'

She hesitated for a split second. 'It might be good for me.'

'Okay, we can meet for lunch someday,' I said, with no intention of following through. I tried to get off the phone.

But she wasn't ready to let me go. It seemed as if she was following a script, and she needed to see it through. Finally, she got to what I believed was the point of contacting me: 'So how did you feel when you heard that Swamiji was arrested?'

There was no way I was going to tell her or anyone else at Barsana Dham that I was thrilled during the entire forty-eight hours he was incarcerated.

'I don't know,' I replied neutrally. 'I guess I felt disassociated from the situation.'

She seemed surprised by my response. Then she rushed to her next question. 'We heard that some people were tipped off that he was going to be arrested. Had you heard anything about it?'

'No, I had no idea,' I lied. Frankly, what I knew and didn't know was none of her – or anyone else's – business.

'Well, there are some rumours going around that someone down at Hays had said something to someone, and some people found out.' Her vague comment was a complete fishing expedition.

'Really?' I said, feigning surprise.

There wasn't much more to say. As much as I liked her, I could not trust Pam now. When we said goodbye, I knew it was for good.

A couple of weeks later, I was having lunch with Carol, a once-dedicated devotee who had moved out so she could have a boyfriend. We had met a couple of times recently, since I thought she was completely out. But I soon realized that she was not, for she told me outright one day: 'There's a rumour going around the ashram that you knew Swamiji was going to be arrested.'

'How would I have known that?'

'You were tipped off by your press contacts.'

I nearly laughed out loud. Typical Barsana Dham, I thought, drawing ridiculous conclusions. I didn't have any press contacts. Plus, why would someone from the press tip *me* off? If they had known about the arrest, they would have reported it before the justice department sent out the press release.

Of course, I was tipped off – just not by the press, as they thought.

My Life as Deep Throat

Digging Deep

FROM 20 MAY to 27 September, my life revolved around Eric Dexheimer. Freshly departed from the ashram, and committed to getting out the truth, I was the perfect person to provide the 'inside' information and contacts he needed.

It was the worst of times and the best of times. The worst part was uncovering many more salacious facts about the gurus and their minions. The best part was that my research connected me to several ex-devotees who had suffered mightily during their years in this organization and afterwards.

Eric made it clear that he was interested in exposing the organization's secret and suspicious activities. He had told me early on: 'When lots of money is involved, there tends to be corruption.' And I wanted to help him expose it as best as I could.

Originally, Eric was only going to write about Prakash. It was not clear to the average outsider that there were actually two 'gurus' running the show. But, in terms of sexual abuse of children and female devotees, Kripalu was more prolific. I told him about Kripalu and provided him with the relevant information. Eric decided that he would investigate both men and their exploitation of their followers.

Newspaper journalists follow a strict code of ethics and standards for obtaining information, confirming its validity and reporting it. I knew that it was going to be a challenge to supply Eric with information that was not only newsworthy, but also could be corroborated. After all, I myself had seen the true face of the gurus only after fifteen years on the inside. Most of what I knew had been gleaned from people who would never confirm the facts to any outsider because they were still devoted to the gurus.

A majority of women who'd had sexual contact with the gurus would not speak out either, for reasons ranging from fear to humiliation to denial and the need to close the chapter. Another problem was that many of them had left suddenly and quietly, and I had no idea where to find them.

I had zero empathy for the women who refused to speak out, for that was the easy way. It was important to speak out because it was the silence of so many for so long that had allowed the gurus to run amok in the world, wreaking havoc in the lives of innocent spiritual seekers around the world and hurting children.

One day, Eric pressed me for the names of any women who might talk about their sexual experiences with the gurus. He told me that he would need to speak to at least three women with stories of abuse by each guru before the newspaper would feel comfortable going to press with stories of sexual improprieties by them. They could stay anonymous if they wished to.

I had decided that I would tell him my experiences with both gurus, as uncomfortable as I knew it would be, if I could stay anonymous. I asked Kate if she would talk about her experiences, and she agreed. But she needed to save the details of her underage sexual experiences with Prakash for the courtroom and so decided to reveal only what had happened to her after she turned eighteen.

I wracked my brain for more names. I remembered one woman from years ago who had once started to tell me a story about being alone with Prakash. I was brand new in the ashram at that point, and years away from allowing my bubble to be burst. It sounded like the tale was going to have an uncomfortable component to it, so I had intentionally changed the subject. It was finally time to find out what she had set out to tell me that day.

There were a couple of other women whom I suspected of having been abused by Prakash but, despite their suspicious behaviour and exit from the ashram, they seemed to believe, outwardly at least, that the men were saints.

In the meantime, Eric also wanted to talk to anyone who might have insider information about the organization's management and money handling. In that area too, I could not compile even a short list of names of people who I thought might speak out.

But my intuition told me that there had to be someone out there besides me who knew the truth and would be willing to talk. One evening, I remembered an encounter that had occurred just a month before I left the ashram. It was a few days before the annual Holi celebration, also called the 'festival of colours'.

I had come across Jack sitting in his truck, talking on his cell phone. I walked up to say hello. As I approached, he was ending his call.

'That damned Wayne won't help park cars on Holi,' he said, irritated.

'Why not?'

'He said he's fed up with the people and the gurus. He told me to tell Prabhakari to park the cars herself.'

Bingo! Wayne had been a devotee for as long as I had, but had dropped away a couple of years earlier. Curiously, his wife, Kathi, still went to the ashram regularly, which is why we still saw him in the premises, even helping out with the chores sometimes. That night, I sent Wayne's contact information to Eric.

He emailed me the next day: 'I reached Wayne. He said to call him back this evening at home.'

The next morning, I got a call. The caller ID said *Austin American-Statesman*. I was alarmed. I had not yet spoken to Eric or even given him my real name.

'Hello?' I said cautiously.

'Hi. You don't know me, but I'm Eric Dexheimer, a reporter with the *Austin American-Statesman*.'

I took a deep breath. 'Well, actually we do know each other.'

He was stumped for a few seconds. Then he said, 'Oh, are you Orianne?' That was my fake name.

'Yes.'

'Hi. Good to meet you finally. I talked to Wayne last night, then to his wife, Kathi. She gave me your name and number after telling me about her experiences with the gurus.'

Kathi and I had never interacted much and I had no idea what her experiences were. But hearing that she had spoken out emboldened me.

It was as good a time as any to tell Eric my own experiences. When I blurted out my personal experiences with the gurus, Eric seemed shocked. I could tell, even over the phone, that he was writing feverishly.

I told him about Prakash French-kissing me and pinching my nipples, about Kripalu trying to get me to touch his penis during charan seva, and how I had seen him touching a woman's breasts and another time witnessed a woman massaging his penis.

After I told Eric everything, I called Kathi. It was a relief to finally have another ex-devotee who felt as upset and traumatized by her experience in the cult as I did. That day Kathi and I formed a bond that helped us both heal from our horrible experience – and which helped ensure that justice was done.

Kathi explained that she was in the room when Wayne was talking to Eric. 'He was hardly saying anything and it was driving me crazy. Just as he was getting off the phone, I said, "Doesn't he want to talk to me?"'

Wayne asked Eric and of course he said yes. The conversation was a reporter's dream come true. Kathi described an encounter when Prakash had touched her inappropriately. Later on, when she felt stronger, she also told him about her interactions with Kripalu, including a bath seva and two other 'private time' encounters. Eric's determined investigative work was finally paying off.

Eric also asked Kathi if she knew of any other women who might talk to him. She did know several women who had had sex with Kripalu, but she also knew that none of them would speak out, as most of them were still staunch devotees. Others were just unwilling to come out of the closet. Ironically, she gave him my name – even though she knew nothing about my experiences, just that I had recently moved out.

Soon Eric came across the name of Rachael (name changed), whose family had been loyal devotees for many years. But they had left suddenly in 2003. When Eric tracked her down, she told him the harrowing tale of how she suspected that Kripalu had abused her daughter. She refused to give him permission to report the daughter's story. However, she did give him permission to report about her own experiences, which included Kripalu trying to touch her inappropriately.

Then she asked him to tell any ex-devotees he was talking to to call her. She had not spoken to anyone from the organization since she had left. He passed her name and number on to me. When I called Rachel, we talked for over three hours. It was another bitter-sweet moment.

Finally, Eric had the sources he needed to report on the gurus' sexual abuse and exploitation of their followers. Even though most people were loath to speak out, enough of us did to help get the truth out to the public.

Suzy's Story

A Near-Bliss Experience

ONE DAY IN the summer of 1994, a fellow believer Suzy and I had driven to downtown Austin to have lunch, chatting about our life before we moved to the ashram. She told me about an intimate experience she'd had with a man when she was younger. Their intertwining had brought her to great heights, which she characterized as 'bliss'.

Then she told me: 'I nearly had a similar encounter with Swamiji.'

My body stiffened as if a radar warning had gone off. I immediately changed the subject. I did not want to hear another word about my guru in such a context.

After I left the cult, the memory of that conversation crept into my mind. Now I was extremely curious, wondering what she would have told me that day if I had not stopped her. Now I was ready to hear everything, but I had no idea where she lived or how to contact her. She and her husband had moved out of the ashram in 1997, and she visited only occasionally after that.

Fortune smiled when I had lunch with Carol that day. Suzy had recently called her, but Carol had not returned the call. Amazingly, I left Carol's apartment with Suzy's phone number.

Once Suzy and I started talking, I heard much more than I had bargained for – she still had pent-up emotional turmoil and pain, especially regarding Prakash's rejection of her after he had made her his 'number one girl' for a few months.

'Remember when we went out to lunch one day and you started to tell me about an intimate encounter you'd had with Prakash?' I asked when I called her up.

'Of course I remember,' she said.

'I'd like to know now what you were going to tell me then.'

'Sure. I had very intimate experiences with him. I'd get called to his bedroom by Ranjana [Vishi], usually after evening satsang. He'd pull me into his bed. We'd French-kiss, and he would touch and kiss my breasts. Not every time, but sometimes he would put his hands down my pants and slide his fingers between my legs and inside of me.'

My ear was glued to the phone as she confessed her sexual experiences with my former guru. I think I nearly stopped breathing.

'How many times were you with him?'

'Several. Maybe eight or ten times.'

It was what I was expecting to hear, but hearing Suzy actually say the words was painful. The anguish in her voice was evident. My mind reeled with the ramifications of her story. I could not believe now what an innocent, naïve person I had been while I lived in the ashram. While Prakash was rolling around with Suzy and many others in bed, I was struggling to be a better devotee, constantly berating myself for being a flawed soul and having sexual thoughts about worldly men.

Then she added the kicker: 'One time I was lying on his bed with him and Diane. He started kissing her and they were getting pretty hot and heavy. So I just slid down the bed, pressed his feet and waited for my turn.'

Oh my God, I thought. So he was into threesomes – and who knows what else. However, I was not the least surprised about Diane. I suspected long ago that she had her period of being the 'special' one. I once saw the two of them coming down the stairs outside of his bedroom together. They were holding hands and she was acting like his lover. At the time, I wondered what they had been doing in his bedroom, but I never let myself think that they were really engaged in sexual activities, at least not in the worldly sense.

Over the years, I chalked up the occasional uncomfortable scene of Prakash and miscellaneous female devotees as innocent. But mostly I just didn't think about it, pushing any uncomfortable thoughts, like so many other thoughts about the guru, to the far back dark corners of my mind – which eventually became a very crowded place.

Suzy said that her experience with Prakash never reached the blissful heights she had experienced with the other man. 'But I felt special.'

Before she knew it, Prakash abruptly ended their encounters, telling her one day: 'We need to let some time pass, and just be friends now.'

'I was broken-hearted,' she said. 'I wondered what I had done wrong. I started working really hard around the ashram, cleaning and gardening, hoping I could regain his attention.'

Suzy had been one of the hardest workers in the ashram, spending hours at a time doing hard manual labour. I always wondered why she was killing herself at all hours of the day and night.

She told me that one day after he had rejected her, she was walking down a hallway and Prakash was walking towards her. She smiled at him. He gave her a disgusted look, turned around and walked in the other direction.

'I almost died in that moment. I felt so dirty and so far from God,' she said, sadly.

When I explained to her about the article Eric was researching and told her that he needed women to share their experiences, she hesitated. She didn't want to embarrass her son, who still lived in Austin. I assured her that all the women would remain anonymous.

'You know,' Suzy said, 'it would be easy to say no to this. But now that I know that Prakash was touching underage girls, I feel that the only moral thing to do is to speak out about something that is not right. I'll do it.'

Kripalu's Secret Lust

Underage Virgins

ONE OF THE most shocking details that came out after the Trinidad incident was the fact that this was not Kripalu's first arrest on rape charges. He had been arrested in the early 1990s for raping three underage girls.

An article published in an Indian newspaper on 27 September 1991 detailed his arrest. The article used his real name: Ram Tripathi and was titled 'Rangeen Mizaaj Sadhu' which can be roughly translated as: 'the hedonistic sadhu'. The following was translated from Hindi:

> It was morning at Nagpur airport. Ten policemen from Delhi went to the airport at 11:00. Inspector Thakur went to the airport for Tripathi. When the plane landed, they were looking for one passenger whose name is Ram Tripathi. The police identified him as soon as he came out of the airport. He was apprehended and taken to the police station. People were saying that he was an 'all-rounder' saint, meaning the one who says he 'knows everything'. Yet Tripathi (aka, Kripalu) didn't know that police were waiting for him.
>
> After being kept in the police station, he was taken to the Nagpur court before First Grade Magistrate Kureshi. They stated his crimes and said they had been looking for him for the past

five months. He was being accused of raping and abducting two underage girls named Meera and Hema, and keeping them in his ashram. He is not a saint; he is a shame on humanity. An investigation had found that he was arrogant, fake and a womanizer. He had touched many ladies and many young girls. Many people in and out of the courthouse were shouting that this Kripalu was fake and arrogant. They said: 'Give him the death penalty.'

In his life, he had access to a lot of young devotee ladies. He gained their faith and trust, so they will do anything he asks. So whenever he wanted to indulge in his desire for sex, he found a way. He could get his sexual desire satisfied at any time. An organization gave him the title of jagadguru. One time he gave a lecture sitting on a silver throne. He announced himself that he is the incarnation of Bhagwan Krishna and Chaitanya Mahaprabhu. He said: 'Whoever is present here, I am your guru. I am already above everything. You accept guru as a higher position; sometimes more than even God. I am every man's father and every woman's husband. Whatever I order, you have to accept. Otherwise it will be meaningless.' Devotees accepted whatever he said.

While giving this lecture, he saw a beautiful girl in the lecture hall and told his servant to take that girl to his bedroom. When she was in his room, Kripalu closed the door. He ordered the girl to take off all her clothes. She got scared and asked why. Kripalu said I am giving you prem dhan. [This means 'gift of love', and is used here as a euphemism for sex.] All your disease, misery and pain will be gone. She said: 'No I will not do that.' Kripalu said: 'If you don't do it, something bad will happen to you. Think about it. Whatever I'm ordering, you do it.' Then she got scared and took off all of her clothes. He raped her. This was in 1970.

In this way, Kripalu gave prem dhan to many young girls. Educated young girls were also getting caught in the trap to get the prem dhan. There was a line to get the prem dhan. He made Mangarh the main centre for prem dhan. At the time of his arrest, 84eighty-four girls were gathered over there to get the prem dhan. Also, in Vrindavan where he built an ashram, other girls were waiting for his prem dhan. The manager of his Vrindavan ashram was his elder daughter. He was not able to give all the prem dhan to all the women who wanted it. So he got some of the devotees to engage in the distribution of some of the prem dhan. He gave the opportunity to do this to people such as Priya Sharan.

In July of 1984, in a small village near Phat Poor, there was a young man name[d] Priya Sharan, who became his devotee. Kripalu selected him to help him with giving the prem dhan, and he did it [for] four years. He then left Kripalu, went to his own village, Sarovari, and opened his own ashram.

Kripalu has many devotees in many cities. But very important ones in Bombay included: Jai Shankar Mathur, Kantibai Patel, Bhagwan Shaw and Videsh Jain. They were in the clothing and diamond businesses. He had devotees who gave lots of money. Some devotees were actresses and politicians. Kripalu's fame was going to the ditch by February 1991 when he went to Nagpur where one of his devotees requested him to give a lecture on 16 February 1991. While giving the lecture, he noticed two very beautiful girls, Meera and Hema. They came with their father to listen to the lecture. Once he saw them, one of his devotees escorted them to his bedroom and Kripalu convinced them both to give him prem dhan. But one devotee created trouble.

One young man named Niteen Pandey was a trusted devotee servant and very faithful. He thought of Kripalu as God. Kripalu changed his name to Swami Nityanand. One of his duties was taking care of a cooler outside one corner of Kripalu's bedroom. Nityanand didn't know about prem dhan. After the two girls had passed many hours alone with Kripalu, Nityanand thought, let me see what this prem dhan is and why it takes so long.

> He climbed on the cooler and from the window crack he saw things that shocked him. Kripalu and the two girls were all naked. He saw Hema and Kripalu naked on the bed and Meera naked on floor. He ran away from that place. He later found out that Kripalu went to Mangarh and at the same time the two girls disappeared. Then, when he found that the girls were in Mangarh with Kripalu, he went and told the father the whole thing. Once he found out exactly what kind of person Kripalu really was, he got very angry.

Unfortunately, the rest of this article is missing from the copy I was given. But the presumption is that this man spoke out about Kripalu's criminal behaviour.

Two other articles published in India in the early 1990s also spoke to the same issues. One reported: 'Kripalu took very expensive sex-enhancing medication all the time so he could have sex at any time. All the devotee preachers have to be ready to satisfy his sexual desires at any time. He had a habit of seeing new movies with the new girls. Every day, he likes to see a new movie with a new young girl.' One of the articles also speaks to his legal troubles: 'With the help of a politician he got out on bond after his arrest for rape.'

Presumably, he paid off even more officials, because eventually the case just went away. Here is a description of his rape of these girls, from official documents in India:

> On 10th May, 1994, Shri Purushottam Wasudeo Deshpande lodged report with the Police Station, Dhantoli, Nagpur, alleging that his two young daughters, namely Hema and Meera, were kidnapped by the applicant No. 1 Priya Sharan Maharaj in connivance with one Sharvaridevi and Suhasini Narkhede. He further stated that his two daughters were attached for the last two years with the movements of Sanatan Dharma Shri Krishna Bhakti, under the auspicious [sic] of the applicant No. 1 i.e. Kripaluji Maharaj of Sadhna Bhawan Trust at village Managarh,

> District Pratapgarh (U.P.). On the basis of the report lodged by Shri Purushottam Deshpande, P.S.O., P.S. Dhantoli, Nagpur, registered an offence on 11-5-1991, punishable under Sections 363 and 366 of the Indian Penal Code, against the applicant No. 1 Shri Priya Sharan Maharaj, vide Crime No. 149/91.
>
> During the investigation, the statements of Hema and Meera came to be recorded. From the statements of these two girls, it is revealed that the applicant No. 2 Kripaluji Maharaj is highly immoral man so also greedy of money. Those who attended the discourses, used to be persuaded and prompted to bring their wives and daughters to attend the discourse of Kripaluji Maharaj. The applicant No. 2 has two female disciples or agents viz. Neelu Chourasia and Sarasvati Yadao, who used to entice the women and girls to attend the discourses as well as pursuing [sic] the women and girls to appear in a lonely place before the applicant No. 2. These two agents used to impress on the girls that the Maharaj is the incarnation of God.
>
> In the lonely place, according to Hema and Meera, Maharaj was most immoral and vulgar person who perforce (by physical coersion) used to commit sexual intercourse with the women and girls. Maharaj committed intercourse with them perforce. It was also impressed on their mind that it is nothing but a 'Prasad' of God and they have been blessed accordingly. In spite of this, the girls continued to stay in the vicinity of the Ashram and thereby they had no other go than to succumb to the desire of the applicant No. 2. Therefore, according to these two girls named above, the applicant No. 2 Kripaluji Maharaj exploited the religious sentiments of the innocent girls in the name of God.

Kripalu's lust for virgins did not end with his arrest in India – it was still going strong when I met him. Like this daily sex factory with willing adult women, Kripalu had an established system for raping virgins. Many people offered virgins to Kripalu – including his personal servants, female devotees, Prakash, and the girls' mothers and grandmothers.

Feeding the Beast

Offering Virgins to the Guru

AS I LEARNT more about the regular deliveries of underage girls to Kripalu by adult female devotees, it reminded me of one of the stories I'd read in the Mahabharata about Bakasura, a cannibalistic, forest-dwelling rakshasa who terrorized the nearby human population. This demon demanded that local villagers take turns bringing him regular loads of food and human sacrifices. Like Bakasura, Kripalu demanded a steady diet from the women willing to give him their bodies. However, his preferred offering was young girls, who were unwilling participants in his gopi–Krishna charade and were forced to comply by adults who wished to garner Kripalu's good graces by providing him with what he craved most – the flesh of virgins.

After I left Barsana Dham, a woman told me that one day she saw a fifty-five-year-old woman devotee sitting despondent outside Kripalu's bedroom.

'What's wrong?' the woman narrating the story to me had asked.

'I'm sad because Maharajji no longer wants me. He only wants young girls now,' the woman replied.

I eventually uncovered about seven girls he had raped, who were all children I had known in the ashram. But I am convinced this is a tiny percentage of the girls he has raped in his half-century career as a 'guru'.

I had travelled to India in the summer of 2000 with several devotees, including a sixteen-year-old Indian girl. I later learnt that Kripalu had taken her virginity – with her mother's full knowledge and consent – that summer before she flew back to the US.

The girl had also been forced to dance for Kripalu every night during the 'entertainment period' at the end of satsang, during which time many devotees performed dances and songs for his amusement. Prakash once said that Kripalu likes it best when women 'shake a lot' while dancing. Later we were told that older women should not perform for him as he preferred the dance of young women and girls.

Years later, this young woman would not publicly speak out about her abuse at the hands of Kripalu, except to one woman, whom I knew. She told the woman that Prakash too had started touching her when she was eight years old. Now she just wanted to be able to marry and have a decent life, and forget everything that the gurus had done to her. She would not talk to anyone else.

I also heard the story about a sixteen-year-old girl from Ireland who was brought to Barsana Dham in 2005 and taken to Kripalu by the woman who was her 'chaperone'. I was told that when the child returned home and her father heard about her sexual activities with Kripalu, he beat his daughter.

Another young girl from the US was raped at the age of thirteen. However, her parents had no knowledge of what their daughter had gone through. This girl was escorted to her nightmare by Prabhakari who waited outside Kripalu's bedroom for the girl to emerge. According to what I was told, when the girl came out crying, Prabhakari told her, 'Consider this your wedding night with Krishna.' She also warned the girl: 'Do not tell anyone, not even your parents.'

There was an eleven-year-old girl in Barsana Dham who was taken to Kripalu's bedroom by an 'experienced' sixteen-year-old girl from Australia, who demonstrated for the young girl what to do when alone with Kripalu by engaging in sexual activities with him in front of the child.

The Australian girl, whose single mother had been taking her to Kripalu since she was three, had a long-running, unusually close relationship with Kripalu. The mother once told me that from her first trip to see Kripalu, her daughter would sit on his lap and hug him for hours. He nicknamed her 'the leech'. I saw her clinging to him myself on my first trip to India. At that time, the pre-teen was obviously his favourite. But it was years before I knew just what that meant.

On the day that this teenager 'performed' with Kripalu in front of the eleven-year-old, the younger girl was so shocked at what she witnessed that she ran to her grandmother's room and told her what happened. Initially upset, the grandmother took her to Prakash and told him the story. He apparently said to them: 'Don't you trust me?'

During Kripalu's second trip to Barsana Dham in 2007, the young girl was thirteen, and immediately became his favourite, a regular fixture by his side. By this time, she was beautiful and nubile, with thick dark hair and white skin. She was frequently in his bedroom and often accompanied him on his outings from the ashram, such as shopping at the mall.

The day I went to Vishi's room to talk to her about private time with Kripalu, she used this girl as an example of someone who had surrendered completely to Kripalu. 'She sees nothing but Maharajji. She cares only about him. She has been his for many lifetimes. Now she is just one step away from the divine world.'

I realized that with this kind of psychology coming from the adults in her life, the girl didn't stand a chance at a normal life.

One day I asked the girl about spending so much time at the ashram and missing so much time from school. She said brazenly: 'I lied to them and told them I have mononucleosis; so they told me that I'm not even allowed to go to school. Isn't that funny?' Then she turned and walked away with a swing of her hips.

During that trip, I couldn't help but notice that the young girl changed from a bright, eager-to-please child into a prima donna – all within the span of a few weeks. One day I happened to overhear a conversation between the girl, her grandmother and another woman. The two older women were telling the girl that she had to learn to lie to her parents.

'You have to be able to look them in the eye and lie,' said the grandmother.

'I know. Don't worry, I will,' said the child with utmost confidence.

Clearly, the grandmother was supportive of the 'relationship' between her granddaughter and Kripalu. In the summer of 2008, the grandmother escorted the child on her first trip to India, along with two other women from Barsana Dham. One of the women, who eventually left the organization, told me that the grandmother said 'Don't let any Indian men near her. She belongs to Maharajji'.

Later during that trip, the young girl told this same woman what she did with Kripalu in his bedroom, including oral sex and intercourse. The girl believed she was a gopi sharing intimate activities with Krishna.

It came to light that two other girls who had been taken to Kripalu in 2005 contracted infections. One of them was crying bitterly about her experience to her mother, who had known Kripalu herself since she was a young girl. The mother said to the woman who later narrated the story to me: 'I had to go through the same thing when I was her age.'

A Rapist's Rituals

Kripalu's Modus Operandi

RITUALS ARE SACRED to Hindus, and each sect in Hinduism has its own. Kripalu too had many rituals, some of which were performed publicly, while others conducted in private. Rather than performing the complicated pujas and ceremonies of most Hindu sects, his public rituals were much simpler. For example, one daily ritual in his ashrams was to make devotees line up each morning during satsang to bow to him and pay a cash seva ($2.50 in India and $10 in the US).

My first clue to Kripalu's private rituals came when I read one of the first reports about his rape of the young woman in Trinidad on the Trinidad and Tobago News Blog, in an article titled 'Visiting Guru Held on Sex Charges'. It told of his arrest on a Friday night after a woman claimed rape. The article detailed her experience:

> The woman went to the home ... [for] spiritual healing. The man [Kripalu] ... told the woman to take off her clothes ... [he] sprayed a liquid on the woman ... then began to fondle her ... she was then made to perform oral sex on the man after which the man had sexual intercourse with her for approximately one hour.

I remembered this description when I heard the other stories about Kripalu's sexual activities – which were highly ritualized. From my research, I arrived at the conclusion that Kripalu's modus operandi for sex at this stage of his life (in his eighties) included three basic rituals. The first was when he had sex with willing adult female devotees. The second was his bath seva. And the third was when he forced himself on underage girls.

For sexual encounters with willing female devotees, the ritual went like this: If it was the woman's first time, she was prepped for the encounter by one of the preachers or helpers. They would tell the women some form of 'this is your chance to be with Kripalu intimately, like the gopis are with Krishna'. The women were instructed to take a shower, shave everything, trim their nails and take off their jewellery.

When they were presented to Kripalu, he would tell them to lie on the bed. He would frequently spray them and himself with perfume. Then he would proceed to French-kiss them and paw at their clothing. If he could not easily get their clothes off, he would tell the women to take them off. Once they were either partially or completely undressed, he would indicate for them to perform oral sex on him. At some point, he would initiate copulation.

If it was not a woman's first time, he would be a little more familiar with them, and usually get to the main event faster. Right away, he would do one of three things: have her perform oral sex on him or he would perform it on her, then he would climb on top of the woman and slide his partially erect penis inside her.

One woman told me that when she walked into his bedroom once, he was already sitting on the edge of the bed, masturbating. He gestured that she should take over the job.

When he was done with a woman, he would tell her he loved her. If it was her first time, he would add a warning: 'Don't tell anyone.'

Many women returned to these private encounters with Kripalu hoping that things would be a little more cosy, and less quick and rigid. But as one woman finally realized, 'Maharajji doesn't cuddle'.

The basic structure of Kripalu's daily bath ritual, which women paid $2,200 to perform, operated like this: Each day, a woman would be selected for the ritual and prepped. Everything had to be just so, from the temperature of the water to the position of his rugs. He would walk in naked and sit down on his bath stool. Using a bucket of water, soap and a washcloth, the woman, with his help, would wash his entire body, including his private parts. When he was clean, he would indicate that it was time for her to perform oral sex on him. When he was done, he would stand up, indicating that it was time for the woman to leave.

Then there was his ritual for raping underage girls. A young girl would be told by a preacher or helper to take a shower and wear loose clothing. She would be taken into Kripalu's bedroom and left alone with him. He would often spray the girl and himself with perfume, then proceed to take off her clothing or tell her to get undressed and then lie on top of her and force his partially erect penis inside, guiding it in with his finger. As with the adult women, when he was finished with a girl, he would indicate that she should leave, telling her that he loved her and not to tell anyone.

Typically, the women who brought young girls to Kripalu the first time would wait outside the bedroom door.

A few times a day, women would remake Kripalu's bed with fresh sheets. That explained the large closet – filled with stacks of sheets, and many bottles of perfume and lotion – next to his bedroom.

The Moral Minority

Our Ex-devotee Network

BEFORE LEAVING BARSANA Dham, I read somewhere that the two most effective ways to get over being in a cult are having a great therapist and having the support of other ex-cult members.

After Steven J. Gelberg left a Hindu organization called the International Society for Krishna Consciousness (ISKCON), he wrote about his experience, including this insight on recovering from a cult.

> It's hard to imagine an experience more wrenching, more potentially disorienting, than leaving a spiritual community or tradition to which one had devoted years of one's life. This re-orientation to self and re-entry into the world is no small task, and it's more easily finessed when one has the support of others who've travelled a similar path.

I already had the perfect therapist in Elise, and she had helped me in ways that were miraculous. But when I read Mr Gelberg's words, I assumed that I would never have an ex-devotee support group. While many people had come and gone over the years, I did not know where they were and so I had no way to reach out to any of the people from the past.

I had few friends in the ashram because, as Prakash instructed, I kept my friendships to a bare minimum, so that 'friends' would not distract me from my devotions.

Although Jane and I had not been friends in the ashram, we bonded once we got out, mainly because all we had was each other. We clung together like the last two survivors on a life raft. Our two-person support system was a long-distance relationship, since she had moved away to a northern state. But we stayed in daily contact via email and occasionally had long phone conversations. It was a relief to know that I had a kindred spirit in the big wide world.

In Austin I was alone, except for my long-time friend, Karen, whom I knew through work. Karen was a wonderful supporter, but she had not been a devotee and so had not 'travelled a similar path'. As a result, she could not truly understand the devastation I was experiencing, and the feelings of fear and loss that I was going through. Only another devotee would be able to understand.

A miracle happened when Kathi and I connected. We formed an impromptu network and slowly expanded our support system to include over a dozen ex-devotees. Of course, Kathi's husband Wayne was a member. He had decided that he was done with JKP the day Kripalu gave him a cookie and told him it cost $2,000. But his wife took a few more years to disengage; basically because she felt like she loved Kripalu, as did many of the female devotees.

Kathi also connected to an Austin Indian couple, Deepak and Sushma, who had been going to Barsana Dham for years. In fact, they had moved their family from California to Austin in the 1990s to be close to the temple. But by 2005 they were beginning to learn about the activities of the gurus and slowly extricated themselves from the organization. They gave our support group a valuable cultural perspective on gurus and Hinduism.

A single man who had moved to Austin to be closer to the temple and who had also been a faithful follower had left the group around the same time, sick of the abuse directed at him despite performing endless hours of free labour. But learning more facts from Deepak and Sushma sealed his decision to leave and never look back.

Kathi had already reached out to a woman who had not been a devotee herself, but had been married to one for many years. When Sue's husband died shortly before Prakash's arrest, Kathi offered her a hand in friendship. Sue's other friends from Barsana Dham had abandoned her once they realized she had taken the girls' side in the criminal charges against Prakash. While she couldn't provide the insight of a true devotee, she was a lawyer and brought a much appreciated legal perspective to our group's regular discussions about Prakash's arrest and legal machinations.

Our network grew to include several more people who were not in Austin, including two families in California, a man who worked in Washington DC, and Suzy and her husband, who now lived in the north-east. We all stayed in touch via email and phone calls. Several ex-devotees declined the invitation to join us, wanting to forget about the whole experience.

At first, we had all believed that devotees would leave the ashram in droves when word got out about the true nature of JKP and its gurus. But the sad reality was that the vast majority of people stayed thoroughly entrenched in the organization, choosing to believe that the gurus were above reproach. We were disappointed. After all, there were children involved, who had been molested by these men.

Our Austin contingent came together regularly to keep each other informed on the latest news and to provide support. We were driven by a shared need to understand the twisted gurus and how we got caught in their trap.

We were a small group, but, as it turned out, a formidable one. Eventually, our little network created a powerful force of advocacy for the girls and women abused at Barsana Dham. We had several great moments of success while doing our part to help expose the gurus' crimes, including an email campaign that kept Prakash out of Barsana Dham until the trial.

We rejoiced at every win for 'our side' and witnessed some miraculous events along the way. The miracles started with Prakash's arrest, and continued through his criminal trial. In fact, we often said to each other: 'This whole thing must be guided by a divine force, because none of us could have created the miracles that we are witnessing on this side of the battle for justice.'

While I was no longer sure what form God took, I could definitely see his handiwork in the perfectness of the execution of Prakash's eventual justice. One time I commented: 'We waited in the ashram for the gurus to perform miracles, which they never did. Now all of the miracles are happening out here. If the people supporting the gurus want to see miracles, they need to get out of there.'

Of all the miracles we witnessed, we longed for one miracle above all: that Prakash be found guilty in a court of law.

Talking to Mary

The Former Sureshwari Surfaces

ONCE KATE REALIZED the truth about the gurus, she started getting in touch with former devotees – and found Mary, the former preacher named Sureshwari.

Actually, Mary was one of the first people to join a private online chat group – where ex-devotees could join and lend support to each other – Kate had started. She had been Prakash's main preacher for nearly thirty years and Barsana Dham's president for nearly ten. Prakash initially gave her the name Meera Devi, but in the early 2000s, Kripalu changed her name and that of many of the other preachers – for no apparent reason, except perhaps to make them 'his'.

A few months after I moved out of the ashram, Mary agreed to speak with me. She told me how she came to realize that JKP was an evil cult and described how her life had descended into a hellish nightmare. But she could not speak out publicly because she feared what the organization might do to her. She had heard, seen and experienced a lot more than most people, and believed that the gurus would retaliate if she spoke out. They were not idle fears, since she had already suffered unimaginable abuses once the gurus realized that she was no longer a malleable, brainwashed follower.

To many of the followers, Mary epitomized the perfect devotee. She was the only preacher who seemed to live the principles that Prakash recited to us. In fact, without her by his side all of those years, Prakash's mission would never have grown to the level it had (which, in comparison to other Hindu organizations that came to the West, was not very large). Many of us assumed she was just a hair's breadth away from achieving God realization – if she hadn't already. But, in the end, she realized that she had been just another victim of these two conmen, along with everyone else.

In February 2004, she left the ashram and the organization. Both gurus called her repeatedly to win her back. She refused their calls and attempted to begin healing and rebuild her life.

But just before she was scheduled to start a new job, she second-guessed herself and thought: 'What am I doing out here? I'm a sanyasi and I should be with my gurus.' She decided to give the gurus another chance. Three months after she left, she wrote a letter to Prakash asking if she could return. He told her to go to India. In hindsight, the trip was a bad idea. Prakash put Sureshwari in a mental hospital, where she received severe treatment. It seemed to me that the purpose of this 'treatment' was to wreck her mind so that she could never speak out against the gurus.

As soon as she could, she left again – this time for good. Her departure left a lot of devotees with questions – questions that were never answered by Prakash. The only thing he ever did was have Peter S. tell us that she left because she was crazy, and she had been crazy for a long time.

However, this story made no sense, because if she had been crazy, why did Prakash let her run the ashram as president and continue to be his primary preacher?

JKP's gurus never bothered themselves over important details like this and their followers never held them accountable for inconsistent and outlandish statements and behaviour.

Hell on Earth

Saving a Soul

EVERY TIME I heard some new insight about the gurus, I would get depressed for days at a time, sinking into a dark space of shock and regret. Every time I thought I had heard the worst, there was always another gruesome secret to discover. Each new disclosure sent me reeling into new depths of hell, from which I always struggled to return. I eventually came to the conclusion that there was no bottom to the gurus' depravity.

Kathi told me about how female devotees who were looking forward to private time with Kripalu would get waxed 'down there' before visiting him. Apparently, once he experienced women with waxed privates, he liked it.

I was floored by this revelation. After all, I had worshipped God with these women, or thought I had. Meanwhile, they were off procuring Brazilians for the guru!

Each time I unearthed something new, I would have nightmares for several nights. In one, I was surrounded by devotees and trying to inform them one at a time about the gurus' secrets. I finally got one man alone and whispered to him: 'The gurus are raping children.'

The next day I was having lunch with Nancy, my former best friend in the ashram. She was still living there and we hadn't talked in months. She had decided that she didn't want to communicate with me after I left, because I had 'gone negative' about the gurus. But several things had happened within the ashram since then that made her increasingly suspicious. She called me one day and said, 'I'm ready to hear the truth.' We planned to meet for lunch in a few days.

We sat down in the restaurant facing each other, with some awkwardness. She looked resolute but afraid to hear what I had to say.

I didn't know where to begin. She was the first person I had talked to from the ashram who had not come to the conclusion on their own that JKP was an evil cult.

Then four words came to mind from my dream: 'The gurus are raping virgins.'

She stared at me with her eyes wide open and her lips pursed. She did not say a word. I talked almost non-stop for the next twenty minutes, filling her in on one gory detail after the next. When her eyes glazed over, I knew she couldn't take any more, so I shut up.

When we parted that day, she was still in shock. I did not hear from her again for another six months – after which she called to tell me that she had moved out of the ashram.

Occasionally, over the next few months, she would want to talk and was open to hearing more. But then she would always reach her limit pretty quickly. It was as if her mind was resisting the dark reality of our former spiritual path. She pushed it away for another two years. It was frustrating to witness a person resist the truth for so long.

Finally, she was strong enough to accept that the two men we had worshipped as representations of the highest form of God were, in fact, nothing but paedophiles, rapists and conmen.

My Awakening

God Realization in the Blink of an Eye

WHEN I RECEIVED God realization, it happened in the blink of an eye – and far from the gurus' grasp.

One afternoon, about three months after I left the cult, I went to see my therapist, Elise. I was depressed that day. I believed there must have been some serious flaw in my character that allowed me to make such a grave error in judgement. I asked myself repeatedly: how *could* you put yourself in a situation where you could be so cruelly tricked and taken advantage of? It did not fit with my image of myself as a smart, independent person, with a reliable gut instinct. How could I have let myself down so horribly?

As I drove to see Elise, I was convinced that nothing could drag me out of my bleak state of mind. I told her about my despair over having wasted a chunk of my life. Thankfully, she gave me some insight that helped me see the situation from another perspective.

'It's not unusual to desire something beyond being human. When we begin searching for that thing, we search outside of ourselves. We look outward, thinking someone else has the thing we do not have, and we believe that person will save us. However, it's not anywhere else, it's within us. The hardest place for us to stay present is within ourselves.'

Something in what she said clicked. I left her office feeling light as a feather, strong and positive. Although I had spent so many years being deceived by truly wicked people, my life was now in my hands and I could make what I wanted of it.

I knew one thing for sure: I would never again allow any other mere mortal to tell me anything about God. I heard everything I ever wanted to hear on the subject. And I no longer believed in 'saints'. I now only believed in a God-energy of some sort that didn't require any intermediary for me to commune with it.

As I pulled into the garage of my new apartment, I suddenly experienced an extraordinary feeling. In that instant, I sensed the power of God. I felt the energy as the dominant force in the universe. I was completely connected to that energy, and realized that I had never truly been disconnected from this 'God-force' in the first place. I now knew that, in the past, I had only failed to make the simple connection that was always there. It was like how, in *The Wizard of Oz*, Dorothy always wanted to go home – not realizing she already was home.

It was the most natural, simple, and quiet experience. Yet it was incredibly powerful – a private nod of acknowledgement from a divine existence to me and from me back to it. That small gesture put me in a state of peace about my relationship to the divine that I retain to this day.

It was not an overwhelming bolt of bliss that knocked me to the ground, or some euphoric high that opened up my vision to God's uncountable forms, as they exist in the divine realm. I think people in the ashram thought that the moment of God realization would be something magical and beyond description, a metaphysical celebration that would mark their entrance into the divine realm forever, and something that would only happen after extreme devotion to a guru.

The funny thing is that during my fifteen years in the ashram I never observed a single person who seemed to have achieved the ever-elusive 'God realization' that the gurus wagged before us like a carrot on a stick that was always out of reach. Now that I had actually experienced God realization, I knew beyond a shadow of a doubt that my connection with God was the most natural thing in the world.

I also knew, with complete clarity, that everything we were told to do in the ashram to find God was just irrelevant busy work. All the hours of chanting, drumming, cymbal playing, video watching, darshan sitting, seva work, going to India – every last bit of it was just the guru's way of keeping the masses occupied. I could see now how one way they kept their con running was to keep us all too busy to pay attention to their lives of luxury, their decadence and their non-spiritual behaviour.

What's more, not only were we kept busy and out of their hair, but our devotional activities were also an important part of their con game's smokescreen. People saw our devotion and worship, and assumed the gurus were as devotional as their devotees. It was a trick, a sleight of hand that had served them well for six decades.

After struggling for a decade and a half in the ashram and always feeling like a spiritual failure, all it took was a single solitary moment to 'find' God, and to realize that I'd never lost Him in the first place. Some might call this experience reaching samadhi, or higher consciousness.

The Hindu theory of non-duality suggests that you cannot experience anything without also experiencing its opposite. As the

Lankavatara Sutra scripture states: 'Light and shade, long and short, black and white can only be experienced in relation to each other: light is not independent of shade, nor black of white. There are no opposites, only relationships.'

Similarly, perhaps I could not experience the divine without first experiencing pure evil.

Witness for the Prosecution

Nothing but the Truth

ONE OF OUR ex-devotee network's first victories was in helping to keep Prakash out of Barsana Dham. After he received his passport in exchange for the $10 million promissory note in May 2008, Prakash had stayed out of the US for three months. But when he returned to Austin in August, he wanted to go back to his ashram, despite the agreement he had made with Hays County. In the meantime, he was staying in a devotee's home, two miles west of the ashram.

His lawyers had requested a hearing on 20 August to seek permission for him to return to Barsana Dham. I immediately emailed our network and asked everyone to send emails of protest to the district attorney. Our number one concern was for all the children who visited the temple for Sunday services, celebrations and family camps. In my email, I included links to online videos of two families staring into the camera and explaining why they loved going to Barsana Dham. To a normal, non-cult person, these videos looked creepy – like the parents were completely brainwashed and the children were forced to go along for the ride. These were Barsana Dham's own videos posted on YouTube.

I later learnt that our comments made a huge impression on the

DA, especially when she realized how many people were supporting the girls. Our emails strengthened her resolve to keep Prakash out of Barsana Dham, but she worried about what defence his lawyers would bring to the judge.

The day before the hearing, I talked to Kate about our email campaign. While we were on the phone, she emailed the DA to make her own request, and received an immediate response: 'I will do my best to keep him out, but they will likely have several witnesses. And I don't have any witnesses.'

I said to Kate: 'Send her my name and phone number right now.'

Two minutes later, my home phone rang.

It was Cathy Compton. She asked me if I would come down to the courthouse the next day to be a witness at Prakash's hearing. She wanted to meet two hours before the hearing.

I agreed and was prepared to tell her whatever I knew.

The next morning, I was a nervous wreck as I drove south on Interstate 35 from Austin to San Marcos. Everyone in our ex-devotee network had sent me emails of support the night before, but I was still terrified at the thought of being on the witness stand in front of Prakash and his devotees.

Cathy asked me many questions about my life in the ashram, how I got there, and why I left. She was particularly interested in a letter I had taken with me – the one I had sent to Prabhakari just four days before I moved out of the ashram. It was clear evidence that I had left Barsana Dham under good circumstances and was not kicked out by them for any reason.

She also wanted to know what life in the ashram was like, what Prakash did when he was there, how often he left for India and how the place functioned when he was gone.

Cathy was a tiny woman, but had a huge personality. Right away, I sensed the brilliance under her southern accent. 'Defence lawyers often think I'm just some little country bumpkin,' she laughed. 'I like it when they do, because that throws them off guard. They're not prepared when I attack.'

The court's victim's advocate, Allison, came to check on us. 'I just want to warn you that their side of the courtroom is completely filled with their people.'

At the news, I burst into tears. The thought of being all alone in front of that mass of diehard Prakash worshipers overwhelmed me. Cathy walked over and stood in front of me, looking at me intently. 'When you are on that stand, just look at me. Don't look at them, okay?'

I looked her in the eye and said exactly what I felt in that moment: 'I trust you.'

Then she left for the courtroom. The plan was to keep me sequestered until she needed me on the witness stand. I stayed in her small office, pacing the floor. I tried to gather strength by thinking of the girls who would one day face Prakash and the devotees with their stories of sexual abuse. That day I wanted to do the best job possible for their sake.

Finally, Allison came to get me. She took my hand and led me into the courtroom. She was protective as she guided me around the phalanx of devotees in the courtroom, all facing the judge's bench. Just as we were about to walk up the centre isle towards the witness stand, Cathy came rushing up to us and said, 'It's done. The judge denied their request.' She told Allison: 'Take her to the corner so she doesn't have to mingle as their people leave the courtroom.'

I sat in a chair in the back of the courtroom with Allison and her muscular husband sitting beside me. She even stood up at one point to block the devotees' view of me. I have never felt so protected in my life. I took refuge in the safety of my protectors, relaxing because I did not have to take centre stage on the witness stand. And we got the win anyway.

I barely looked at the devotees, not wanting to make eye contact with any of them. I noticed a few familiar faces here and there. They looked confused and shocked by the outcome of the hearing. I'm sure they thought that their great and powerful guru would successfully get whatever he wanted from a mere worldly judge.

When most of the devotees had left the courtroom, Cathy and

the head DA, Sherri Tibbe, came over and thanked me. Cathy said, 'The information you shared with me before the hearing helped me effectively cross-examine their witnesses. Right after I called you as a witness, Judge Ramsay said "Motion denied", then stood up and left the room.'

I was happy and relieved. The victory for our side felt wonderful. Maybe Prakash wasn't in jail yet, but at least he could not return to the kingdom were he molested young girls.

As we were talking, Prabhakari walked out of the room, pushing the door open with disgust. Sherri said to Cathy, 'There she goes.'

I said, 'Yeah, she's leaving in a huff.' They laughed.

Then she came back in the room, her back ramrod straight and face pinched. She marched over to the table where Prakash and the lawyers had been sitting and grabbed a handful of papers. Then she repeated her huffy exit from the room. We all laughed again.

When we returned to Cathy's office, she dashed off a note to the girls. 'Great news! The judge denied their motion. Prakash cannot return to the ashram. Karen wanted me to tell you that Prabhakari walked out of the courtroom in a huff – twice.'

I was elated as I drove home. When Kate called, I happily told her every detail – including how brilliant Cathy Compton had been.

'You girls have an incredible woman in your corner,' I said to Kate.

Appealing to a Higher Power

The Guru Can't Take No for an Answer

PRAKASH'S ATTEMPT TO get back into Barsana Dham did not end with his denial in the Hays County courtroom that August – not by a long shot. His efforts to return continued for almost fifteen months. I'm sure it was both a personal indignity and a public relations nightmare for him not to be able to enter his own ashram. After all, he led his followers to believe that he was a form of God incarnate, with powers that included dominion over the mundane world. But now he could not even step into the ashram property.

This was a problem he clearly hoped to remedy as soon as possible. Janet, my friend, told me that Heather – another woman in the ashram who was close friends with Vishi – had said that the case was going to be resolved very soon because Prakash was 'taking it all the way to the Supreme Court'.

Unless she meant the US Supreme Court, my guess is that Heather mixed up the names of the highest state court in which Prakash would be allowed to appeal. For criminal cases, the highest appellate court in Texas is called the Texas Court of Appeals.

But Prakash's lawyers could not simply go straight to the top. They first had to follow standard procedure, which required them to make their request to the county court a second time. However, to do this, they needed to bring something new to the bench – which they did, in the form of a creative motion.

Almost immediately following the first hearing, Prakash's lawyers filed a new motion containing a writ of habeas corpus. A habeas corpus is a summons with the force of a court order, addressed to the custodian (a judge, for example), demanding that a prisoner be taken before the court and that the custodian present proof of authority, allowing the court to determine if the custodian has lawful authority to detain the prisoner. If the custodian does not have authority to detain the prisoner, he or she must be released from custody. Although this seemed irrelevant to Prakash's situation (after all, he was not being kept *in* a place, he was being kept *out* of a place), his lawyers were able to use it as an excuse to obtain a second hearing, which was all they wanted.

It was obvious that his lawyers knew their motion would be denied. What they were really after was access to the Texas Third Court of Appeals, which does not allow just any case through its doors. But one of the types of cases it will hear is a habeas corpus case.

As if on cue, at the next hearing on 2 December, Judge Ramsay delivered a judgment of *nunc pro tunc* (a Latin legal term meaning 'now for then'). In general, a court ruling of *nunc pro tunc* applies retroactively to correct or uphold an earlier ruling. In this case, it meant that the earlier decision of the Hays County court would still hold. In other words, Prakash's new motion was denied.

The very next day, on 3 December, Prakash's lawyers notified the Hays County court that it was filing a writ of habeas corpus with the Texas Third Court of Appeals. On 15 December, Prakash's lawyers filed the case.

In Prakash's fifty-five-page appellant brief, his lawyers cited the following issue: 'Continued imposition of bond conditions which prevent appellant from residing in his home, leading religious ceremonies, and ministering to his congregation, constitutes a violation of appellant's rights under the first, eighth, and fourteenth amendments to the Constitution of the United States.'

Basically, they were playing the 'freedom of religion' card – and playing it hard.

Several months later, in May 2009, the appeals court heard his case. The Hays County attorney made several compelling arguments: the defendant's (appellant) appeal should be dismissed for want of jurisdiction, because it is essentially an appeal of an interlocutory pre-trial order and a 'court of appeals does not have jurisdiction to review interlocutory orders'. An interlocutory order basically means an interim order rendered in the midst of trial proceedings, which have not yet received a final judgment.

On 24 June 2009, the Texas Third Court of Appeals denied Prakash's bid to gain access to his ashram: 'There is no allegation that [the guru] did not understand the agreed conditions of his bond or that [his] acceptance of those conditions was involuntary.'

In the third court's judgment document, I particularly liked a comment made by Chief Justice J. Woodfin Jones: 'Appellant's inability to return to Barsana Dham was no less a hindrance to his ability to practice his religion or associate with his followers in May than it was in August, or than it is today.' It was refreshing to know there were people who saw right through his con game.

Prakash's team had one final option: the Texas Court of Criminal Appeals. But on 17 November 2009, the court declined to even hear his case and upheld the decision of the Texas Third Court of Appeals, which had upheld the decision of the Hays County court.

Finally, Prakash was out of appeals and had to give up on returning to Barsana Dham before his trial. The only way he would be free to once again reign over his kingdom was if he were found innocent at this criminal trial. Being found guilty, he would be an accused sex offender and likely to be taken to a new, less luxurious home – jail.

Prakash left Austin two days later. Apparently, he had been scheduled to stay a bit longer, because an insider emailed me after I told him about the court of criminal appeals decision: 'Probably that was the reason for his early departure to India this morning!'

Prakash did not return to the US again until early October 2010 – over ten months later.

Publication Day

The Power of the Press

I BOTH CRAVED and dreaded seeing Eric's articles in the *Austin American-Statesman*. I wanted the public to know the true nature of the temple sitting behind an eight-foot-high fence. But I was also afraid of being identified as someone once involved with such a despicable place.

Four months after my first contact with Eric, the articles were published in a two-day weekend exposé on 28 and 29 September 2008.

Both appeared on the front page. The first article, on Saturday, was about the sexual allegations. It was titled: 'Women Say Temple Guru Made Sexual Advances.'

In order to keep us anonymous, Eric had created a system of numbering each of the five women he interviewed.

Suzy was Woman No. 1. And she recounted her experiences with Prakash. Kathi was Woman No. 2 and she revealed her one limited encounter with Prakash in which he groped her right before her dance performance, and also several more intimate experiences with Kripalu, including performing oral sex on him.

I was Woman No. 3 and Eric had interviewed me about an encounter in which Prakash had pulled me close, kissed me and fondled my breasts. Kripalu's body-pressing incident was included as well.

Kate and Rachel were Women Nos 4 and 5 and they recounted instances of being groped and fondled by Swamiji and Kripalu respectively.

The 2,600-word article ended with the following commentary:

> N. Kumar, a California devotee since 1992, had hosted prayer sessions at his home. 'We were shocked,' he said. 'This is absolutely not acceptable in the religion, in India, in the culture.'

Eric's writing was brilliant. One person told me the article was worthy of a Pulitzer Prize. I was very happy, and wanted to walk around Austin and watch people reading the newspaper; perhaps overhear them discussing the article.

But mostly I just wanted people to be appalled, to be morally outraged, and to never set foot inside that place – especially with their children.

The Infomercial Guru

Mixing Spiritual and Secular

ALONG WITH THE guru's sexual misdeeds, Eric uncovered the curious relationships between Prakash and some of his devotees' businesses in the infomercial industry.

Sunday's story was headlined 'Infomercial Executives Help Support Hindu Temple':

> In the mid-1980s, the leaders of a Hindu organization trying to gain a foothold in the United States contemplated how to raise money. Eventually, Prakashanand Saraswati and his devotees within the International Society of Divine Love – later called Barsana Dham, after they'd established themselves in Austin – ended up with an unorthodox source of support: infomercials.
>
> The result has been a peculiar but apparently profitable alliance between the sacred and secular. Through overlaps between temple leaders and direct marketing executives and their companies, it has paired Prakashanand, a 79-year-old Hindu holy man also known as Shree Swamiji, with such late-night fare as promotions for the Miracle Blade, Abflex, homeopathic impotency treatments and the Ionic Pro air purifier.

Few people who had worked in the devotee-run businesses and knew the secrets would talk to Eric. But that didn't stop him from finding the facts that produced a complete picture of a so-called spiritual guru with his hands involved directly in several very profitable business operations.

I had done my best to help him research the financial activities of the organization. It was common knowledge among the devotees that Prakash was active in their operations and management – advising the owners in most major decisions, from naming products to hiring executives to opening new offices. Over the years, the businesses had some incredible successes, where they were practically minting money by selling items like the Miracle Blade (named by Prakash himself) in late-night infomercials.

From the beginning of his mission in the US, Prakash looked to his devotees to start businesses that would support his plans to build a US ashram. Sometime in the 1980s, Katie W. and Peter S., both former members of Transcendental Meditation (TM) and a couple, brought him the idea to start an infomercial media-buying company, because Katie had worked for an infomercial company in Fairfield, Iowa, when she was in TM. Prakash thought it sounded like a good way to make him some money. Another long-time female devotee joined them and started an infomercial production company. When these three high rollers were staying in the ashram, they had standing meetings with Prakash in his bedroom at 10:00 p.m. every night to discuss business matters.

When I discovered that Prakash had an infomercial business running on the Barsana Dham property, I got a sick feeling in my stomach. After all, infomercials are often viewed as one of the lowest form of product sales, rife with the potential for scams.

The first devotee-run business on the property shipped products to people who purchased the infomercial products sold by the original company. A second company bought media time for other companies peddling products in thirty-minute advertisements. Both companies located in the ashram grew during the early 1990s. But both crashed by the 2000s, when the executives of the main companies working out of Los Angeles went bankrupt for the first time (they would file bankruptcy a second time in 2007).

I had some level of inside information on the businesses because I had freelanced as a writer for one of them. In fact, I was once assigned to help smooth over a PR crisis when one of the companies went bankrupt – and almost immediately, a new devotee-run company picked up where the other had left off. It led to a court trial with an industry publication. The president of the new company tried to claim 'freedom of religion' as a reason for not submitting to a deposition, but was denied. So, instead, she was less than truthful and forthcoming in her deposition.

Of course, Prakash wanted to keep his business activities a secret – if for no other reason – to avoid issues with the temple's tax-exempt status. As a result, the businesses took great pains to act as if they were disconnected from the temple. The party line about the businesses housed on the property was that they were simply 'renting office space' from Barsana Dham (even though the companies themselves paid to build the buildings).

I also informed Eric about JKP's highly unusual system of collecting donations – they charged devotees for seva. I sent Eric a long price list of the costs for different sevas. He was happy to receive it, and I knew he was shocked. After all, what kind of organization charges people to push the spiritual teacher on a swing ($200), or wash his feet ($600), or celebrate your birthday with him ($2,500)!

I laughed out loud when Eric commented on the price to receive a cookie from the guru ($220). 'What kind of cookie?' he asked, incredulously.

One Indian man made it perfectly clear in one of Eric Dexheimer's articles in *Austin American-Statesman* that JKP's seva activities were extremely unorthodox in traditional Hinduism:

> Some temples accept sizable donations from devotees who, in exchange, are given a place of honor at large celebrations and ceremonies, said Sannyasin Arumugaswami, managing editor of *Hinduism Today* magazine. But, he added, 'While the practice of being with, serving and honoring the guru is a central Hindu tradition, the idea of putting detailed price tags on interacting with the spiritual teacher would be regarded by most Hindus as inappropriate, even reprehensible.'

By sheer coincidence, I was soon to discover evidence indicating that Prakash and Kripalu had planned – right from the beginning – on making millions in the US from westerners.

Conmen's Correspondence

The Forgotten Tree House

THERE ARE TWO letters in a certain safe deposit box in Austin that speak to the monetary side of the con game that Prakash and Kripalu brought to the US shores from India. One is from Kripalu in India to Prakash in Barsana Dham. Postmarked 9 March 1993, it contains a handwritten note from Kripalu to Prakash, firmly requesting money from him for the construction of another ashram in India. The second letter (draft) contains Prakash's sternly worded reply on lined college notebook paper.

Unlike English, the Hindi language allows people to speak to others in ways that connote the relationship between the two parties, such as adult to child, peer to peer, and superior to subordinate. In public, Prakash showed great reverence to Kripalu, addressing him in the most formal, respectful and subservient mode of Hindi dialogue. But the tone of the letters portrayed a very different relationship between the men. They read as one businessman talking to another – with a detectable level of contempt between them.

What's more, the letters proved that Prakash and Kripalu viewed the US as the goose that was going to lay the golden egg – and keep laying it to the tune of 'millions of dollars'. In Kripalu's letter, he insisted that Prakash was not sending him enough money. He wanted more, and he wanted it soon. And he wanted it in India. But Prakash's letter to his 'guru' was the real smoking gun. He basically ranted to Kripalu about asking for too much money and stated that the constant haranguing could get him in trouble, including with the Internal Revenue Service (IRS). Then, in one fateful sentence, Prakash revealed their true intent: 'So if this happens, our planning to collect millions of dollars for Barsana [India] will be finished.'

I could not believe that I had such incriminating evidence in my possession. I had found the letters in a pile of discarded newspapers in a tree house at Barsana Dham years before. I had asked to use the tree house as a place to study Hindi. Built on a whim, at Prakash's request, it was just big enough for a single bed, an end table and a small cupboard. For a while, Prakash was rumoured to occasionally spend time up there with female devotees, but the novelty wore off quickly. Apparently, he had left the letters there and forgotten about them.

Since both letters were written in Hindi, I had no idea what they said, but I did know that the airmail letter was *to* Prakash, because it was addressed in English. I also knew the longer hand-drafted letter was *from* Prakash, because I recognized his handwriting.

I thought perhaps someone in India had written Prakash a love letter. I knew he received many such letters from devotees. I had written him a few myself. But, despite studying Hindi, I could never decipher handwritten Hindi. So I had kept the letters in a shoebox along with other devotional notes I collected over the years, thinking that I would one day be able to read them.

Once I moved to my new apartment, I pulled the letters out one day and tried to read them again. But it was impossible. Then I heard that Eric had asked Deepak and Sushma to translate some articles written in Hindi that someone had sent him about Kripalu. I realized that I could ask them to translate the letters I had as well.

When Sushma read them the next day, she was beside herself with excitement. 'They are very bad,' she said. 'They are very revealing about the true nature of Kripalu and Prakash.'

I was jumping with joy. She asked me to keep the letters in a safe place, like a safe deposit box.

In Kripalu's airmail letter to Prakash, he wrote:

> My Dear Prakashanand, Your brief description didn't explain everything. Send us the drawing, then it will be clear. In Shyam Dham they are putting granite. But in the trust we have no money. Your 2.5 lakh rupees [$5,600 US] in black money is gone. Now we have to put tiles. Please send 15 lakh rupees [$33,600 US] in the name of the trust so that the work does not stop. The other side is already finished. It will take 15 lakh more. Granite costs have gone up one-and-a-half times. If you can, send it fast. The Barsana Hall [in India] is not a rush. Kripalu

In Prakash's handwritten draft of a letter to Kripalu, he wrote:

> My Dear Kripalu, 1. Today you called me to send some more money. Now I cannot send more than 2 lakh [$4,400 US]. I'm sorry to say this, but I have told you several times before that anytime for special expenditures we have to make a plan at least one year in advance. If you want something suddenly, I can make an arrangement for only 1 to 2 lakh. Last time you asked me, I promised 10 lakh [$22,000] and I fulfilled my promise. The only cash money I have in a year's time in my possession is 3 to 4 lakh, which I receive in donations. The rest belongs to the Society [ISDL].
>
> 2. In this country, if something goes wrong, you cannot pay a bribe and get away. Here if you bribe someone, you will go to jail for two years. In Canada, the licence of a famous, reputable person was taken away because of a simple mistake. If you do anything wrong in this society [don't follow the law], they will finish you forever. So if this happens, our planning to collect millions of dollars for Barsana [India] will be finished.
>
> Last year, I sent you 10 lakh from the US and before that I also gave you 10 lakh in Vrindavan. For that we wanted some type of journal entry, which was not given to me. So we had to answer a lot of questions from an income tax officer [in Delhi] because everything was not documented. The IRS also

> questioned me here [in the US]. I had to answer the question: how come you get so much cash with no accounting?
>
> Last time also when I sent you money from here and I told you in Vrindavan to show me the accounting, you never did. I told the people in Vrindavan about the money, but they have never showed me anything yet. For the last two years, I had to tell you not only one or two times, but twenty-five times. This time when I told you 'No' over the phone, you got very angry. Right now I don't have any money, but even if I have, how should I send you. Prakashanand

This part was scratched out:

> You will also not want me to do illegal things over and over, or I will ruin the Society. How many, how many, how many times do I have to repeat for one simple thing. Same thing I say over and over. Because of those people's foolishness, now I cannot give any money to Vrindavan Society. Because of those people now I cannot give because I have done so much illegal work. But I cannot do over and over. You get very upset with me; always it happens when things go wrong. Then everyone lies to each other. Then more bad comes and everyone lies.

I was frantic to get those two incriminating letters – which had been lying around for years in a tiny forgotten tree house and then a shoebox – into a bank safety deposit box.

The Truth Project

Exposing the Gurus' Dark Side

A FRIEND WAS flipping through the May 2010 issue of *Austin Monthly* at my home one day, when she stopped suddenly. 'They've mentioned Barsana Dham in this article.'

'What?'

And there it was. In an article titled '110 Fun Things to Do in the Summer,' number 90 was: 'Tour a Temple'. The blurb read:

> Heading toward the Salt Lick on FM 1826, you wouldn't expect to pass a gorgeous Hindu temple perched on a hill. And yet, Driftwood is home to Barsana Dham, an ashram complex sitting on 200 acres of gardens. Visitors are welcome to tour the grounds and temples. They can even participate in the morning chanting, a ritual called darshan.

'Are they out of their minds?' I said. 'Don't the editors read the local newspaper? If they had, they'd know the main guru is an accused paedophile and the main guy in India is an accused ritual rapist. And they want to send families with children out there?'

The next day, I emailed to the editor and publisher. On May 25 I received a response:

> Hi Karen,
>
> Thanks for contacting us and bringing this to our attention. We're looking more closely into this situation right now, and we certainly will keep this in mind for the future.
>
> Best,
> Melissa

On 22 June, I received an email from a freelance writer for the magazine. He wanted to meet me to do research for an article.

I met John at a local coffee shop and answered all his questions about my life in the ashram, why I moved there, what life was like and why I left. I thought the article was going to be published right away, but when I contacted the editor a few months later, she said they had decided to wait until the outcome of the trial to publish anything. In the end, the magazine never did repair the damage it did by promoting the ashram.

Despite the revealing articles in the *Austin American-Statesman*, it was an uphill battle to inform the public about the true nature of Barsana Dham. Various media outlets would occasionally run small stories about events being held there, as if the organization was a benevolent religious and cultural centre. I knew that Barsana Dham had spent big bucks to hire a large local PR firm to steadily work on its public image. I felt like David facing off with Goliath.

Meanwhile, I had been keeping our ex-devotee group updated about everything I was gathering about the fake gurus. The list of deception just kept growing – for example, I discovered that, contrary to his claim, Prakash was never really offered a prestigious religious seat when he was twenty-three; the organization that supposedly gave Kripalu the title of Jagadguru did not actually exist; and several Hindu organizations were against an ill-fated campaign in the mid-1990s to change the depiction of Hinduism in school history books in California. I forwarded the information to a well-known cult-awareness website, but unfortunately Prakash got lost in the sheer number of cults exposed there.

I had been doing my best to inform the public by blogging, talking to local university professors of religious science, and meeting local Hindu leaders. But I was fighting an uphill battle to educate the public at large.

I wasn't the only one trying to get the word out. Vijay Mehta, an Indian in Temple, Texas, reported on the cult regularly on his blog. Others had tried to get the Wikipedia pages about the organization and its gurus corrected to reflect the truth. Some of us were doing what we could to prevent more people from being hurt by JKP.

I realized that I needed a more effective way to distribute the information I was collecting. I started a Facebook page called 'The Truth Project for Barsana Dham and JKP'. As soon as the page was up, other people started adding their stories, such as a young man who had participated in temple events when he was young and felt used by the experience. A man from India posted a document that had circulated around India about Kripalu's rapist past. I received many comments from people thanking me for sharing the information and telling me they thought I was brave for standing up to such a corrupt organization.

I sent a press release to the local media with a link to the page, after which I finally stopped finding upbeat articles about the temple and ashram. Eventually, the tables turned and some reporters started contacting me because of 'The Truth Project'.

I received a great deal of support from many people for the Facebook page. I even received some great information from others, including a document that had been sent out years ago in India by people concerned about Kripalu. An Indian friend translated the document for me.

> Alert. Alert. Alert. Here is information about the human demon – Kaliyug Chaitanya Mahaprabhu – the fake Jagadguru, Kripalu's deceptive conduct. This notice is for all religious people in this area to inform them that a man calling himself a 'Jagadguru' is living here and there in these places (Raigarh, Bilaspur, Mungeli, Raipur, Rajnandgaon, and Bhatapara). This Alert is to inform good people about him. A pundit from Kashi was contacted to confirm this information. Kripalu does kirtan and has a little knowledge of Sanskrit. So people go to hear him. It is known that during one kirtan in Kanpur, he claimed to make a girl feel like a gopi and himself to feel like Krishna. Then he kissed her and engaged in immoral behaviour with

her [had sex]. When this happened, many people got angry. So someone threw acid in his face during a ras leela. The skin around his eyes was damaged, but he got treatment. However, there is still one small spot from the acid below his left eye. That is the mark that identifies him as the one who performed these immoral activities [with underage girls]. He tried to pretend that that mark is some disease. He has used the title of 'Jagadguru', which he had never received, but with which he's trying to cheat people. According to the Kashi Vidwat Parishat [which he claims gave him the title], he was never given the designation of Jagadguru. He made it up. He artificially awarded this upadhi [title] to himself. Related to this man, on 28 February [year unknown], a journal article (page 853) was published to inform the world [about him]. The title of the article was: 'God Save Us From This Extremely Demonic Mahatma'.

A journalist received a letter written by one devotee and it's described here. The person who wrote the letter one time saw this mahatma doing kirtan, during which he became unconscious, fell on the ground and had tears coming out of his eyes. So the man became impressed and accepted him as his guru, and he [Kripalu] accepted him as his devotee. But later he saw the man's true character and behaviour and was shocked. Then he started thinking all kinds of thoughts about him; then he got scared. He felt that if he told anyone he would be committing 'guru aparadh' [a transgression against a guru]. At that time, Kripalu was staying at many rich people's homes and giving a lot of eloquent lectures, and he was impressing people. But he was playing with the people's emotions and saying that he was an avatar of Chaitanya Mahaprabhu. When that devotee [who wrote the letter] was staying with him day and night very close to him, he realized his character and manner of dressing, which was exactly like that of a family man. But his lustful behaviour was at its peak. During the day, he was eating 100 paans [betel leaves] with nicotine. And he was raping beautiful pious young girls and taking their virginity. All these things he saw with his own eyes and quit his association and went away from him. After three months, this devotee wrote the letter. At that time, the guru was staying at a lawyer's home. The devotee wrote to Kripalu: he stated that his behaviour is not that of a real mahaprabhu and he gave the example of a true mahaprabhu from Gosai Challisa [Ram Charan Pankaj Anurag ...].

Because of his eloquent lectures, people were becoming impressed and inviting him to stay in their homes. But at that time he was taking advantage of the innocent beautiful young girls and destroying their virginity after telling them: 'I will destroy your material desire and I will reveal God to you.' Innocent girls did not understand, and under his influence were having sex with him. Wherever he was staying, his sexual behaviour with the girls was getting worse and worse. Those innocent people did not see through his actions and were afraid of performing guru aparadh and so did not expose his behaviour.

You can check out this particular article and whatever is described here in the *Kalyan* journal. It was published by Gita Press. After noticing this article, it was made public. Now we are sharing this information to alert people about this bad demonic person. If you go for kirtan, be aware of the true nature of this 'religion'. Do not let your mothers and sisters anywhere near this deceptive person, who has obsessive sexual desires. You can identify him by the mark below his left eye. [Signed by the authors of this alert: the names were illegible.]

Clearly, Barsana Dham was not happy about the Facebook page. On 1 September 2010, I received an email from a woman living in the ashram. She had written, 'You don't know what you are talking about', in the subject line. This is what the rest of the mail said: 'You are part of spreading poison about Barsana Dham. It's such a shame when you don't know any facts, just the rantings of disgruntled people. You're taking their words as facts. Why don't you get the facts first?' I wrote back to her: 'What are the facts? Please provide your sources as well. Thanks.'

Of course, she never did send me any facts to support her claim. We exchanged a few more emails, but she continued to claim that I was 'out to do as much damage as possible to Barsana Dham'. What she failed to understand was that the gurus had done the damage themselves.

Uncivil Behaviour

When Lawyers Play Dirty

I LEARNT THE hard way about the differences between criminal and civil court cases. In criminal cases, there are strict rules regarding whom the defence lawyers can interview or examine and whom they cannot. For example, defence lawyers do not have access to the state's witnesses. In civil cases, however, the defence lawyers can examine almost anyone they want to, no matter how remotely related the person may be to the case. As one lawyer told me, they could interview a neighbour's gardener if they wanted to.

Despite the rules, Prakash's defence lawyers tried to talk to two of the state's female witnesses in his criminal case. They attempted to contact both women, even hiring private detectives in Seattle to track them down. They became so aggressive that the DA finally told them point-blank to leave her witnesses alone.

And they did – for two years. Then a potential jackpot fell into their laps. In March 2010, an ex-JKP devotee launched a civil suit against Prakash and seven members of the Barsana Dham organization. Since she could not find a lawyer to take on what some characterized a frivolous lawsuit, the woman filed *pro se*, which means she advocated on her own behalf, rather than being represented by a lawyer.

With the filing of that civil complaint, all bets were off from Barsana Dham's perspective. They could interview or examine anyone they wanted to, and claim that it was for the civil suit. One of Prakash's lawyers, Randy Levitt, immediately sent out subpoenas to six people – the three women, related to the criminal trial, who were allegedly abused by Prakash as children (Kate, Shyama and Vesla) and their significant others.

Five of the six people subpoenaed had absolutely nothing to do with the ex-devotee filing the civil case. In fact, the three men subpoenaed didn't even know her. It was clear that Randy, the attorney for Barsana Dham, was exploiting the more lenient rules of civil law to gain access to the witnesses involved in the criminal case. What Prakash's defence team did not count on was the determination of the three girls to not simply roll over and play dead.

The depositions for Kate and her husband were scheduled first. I emailed Melina, a lawyer I had met along the way who had once been a prosecutor in San Antonio. I explained the situation and asked what Kate should do.

She wrote back saying: 'Maybe they can quash the depositions.' 'Quash' means to legally deny an action requested.

Kate began researching how to quash a deposition, and found a lawsuit in which the wife of a CEO of a large energy company in Texas had successfully quashed a deposition that lawyers had requested of her, related to her husband's legal problems.

Kate used the document as her template and created motions to quash for herself and her husband, which she then filed with the state of Washington, where she lived. The motions to quash were simple and straightforward:

> Kate does not have any knowledge of the events alleged in the Plaintiff's civil action and JKP Barsana Dham has failed to show that she has. Kate's only significant interaction with the Plaintiff

> was as a child neighbor before the year 1997 when she moved away at 18 years old. Kate had no association with the Plaintiff as an adult between the years of 1997 and 2007 and has not lived near her or had any interaction with the Plaintiff as an adult during the years she has made her claims.

Kate notified Randy that she had filed the motions and, as such, would not be appearing for the scheduled deposition until she heard back from the Washington judge. But Randy did not want to let her off the hook, even though she was following legal procedure. He wrote back, insisting that Kate did not understand the rules of law and that she and her husband were still required to appear at the deposition as scheduled, despite her motions to quash. Finally, Kate just ignored his manipulative emails. Nonetheless, Randy flew to Washington, wasting his time and Barsana Dham's money, and even tried to charge Kate and her husband for the trip – and he filed a motion to that end.

Within a few weeks, Kate received news from the Washington court. Both her deposition and her husband's had successfully been quashed. Kate accomplished this out of sheer determination not to let Prakash's lawyers push her around. The depositions for her sister and brother-in-law too were successfully quashed. The letter she received from the Washington judge is worthy of being framed. One paragraph summed up what he thought of the matter:

> Defendants sought attorney fees and expenses because their counsel flew from Texas to Seattle to take the depositions of Kathryn Tonnessen and Dylan Peterson. Defendants also sought an order of contempt. The court declines to award attorney fees or to hold the witnesses in contempt. They properly filed motions to quash the subpoenas, and did not act unreasonably in failing to appear for depositions before the court had ruled on their motions to quash.

After her victory, Kate joked, 'I had the best lawyers money could buy' – which was more than Prakash could say.

Justice Delayed

Out of Sight, Out of Mind

CRIMINAL TRIAL DELAYS are like a punch in the gut. Once a date is set, your consciousness becomes totally focused on that date. When it is suddenly cancelled and reset, you feel deflated, empty and off centre.

We eventually understood that a few delays are expected in every trial. Cancellations can happen for any number of reasons, and often result from scheduling conflicts between the various lawyers, prosecutors, judge and witnesses. Sometimes trials are delayed at the request of the defendant who hires a new lawyer or finds new evidence. Rarely do witnesses for the state request delays. In our case, neither of the two young women who were official witnesses, nor any potential supporting witnesses, ever requested a trial delay.

Meanwhile, the defence team sought every possible manner of delay. For starters, during the entire first year following his arrest, Prakash's lawyers spent hours of the court's time and resources on a fruitless quest to allow him back into Barsana Dham. During that time, pre-trial hearings for the criminal case were repeatedly cancelled.

The first trial date was finally set for 2 November 2009 – about a year and a half from the day of his arrest. I occasionally checked the Hays County website for updates. About a month before the trial date, there was a flurry of paper shuffling, instigated by Prakash's lawyers. When I checked back a few days later, I was unnerved to find the word 'cancelled' next to the date of his trial, with a listing for a new date – 11 January 2010.

What had happened? What did this mean? Everyone in our ex-devotee network was worried. We heard that Barsana Dham was publicly blaming the witnesses, claiming that the trial was delayed because Kate had just had a baby. It was true that Kate had given birth to her first child in mid-September. We'd had many discussions about the issues of her travelling cross-country so soon, with a newborn baby. But at no time did she or any other witnesses request a delay. In fact, the prosecution was clearly planning to move forward, because the DA had just filed subpoenas for fourteen witnesses. But we soothed ourselves with the knowledge that it would all be over in just a few more months.

Then the trial was again pushed back – this time, all the way to April for, according to his lawyers, Prakash had undergone back surgery in India and was now bedridden. The timing, of course, was suspicious, and so was the fact that Prakash had received *all* major medical care in the US, never in India. Our prediction that Prakash would have a 'medical crisis' at some point before the trial had come true.

A 25 February article in the *Austin American-Statesman* under the headline 'Swami Lawyers Ask for Another Delay' reported on the trial date change:

> Attorneys for Prakashanand Saraswati, the Hindu leader who stands accused of groping two under-aged girls in the 1990s, have asked for another delay in the holy man's trial in Hays County.
>
> According to court documents filed last week, the founder and spiritual leader of Barsana Dham, the 200-acre ashram south of Austin, has been spending most of his time in India where, the filings say, he underwent surgery on his lower back. A note from Dr S.S. Kale of the All India Institute of Medical Science described the January operation as 'serious' and said it took five hours to complete.
>
> Kale added that Prakashanand, also known to his followers as Shree Swamiji, should 'avoid travelling and have complete

> rest for the next three to four months' and shouldn't sit for more than a half-hour at a time.
>
> 'The defendant is a very elderly individual,' the filing said. 'Travelling from India to the United States takes approximately 18 hours' and thus 'renders a trial in April 2010 a virtual impossibility'.

The trial date was reset for 20 September 2010, but that was eventually cancelled due to a scheduling conflict with the judge. The next trial was set for 1 November 2010 – one year after the original trial date and two-and-a-half years since Prakash's arrest.

Incredibly enough, the date was changed yet again. Prakash was still sending letters saying that he was unable to fly to the US due to ongoing back pain. The new trial date was now 24 January 2011.

By this time, we had almost completely lost hope that a trial would ever take place. It seemed that the Hays County court was going to grant Prakash every delay, now that he allegedly had permanent 'health issues'. We were sick with worry that he would never actually have to sit in a courtroom and be judged by a jury of his peers.

Then Prakash did something unbelievably stupid.

Caught!

Prakash's Critical Misstep

IN EARLY OCTOBER 2010, Prakash flew back to the US. Barsana Dham had scheduled its annual Intensive programme for one week in early October. The greatly diminished event, which had formerly been three weeks long, was to feature a special guest: Prakash himself. His devotees from various countries, including Ireland and New Zealand, were called and told to come and see him, because 'it could be their last chance'.

In the summer of 2010, I heard that followers were being assured that Prakash would attend the Intensive. I assumed they were just saying this to bolster confidence among the devotees, and that they would simply pull the plug on his trip at the last minute, citing his alleged health issues. In the meantime, devotees would be happy thinking that he was coming to Austin.

Late in the summer, an anonymous contact in India sent me links to photos of Prakash in various places in north India – places that were clearly *not* his bed. The photos clearly showed him in satsang in his Barsana ashram. In one, he was sitting in a chair close to Kripalu, and standing right behind him during the arti ceremony in another. Two other photos showed him standing next to Kripalu at an event in Kunda, 200 miles from Barsana.

I sent the links to the assistant DA, Cathy Compton, who was very interested in this new evidence. She even went online herself and discovered a few more photos of him gallivanting around India, including in Mussoorie, which is several hours from both Barsana and Kunda, and only accessible by car. He looked healthy and happy.

I informed Cathy that we were hearing rumours about him coming to Austin for the October event. She told me to keep her posted if I heard anything else. But neither of us ever dreamed he would actually return.

On Saturday, 2 October, on the way to Kathi's house for a visit, I drove by the house where Prakash stayed when he was in Austin. There were four cars parked in the back of the house and obvious activity inside. Was he really going to fly in?

The next day, I received a message from my contact inside the ashram: 'He's here.'

I was in shock. I couldn't believe he'd actually done it – cocked a snook at the law and returned to the US.

My heart raced and my brain whirred. I emailed our network, then wrote to Cathy Compton: 'Prakash is in Austin right now – staying at Marsha's house on Rural Route 1826. He arrived either yesterday or today. He is here for Barsana Dham's annual Intensive. The dates of the event are Oct 2 to 9. He'll likely leave Austin on the 9th or 10th. So if you are going to do anything you have to act fast.'

Kathi called, fired up by the news. 'How dare he think he can just fly into the US and fly out again, while lying to the authorities!' She said she had just sent emails to Cathy, Sherri Tibbe (the head district attorney), the judge and the Texas Attorney General.

I awoke the next morning at 5:00, on fire to get back into action. I wrote a long email to Sherri Tibbe, who wrote back asking for the address of the house where Prakash might be found.

All day long, we wondered what was happening at Sherri's end, and also what the hell Prakash was thinking when he returned to the US. Was he really that stupid? Or was he just that narcissistic and confident in his invincibility as a god?

We finally heard that the DA had contacted Prakash's lawyers, and that they were claiming to have no knowledge of him being in the US.

Hays County then scheduled an emergency hearing before Judge Charles Ramsay on Tuesday, 5 October. At the hearing, the state asked to amend the conditions of Prakash's bond to include taking his passport back. They also asked that Prakash be required to submit to an independent medical exam to determine if he was fit to stand trial. Judge Ramsay agreed to the medical exam and said that he would make a decision about the passport pending the doctor's review.

The doctor found that Prakash was perfectly able to sit through a trial, even if he needed a special chair. At a follow-up hearing on 27 October, the state requested to have Prakash's passport surrendered to the court. The judge agreed and his passport was placed in a vault in Hays County.

Cathy called to give me the news. She noted one interesting fact: 'Guess where else he was while his lawyers were telling us he was bedridden? He was in Nepal. According to his passport, he flew there in March.'

Prakash had never been bedridden at all, just as we had all suspected.

I emailed Eric with the news. On 27 October, he published another update in the *Austin American-Statesman:*

> A state district court judge on Wednesday revoked the passport of a Hindu guru who claimed he was too frail to withstand a trial scheduled for earlier this year, but who prosecutors said has maintained an active travel schedule overseas.
>
> But on Wednesday in San Marcos, prosecutors cited evidence – including photographs on websites documenting the guru's travels and stamps from his passport showing his movements between countries – that Prakashanand had managed to take several trips during the time he claimed to be incapacitated.
>
> Speaking for Prakashanand, who arrived in court wearing a saffron robe and seated in a wheelchair, Austin attorney David Botsford ... said the swami's travelled exclusively on first-class flights so the elderly religious leader could lie down. 'Every time he travels, he travels in the recumbent position,' Botsford said.
>
> Botsford added ... taking away the holy man's passport would 'impede his ability to practice his religion'.
>
> But Compton said Prakashanand had abused that privilege by misleading the court. 'The victims in this case have been waiting three years to get to trial,' she said. 'Every single time somebody came here seeking delay, it was because he was too ill to travel. Enough is enough.'
>
> In a written statement, Katie Williams, an executive at the ashram, said Prakashanand's followers welcomed the trial. 'We are eager for Shree Swamiji to have his day in court. The sooner the truth can be told in a fair and impartial setting, the sooner justice will be served and he can finally be vindicated.'

I thought that Katie Williams's comment was interesting because, despite her claim, it sure didn't look like they were 'eager ... to have his day in court'.

PART SIX

In the Trial

Truth and Consequences

'One sannyasin once told me, "Unfortunately, not every Sannyasin has lost his attachment to maya and its effects."'
– Dr Vidyasankar Sundaresan, independent scholar of Indian history and philosophy

'What it lies in our power to do,
It lies in our power not to do.'
– Aristotle, Greek philosopher and scientist

'Lawyering Up'

Mounting a High-Priced Defence

I CALLED PRAKASH'S defence team 'The Dirty Dozen'.

When the powers-that-be at the ashram finally acknowledged the criminal charges against Prakash, the devotees were told: 'Barsana Dham is lawyering up.'

They were not kidding.

No expense was spared to surround Prakash with high-dollar legal representation. By the time the criminal case reached trial, almost three years after Prakash's arrest, they had hired nine attorneys, none of whom came cheap. The defence team also included a private detective (on the case for nearly three years), a public relations specialist (one of the most expensive in Austin) and a jury selection specialist.

Despite having high-priced lawyers from the start, once Prakash was caught in Austin in October 2010, there was a lot of lawyer shuffling, which continued right up until just weeks before his trial started. I assumed that their scramble meant that they were scared.

Prakash's first new lawyer was Joe Turner, who was apparently one of the most expensive defence lawyers in Texas. The *Austin American-Statesman* had run an article about him in August 1998, in which he was reported to be friends with the famous American country singer Willie Nelson, whom he had successfully defended on drug charges.

The article also stated that he called himself 'Mad Dog', based on his courtroom style. He was quoted as saying, 'I can be ruthless ... And I've been known to cheat.' Many referred to him as a snake in the courtroom – a perfect fit for Prakash, I thought.

So I was surprised to learn that by late December 'Mad Dog' was out and an Indian lawyer from Houston was in. It was a strange choice, because the Indian attorney did not appear to have much trial experience, if any. I wondered why Turner had been booted. My guess is that it was due to a strategy conflict between the attorney and the client – maybe even over the generous plea deal offered to Prakash by the state. To accept the plea deal and avoid a trial, Prakash would have to admit to one count of 'indecency with a child by sexual contact' for each girl (he had been charged with ten counts per girl), accept probation (with continuous monitoring by a probation officer), and be registered as a sex offender. Word came back from his defence team that Prakash would admit only to one count of 'assault' per girl and take probation. The state passed.

By early January, Prakash was again hiring new attorneys. In fact, it wasn't clear until just days before the trial which lawyers would be representing him. The final decision was Jeff Kearney from Fort Worth, Texas, and Jo Angelyn Gates from San Diego, California.

If we thought Joe 'Mad Dog' Turner was bad, we were in for some surprises.

Cathy Compton

A Warrior for the Prosecution

CATHY COMPTON HAS little patience for people who hurt children, and it shows in her high conviction rate of child molesters. 'I prosecute the cases of the creepy dirt bags of the world,' she told me when I met her in August 2008.

Within an hour of meeting her, I knew she was exactly the person we needed. She had incredible insight, unshakeable confidence and complete faith in the girls' case. She could see right through Barsana Dham's media hype surrounding the 'holy' guru. 'He's no saint,' she said. 'He's no different than the rest of the child molesters I prosecute.'

Despite her obvious intellect, Cathy was very down-to-earth. She had none of the condescending 'I'm the smartest person in the room' attitude common to some trial attorneys.

Once Prakash was caught in the US in October 2010, the gloves were off and it was game on! 'The first thing I did,' Cathy said, 'was tell his lawyers, "Your client is not getting any more special treatment."'

Up until that point, Prakash's lawyers had finagled special conditions for their client, such as hearings in the afternoon when the courtroom was less crowded. 'Now he's going to be treated just like any other defendant,' Cathy informed them.

It was clear that Prakash's entourage did not like Cathy at all. At one of the pre-trial hearings, one devotee flipped Cathy the finger. After a later hearing, another hissed at her.

Three weeks before the trial, Kate and I had lunch with Cathy. We tried to get some insight into her strategy for the trial, but all she would say was, 'I won't know how it's going to play out until the trial starts. I need to see what the other side does first.'

'How will you stand up to his nine lawyers?' I asked.

She laughed. 'I'll be the last man standing – and still have more energy left than the rest of them.'

On the first day of the trial, while we were waiting in the witness room, we could see Prakash's entourage meandering aimlessly in the hallway. Finally, his people made their way into the courtroom and the hall settled down. Then we saw Cathy walking towards the courtroom, pulling a cart of files behind her – like she was going into battle with her own little arsenal of weapons. She and her assistant, Amy Lockhart, also a fierce defender of children, walked purposefully side by side, both of them looking forward. Cathy's back was ramrod straight and her body language said: 'Bring it on.'

The battle was about to begin – and the girls' lead warrior was ready.

Pre-trial Shenanigans

By Hook or by Crook

PRAKASH'S DEFENCE LAWYERS thought they had caught a break in mid-December 2010 when they claimed that they had been denied key evidence for the trial by Hays County.

They wanted the case thrown out of court because there was a missing tape of the initial interview with one of the two girls cited in the case. Prakash's original lawyers had requested the tapes in 2009 and had been told then that one of the tapes was missing. But no one seemed to care much about it until a year later, when Prakash was caught in the US.

Eric Dexheimer reported the events from the hearing about the missing tape on 15 December 2010.

> Though the Hays County sheriff's department has lost key evidence in the case against Prakashanand Saraswati, the religious leader charged with groping two underage girls in the 1990s, a state district judge ruled Wednesday that the case against the guru can proceed. Attorneys for Prakashanand, also known as Shree Swamiji, argued that the loss of a 1 1/2-hour recorded interview with one of the two women who said they were groped by the guru should have disqualified her statements implicating him.
>
> 'The bottom line is, whether you believe the sheriff's

office destroyed the evidence or lost the evidence, it creates a significant problem for the prosecution of this case,' said Joe Turner, one of a half-dozen attorneys representing Prakashanand. Prosecutors in Hays County argued that a detective's summary of the interview was sufficient for the case to proceed, and District Judge Charles Ramsay agreed. The trial is scheduled to begin in late February.

In a hearing that stretched for more than two hours Wednesday, Sgt Jeri Skrocki explained that she discovered that the original DVD recording of the interview had disappeared in late 2009. The judge had ordered prosecutors to turn over a copy to defense attorneys, but they found that the copy was unviewable. When she went to the sheriff's department records room to retrieve the original, Skrocki said, it was gone. A thorough search of the room by records custodians came up empty, she said.

Prakashanand's attorneys contend that the absence of a video record of the interview would deprive them of information and nuance crucial to the defense of Swamiji, including the young woman's demeanour and whether her interviewer asked leading questions. Without it, 'the court must strike the testimony or declare a mistrial', said Gerry Goldstein, a San Antonio attorney who is part of Prakashanand's defense team.

Assistant District Attorney Cathy Compton responded that Skrocki's report of the interview was an accurate and sufficient representation of the accuser's testimony and that the guru's lawyers would have ample opportunity to question her during the trial.

Round One in Prakash's pre-trial battle had been lost.

Their next move was to offer Hays County another \$1 to \$2 million for his passport back, a fact that Cathy mentioned in the trial: '... As much as another \$2 million were offered for the return of the defendant's passport.' Hays County declined.

The next attempt to spring Prakash occurred when some mysterious person from California sent a letter to thirty-six Hays County officials insisting that, in his opinion, Prakash was being persecuted solely because he was a Hindu. In the letters, the man demanded an immediate dismissal of the case. He also posted the same message on a website. Part of the rambling diatribe included the following remarks:

> The Critical Mass Of Truth Committee reviewed the State vs. Saraswati case (Cause Nos. CR-08-272, CR-08-273). It is our opinion that this case represents multiple levels of dishonesty, fraud, deceit and misrepresentation on the part of the complainants and law enforcement officials. Firstly, the complainants have made false and unsubstantiated accusations based on desires for revenge, the need for attention and possible monetary gain.
>
> Secondly, law enforcement, including the Sheriff's Department, the District Attorney's Office and the presiding Judge have abused their powers and grossly overreacted given the charges involved and the facts in evidence. Before this case goes to trial and hits the media, there is a window of opportunity for saner heads to prevail. Hays County and the State of Texas have opened themselves up for major embarrassments including charges of racism and religious persecution. In order to restore fairness and justice, I suggest the following possible remedies: immediate settlement by mediation with other Texas State and Federal Officials participating.

The communiqué was signed by a single name.

When no one from Hays County responded, a second letter was sent out – this one threatening Hays County with a worldwide negative media blitz if the court did not return Prakash's passport to him by the first of February.

The day came and went with no media attention whatsoever.

The next threat escalated to include bodily harm. Around a week before the trial, an anonymous man with an Indian accent called a member of the prosecution team to say, 'These people are dangerous, and Cathy Compton is potentially in danger.'

Hays County immediately implemented pre-emptive safety measures that included extra security in the courthouse and an undercover officer shadowing Cathy throughout the trial. The extra security was reassuring to the three girls, who had only their husbands, one brother, and a few others around to support them. Meanwhile, the courthouse was mobbed by the guru's followers, which included more devotees than could fit in the courtroom. The spillover loitered in the hallway. A few of them stared at the witness room and gave us dirty looks.

On 11 February, Prakash's new lawyers tried one last time to get the trial delayed by filing a motion for continuance, requesting more time to prepare. After that hearing, we heard from Cathy via email that Judge Ramsay had denied the request: 'We are going to trial, ladies.'

His Day(s) in Court

The Guru Has Entered the Building

WHEN YOU HIRE high-priced attorneys to defend you, they don't just put on a minimal defence – they shoot for the moon. Prakash's lawyers were no exception. Their witness subpoena list included over a hundred people. Cathy had told the judge that the prosecution would need two or three days for its part of the trial. The defence lawyers said they would need two to three weeks.

After so many delays over the past three years, it was hard to believe that the trial was finally going to happen. Surely, Prakash would pull some last-minute stunt – like another feigned surgery or a faked heart attack. When I mentioned my fears to Cathy, she assured me: 'Then he better produce a confirmable doctor's excuse.'

Just before the trial got under way, I dreamt that we were in the courtroom on the first day of the trial. It was 9:00 a.m. and no one from the defence side had arrived yet. Sixty minutes ticked by as we waited for them to show up. At 10:00 a.m., just as the judge was about to dismiss everyone, Prakash entered the room with all his preachers and devotees. They set up an altar towards the front of the courtroom and proceeded to do arti. Then they passed out raisin and nuts for prasad to the stunned jury and prosecution.

While Barsana Dham's people did not perform arti at the actual trial, they did impose their will on the courtroom, taking up the majority of chairs, ignoring the rule about cell phone use and even bringing a special reclining chair for the defendant. Although the doctor who conducted the medical review said he was fit enough to attend his trial, *even if he needed a special chair*, I'm sure no one expected the huge, overstuffed, brown Lazy Boy–type recliner that appeared on the scene.

To add insult to injury, Prakash often reclined all the way back until he was almost horizontal. He even fell asleep a few times. And to make sure he was comfortable, he took off his shoes – while court was in session.

The ridiculous special seating arrangement was bad enough, but his lawyers had also been granted permission for Prakash to take breaks whenever his 'back pain' was too much to bear. He abused this leniency on the first couple of days by taking ten-minute breaks about every hour. It was clear he was going to make damn sure that everyone knew he was the most important person in the room. However, the breaks decreased as the trial wore on, perhaps because his jury specialist was worried about irritating the jury members who had to be excused from the courtroom for every break.

Cathy later decribed the scene when Prakash entered his plea. She said he stood up, turned around, looked at the roomful of devotees, waved to them with both hands, grinned, and pleaded 'not guilty' in a sing-song voice. All the while, the devotees in attendance giggled quietly or smiled lovingly at their lord and master.

I'm sure that his faithful flock believed he would be found innocent of all charges. They no doubt believed this was just another leela that Prakash needed to perform to fulfil his divine destiny.

Of course, they would never admit that in a court of law.

Day One

A Jury of His Peers

Tuesday, 22 February 2011

EVERY PERSON ACCUSED of a crime in the United States is entitled to a fair trial with an impartial jury – and Prakash was no exception.

The first component of any trial is jury selection. Lawyers for both sides sort through a random pool of citizens to select a final panel of twelve jurors. After hearing testimony from both sides, these men and women ultimately determine the defendant's fate.

For this trial, the lawyers interviewed seventy potential jurors before agreeing on the final panel of twelve.

The day of jury selection for Prakash was both an ordinary and unusual day at the Hays County courthouse. Ordinary in the sense that the process for choosing the jury proceeded like any other selection procedure for a criminal trial. Unusual because of the defendant – a short, pot-bellied, white-bearded Indian man dressed head-to-toe in saffron, navigating the courtroom in a wheelchair.

Cathy Compton was the first lawyer to question potential jurors. Right away, she identified the defendant to the jurors: 'He's the gentleman you see seated here in his chair in the saffron-coloured robes. That's our defendant.'

Jeff Kearney, lead counsel for defence, ignored the issue of his unusual defendant for the first part of his address to the potential jurors; then he finally faced the music: 'I'd like to know, kind of an unfiltered first response ... what did you feel? What was your first thought when you first saw Swamiji rolling in here?'

Responses varied from thinking he was 'a feeble old man' to 'a Hindu Santa Claus'.

His next question addressed the potential for discrimination: 'Another thing I'd like to know ... has anybody ever had any kind of negative feelings about people from India for any reason?'

Responses ranged from having good experiences to working with Indian co-workers 'who have become close friends'.

Kearney's next line of questioning concerned the news coverage about Prakash's arrest and trial, and the potential unfair bias against his client. He asked, for example: 'Who saw the article in this morning's *Austin American-Statesman*? Anybody who did, if you will please raise your hand tall so that we can see it.'

Cathy emphasized to the jury the importance of a fair trial: 'The goal for everyone here, for myself, for all of the people who work for the state, for all of the people who are here on behalf of the defendant – our goal is all the same, and I hope it's your goal too – is to be able to say at the end: "It was fair. I know that because I was there."'

She also wanted to be sure that the people who were selected could convict a person of criminal charges with only the witnesses' testimony as evidence, because in child sex abuse cases, there typically is no other evidence. Knowing the defence would jump all over the 'lack of evidence' as a reason to dismiss the charges, she told the potential jury members: 'If you believe the testimony of one witness, the victim witness, beyond a reasonable doubt – and, again, that doesn't have to be beyond all possible doubt, not to 100 per cent. But if you believe that witness beyond a reasonable doubt, you have to follow the law, and you have to convict. That is the law. In a lot of cases – most of these types of cases – you're only going to hear testimony. That's it. That's going to be the case. You're going to hear testimony. You're going to have to judge the credibility of the witnesses that you hear from, and you're going to have to decide what you believe. You're going to have to decide who's telling the truth.'

After each side weeded out potential jurors who appeared biased in any way with regard to the defendant, his religion, his nationality, or the charges against him, they ended up with twelve citizens of Hays County. Eight men and four women, with a mix of Hispanic, Black and White.

The irony of this was lost to all but a handful of people in the courtroom that day: in Prakash's mind, not a single person in the courtroom – including Judge Ramsay or his own lawyers – was his peer. For nearly sixty years, he had projected himself as a god in human form and been treated as such by his followers. He regarded everyone except his guru, Kripalu, as inferior or subordinate to him. In Prakash's view, he was all but peerless.

Day Two

Back-Room Confidential

Wednesday, 23 February 2011

'THIS IS A very simple case. This is a case about one man and his choices,' said Amy Lockhart, assistant district attorney for Hays County. 'This case is simply about what he did, as a man, to two young girls.'

Thus began the criminal trial of the state of Texas versus Prakashanand Saraswati.

I wasn't allowed in the courtroom during the trial because I was a potential witness. Cathy thought that it would be good to have a witness handy in case she needed to refute something incriminating that one of the defence witnesses might claim about ashram life. I had not witnessed the crimes, but I had experienced life in the ashram for fifteen years. That is how I ended up in the tiny witness room with the girls for the first few days of the trial.

During the time I was in the courthouse, I stayed at Kathi and Wayne's home, and drove the back roads through the Texas Hill country to the San Marcos courthouse every day, stopping at Whataburger for coffee and breakfast.

On the first day of the trial, I arrived early – only to discover that the parking lot was already filling with devotees who were lining up in front of the building. I had no idea how I would feel being around those people, most of whom I had not seen in almost three years. I locked my car, took a deep breath and walked to the front entrance of the courthouse.

As I reached the main doors, I was surrounded by devotees. None of them looked directly at me, but I could sense their furtive glances. I felt nothing. I could have been in line at a grocery store among people I had never met before. These people, whom I had once known so well, were strangers to me now. I was surprised – but very, very pleased – that they no longer had the power to intimidate me.

Once inside, I met the girls in Cathy's office. All three of them were dressed beautifully in prim outfits, much more business-like than the clothes they usually wore. But their smart attire could not hide their extreme nervousness. A few minutes before 9:00 a.m., Allison and an armed guard escorted us to the witness room. We walked down a long, narrow hallway that opened into a large square space with high ceilings near the courtroom. There were a few chairs along the walls. Another shorter hallway led to the doors of a second courtroom, where Prakash's trial was about to begin.

The tiny witness room – crowded with a few chairs, books, a refrigerator and a television – just off the large square hallway would be the girls' new home for the next seven days, and mine, for the next four days. Allison kept the door open to keep the air circulating in the stuffy, small space, because of which we could see everyone going into or coming out of the courtroom.

The girls could not relax and sat like wound up springs, ready to bounce. The first day was the worst, because they had no idea when they would be called to testify. Cathy had not revealed her trial strategy in advance and had only said that she thought the order would be Vesla, Shyama, then Kate.

There was no bathroom in the witness room. Rather than risk running into devotees in the public restroom, we used a private bathroom located near the prosecution offices. At about 10:00 a.m., Vesla and Shyama asked Allison to take them to the bathroom.

Two minutes later, one of the assistants came in looking for Kate. 'Cathy just asked for you in the courtroom.' Kate stood straight up, eyes wide like the proverbial deer in the headlights.

'Do you want a hug?' I asked.

'Sure,' she said, turning around with a leap. I gave her a quick hug of encouragement. She was stiff, like a soldier called to duty, as she marched down the hallway towards the courtroom.

The girls and Allison returned minutes later. 'Where's Kate?'

'She was just called into the courtroom,' I said. 'As it turns out, she's the first witness.'

Kate returned to the witness room at about 11:30 a.m., a bundle of nerves. The worst part now was that she could not talk about anything with us.

Allison had us leave early for lunch so we could beat the devotees out of the building. Kate was still so worked up that she couldn't eat. She had us stop for cigarettes, and smoked outside while the rest of us ate.

She was called back into the courtroom right after lunch, and was inside for the next three hours. To pass the time, I started working on my computer. Shyama and Allison started playing a computer game called 'Angry Birds' which helped pass the time and calmed Shyama's nerves. Vesla sat quietly in one of the overstuffed chairs, lost in her thoughts.

Later, from the court transcriptions, I gathered the details of the trial proceedings. It began with the two sides making their opening statements, including the prosecution detailing the twenty charges of indecency with children against Prakash. Then Cathy called in Kate.

The defence was not happy when Cathy called Kate as her first witness, as evidenced by the dialogue between Cathy and the two lead defence lawyers, Jo Angelyn Gates and Jeff Kearney.

> Gates: We would like an offer of proof as to what Kate Tonnessen is going to testify to and a hearing if there's going to be any allegations under 404(b). That has not been determined. She is not a victim in this case.
> Cathy: Well, Your Honour, we put them on notice, and the law clearly states that if their defence is fabrication that we can bring in other witnesses to talk about his acts with them. And I think clearly, from counsel's opening, that shows their defence certainly is fabrication.
> Judge Ramsay: Defence request is denied.
> Kearney: Your Honour.
> Judge Ramsay: Proceed.

Amy Lockhart interviewed Kate.

> Amy: Can you tell the jury about the circumstances for the first time he did something to you?
> Kate: Yes. I was 14 years old. And as we did every day, we watched him eat his morning meal and his evening meal in a large group. And on this day, he was sitting in a room aside from where he normally did on a large papasan chair. It's a big, round chair. And all the children always would sit as close as possible to him. And I was sitting to his side, and he grabbed me and pulled me in so I was leaning onto the papasan and him on his lap when, with a whole audience, he somehow was able to – he wrapped his arm around me and put it up my shirt and

> began pinching my nipples and fondling my breasts. I believed that that – because we were in front of so many people, I mean, I was just shocked. Now, prior to this he had been – he had started kissing me in a more passionate way. He would never – his tongue never penetrated my mouth, but he would kiss me where when – and for prolonged periods of time and rub his – his tongue against my lips.
> Amy: Okay. Kate, how old were you when he started doing that?
> Kate: 12 to 13.

Kate then described how she had shut herself in her bedroom for three days in despair after the papasan chair incident, how her mother had read her diary, and how her mother had forced her to go to Prakash to 'work things out'.

> Amy: So you were able to tell Swami Ji how he had made you feel?
> Kate: Yes.
> Amy: And what did he say to you?
> Kate: He said it was a test.

Day Three

Cruella de Vil

Thursday, 24 February 2011

ACCORDING TO HER biography, Jo Angelyn Gates has a history of getting people off for crimes such as child sex abuse, selling drugs and first-degree murder. My guess, based on what I saw during

Prakash's trial, is that her defence strategy leans heavily on two tactics: discrediting experts called by the prosecution and using paid 'experts' to discredit the prosecution's witnesses. Both these tactics took up significant amounts of time at Prakash's criminal trial.

On the third day of the trial, Gates spent most of the day trying to discredit the Hays County detective, Sgt Jeri Skrocki, who had recorded the two girls' initial complaints. Gates made it clear that she wanted to see every bit of training material, including every book Sgt Skrocki had ever used and every certificate she had ever received during training, even though this request was clearly impossible to fulfil. She expected Sgt Skrocki to remember details like the names of the authors of the books she had read to train for her position.

Just before Sgt Skrocki left the courtroom at about 2:00 p.m., Shyama was starting to melt down in the witness room at the thought of telling a roomful of people about her abuse. I put down my computer and focused all my attention on her, trying to give her strength. 'You've made it this far, Shyama. Please do not give up now, or you will regret it for the rest of your life. This is your moment. You have to do what you've waited three years to do – face your abuser.'

She was listening intently, but looked like she was barely hanging on. Then Allison said something that jolted her out of her terror: 'Draw an angry bird on your hand, so you can look at it in the courtroom.'

Shyama stood up abruptly. 'Yes, that's what I'm going to do.' Allison handed her a pen and Shyama proceeded to draw a bird on the edge of her hand. She had a smile on her face.

The next morning, we saw Sgt Skrocki head for the courtroom. She had a single file under her arm. When Gates was finally done with her, she came to the witness room and collapsed into an empty armchair. 'What a bitch!'

'I know, she's evil,' said Kate.

'She's nasty. But I only care that I didn't say anything to blow it for the girls.'

'That's exactly how I feel too,' said Kate.

Meanwhile, Shyama was now in the courtroom, being questioned by Cathy. Gates made many objections, including any mention of Kripalu Maharaj – even though the news of his rape charges was what initially motivated the girls to speak out about their own abuse.

Cathy: When was it – and, you know, if you can't remember a specific date, it's okay. But – well, let me ask you this: why did you finally decide that you were going to come and talk to the police about what this man did to you?
Shyama: I read a news article.
Gates: Objection, Your Honour, to any hearsay in the news article.
Judge Ramsay: Overrule the objection.

Gates then objected when Cathy addressed the defence's claim that the girls had hatched a plot against Prakash.

Cathy: Okay. So this wasn't some kind of plan that y'all hatched to somehow hurt this defendant or Barsana Dham or any of these people sitting around here.
Shyama: No. It was not at all. We all came to the decision on our own. I came to the decision on my own.
Gates: Your Honour, objection with regard to any other people's decisions.
Judge Ramsay: Sustain the objection.
Shyama: I came to the decision on my own with no input from anyone else.

Then Shyama described her incidents of sexual assault, beginning with the first one.

Shyama: We were in the kitchen, and he was fixing my sari because at the time I was – saris are generally meant for adults. And I'm – I'm petite, and I've always been petite. And I've always been too small – or was, at the time, too small to wear one. So it

> wasn't fitting correctly. And he was adjusting it to make – they were – him and Ranjana, who is also named Vishwambhari, who's not in this room – she was standing behind me, and he was standing in front of me. And I wasn't very developed at the time, but he was adjusting my sari, pulling it across my chest and was more than just pulling it across my chest. He was openhandedly groping my breasts at the time. But there – I mean, there wasn't much there to grope, but he was still touching me in a very sexual manner across my breasts, squeezing and massaging.

Shyama returned from the witness room just after 5:00 p.m.

'How did it go?' I asked.

She sat up straight and strong in her chair: 'I'm not afraid of that bitch.'

Gates had the unusual habit of wearing short skirts with slits up the back in the courtroom. She also wore spiked high heels that clicked when she walked, so you always knew when she was coming.

Her style reminded me of Cruella de Vil – the wicked witch who likes to kill puppies in the Disney movie, *101 Dalmatians*.

Day Four

The 'Hotshot' Cult Lawyer

Friday, 25 February 2011

WHEN I FIRST heard that Prakash had hired a new lead defence attorney, I googled him, only to learn that Jeff Kearney had a history of working with cults. In fact, according to one article, one case in particular established him as a 'hotshot' lawyer. He was defending a member of the Branch Davidian cult. The man was one of the eleven Davidians charged with conspiracy to murder the four federal agents who died in 1993 during a raid on the religious compound in Waco, Texas. His client was acquitted of murder, but found guilty of gun charges.

In late 2010, Kearney was hired by the infamous Warren Jeffs, leader of a polygamous fundamentalist branch of the Mormon religion, known as the Fundamentalist Church of Jesus Christ of Latter-Day Saints (FLDS). Jeffs had established a 2,000-acre guarded compound in Eldorado, Texas, which was raided by federal marshals in 2008, not long before Prakash's arrest. The raid received international attention, due primarily to the fact that over 200 children had been removed from the complex.

On 1 February 2010, Examiner.com reported the following:

> **Jeff Kearney,** high-profile Texas defense attorney, strode into the courtroom Tuesday with Warren Jeffs to announce he was taking over the defense. Kearney was successful in persuading a jury to find one of the Branch Davidians not guilty of murder in a case which increased his national reputation. He has had several other well-known victories in courtrooms across the country.

I assume that Kearney's experience with other notorious religious organizations is what prompted Barsana Dham to hire him. But in this unusual case, Kearney seemed to be all hat and no cattle (as they say in Texas).

The day began with Amy continuing her direct examination of Shyama. Then it was Gates's turn to cross-examine.

During Shyama's morning testimony, the defence introduced numerous photographs of Shyama dancing and performing in special events at Barsana Dham. Gates used the photos to push one issue: if Shyama had been abused as she claimed, why had she returned to Barsana Dham to participate in these events?

However, they could not nail down the actual dates of the events pictured, which allowed for the possibility that Shyama was still under eighteen and still living in Barsana Dham in all the photos. In the end, the defence's long, tedious production of 'photo evidence' amounted to nothing more than a complete waste of time.

The trial took a dramatic turn when Vesla took the stand – mainly because she was so emotional during most of her testimony, often breaking down into tears. First, under direct testimony, she described ten separate incidents of sexual abuse by Prakash.

> Cathy: The first time that you were ever alone with him that you recall in the bedroom, what, if anything, do you recall him doing?
> Vesla: I was seated on the floor to the right of the chair and looking at it. He was in the chair. He began touching my shirt, my shoulders in my shirt area. Then he started playing with my bra strap, and then slowly moved down into touching my breasts. It was a pretty quick encounter. He then gave me candy. He told me I was a good girl and excused me from the room.
> Cathy: Okay. When you say he excused you from the room, how would he do that? How did you know that you were excused from the room?
> Vesla: He told me I could go. He waved me out.
> Cathy: Okay. And so this was the very first time, and he touched your breasts over your clothes?
> Vesla: Yes.

Cathy was quick to squash the defence's assertion that the girls had brought these charges for revenge and potential monetary gain, which the defence had claimed.

> Cathy: And as we sit here today, nobody – you, Shyama, Kate – none of you all have filed suits or have any plans to file suits?
> Vesla: No.
> Cathy: Is that correct?
> Vesla: Yes, that's correct.

Cathy: Okay. And just hypothetically speaking, if the jury comes back with guilty verdicts on this man, do you have any plans to sue anybody?
Vesla: No.
Cathy: What do you want to do?
Vesla: I want to move on. I want to not be scared in my house. I want my parents back.
Cathy: Do you want these people to believe your truth?
Vesla: Yes.
Cathy: Pass the witness.

Day Five

The Prosecution Rests and the Defence Begins

Monday, 28 February 2011

VESLA RETURNED TO the stand and Jeff Kearney proceeded to ask her a series of vague questions that seemed to go nowhere.

Cathy had always said that one measure of truth is the cost to the victims to speak out. When Kearney passed the witness, Cathy asked Vesla just one question on redirect.

Cathy: What's been the hardest part of this whole experience for you?
Vesla: Losing my family, my dad, my mom, and then being thrown under the bus for this. Not feeling safe, having an unregistered address, my parents not coming to my wedding even though I invited them, not knowing that I'm carrying their granddaughter.

Cathy: Thank you. Pass the witness.

As Vesla made her last statement in tears, it was obvious that she was telling the truth, not out of rebellion or revenge, as the defence had clumsily claimed, but because it was the right thing to do.

Cathy rested her case at about 10:30 a.m. Kearney requested a break until after lunch to gather his witnesses. Cathy objected to the delay, but the judge granted the extra time.

After the long lunch break, we returned to find Divakari Devi, Barsana Dham's then president, waiting outside the courtroom with a scowl on her face. When she glanced our way, she shot the proverbial daggers at us. However, she also looked very nervous.

In the next day's *Austin American-Statesman*, Eric Dexheimer summed up the afternoon's testimony from the day's five defence witnesses.

> Prakashanand's lawyers on Monday quizzed five women who'd had lengthy experience with the ashram, either as devotees or residents themselves, or who have been otherwise close to the goings-on at the 200-acre facility on RM 1826 in Driftwood. In sum, their recollections were presented to cast doubt on the claims and remembrances – and credibility – of the guru's accusers.
>
> 'I never saw a child alone with Swamiji,' said Emily Roberts, a 27-year-old who, like the three women claiming abuse, grew up at Barsana Dham.
>
> 'Prakashanand was almost always surrounded by people,' said Sharlini Saksena, a resident of New Delhi and long-time devotee. She added that she never saw him alone with a teenage girl.
>
> Alexandra Roberts, 17, said that she has been following Prakashanand since she was a very young girl and that she had 'absolutely not' ever been alone with him, nor was she aware of any children being alone with the holy man in his bedroom.

That's where Prakashanand's accusers have said several instances of his molesting occurred.

Responding to questions from the guru's attorneys, Diwakari Devi, who has lived at the ashram since 1993 and who was then president of Barsana Dham, reported different furniture in different locations from that reported by the accusing women. She, too, insisted Prakashanand could not have been alone with the young girls in his bedroom. 'It never happened.'

In her questioning of the witnesses, Hays County Assistant District Attorney Cathy Compton asked whether they could reasonably claim that they knew what Prakashanand was doing every hour of every day. Most agreed they could not.

One of the witnesses, Sharlini, had never even been to the Barsana Dham ashram in Texas.

Amy: Okay. Now, you never were in Texas in the 1990s, right?
Sharlini: No.
Amy: So you would not be able to testify at all about what life was like at Barsana Dham in the 1990s?
Sharlini: That's right.
Amy: And you don't know how Swami Ji was with children in the 1990s in Texas?
Sharlini: That's right.
Amy: And you would agree that if Swami Ji was alone with a teenage girl that he would have been alone and you would not have been able to see that? So it's not significant that you didn't see him alone with a teenage girl because then he wouldn't have been alone if you were there, correct?
Sharlini: That's right.

Jean Roberts, the mother of Alexandra Roberts and daughter of Lois, a long-time Barsana Dham resident, described herself as a 'social devotee of the ashram' (although in all my years there, I'd never heard of such a description). It was true, however, that she only visited sporadically and usually during events. But she claimed to have slept over many times.

Cathy: Okay. And on the overnights, where – when you were there, where was the defendant, if you know?
Jean: Sometimes he wasn't there. He was sometimes in India when I was there. Typically, if he was in residence, he was in his room.
Cathy: How do you know?
Jean: I'm presuming.
Cathy: Okay. You're presuming. But you don't know really, at night, after you were not with him what he was doing, correct?
Jean: No, ma'am.
Cathy: Okay. So you don't have any way to really know on probably multiple occasions what he did or did not do?
Jean: No, ma'am.
Cathy: Okay. So you're not here to testify about any personal knowledge with regard to what this defendant may have done or not done with any of the alleged victims in this case? You don't have any personal knowledge, you didn't see anything, you weren't there for any of the events that have been alleged, right?
Jean: Correct.
Cathy: Okay. Pass the witness.

An ongoing tactic of the defence team was to try to downplay Prakash's role as a 'saint' or a being higher than the rest of us – even though that's exactly what he sought to teach us. Divakari tried to not claim the truth of this point.

Cathy: Okay. But you're the president of this organization. And isn't it true that actually some of your literature refers to him as a living saint?
Divakari: No.
Cathy: That's not true?

Divakari: (Moving head side to side).
Cathy: So nobody from your organization has referred to him in that way?
Divakari: Maybe based on their experience.
Cathy: Okay. And you don't – so it's your testimony that nothing in any of the materials that you as – that the organization puts out with regard to him refers to him as being a divine—
Divakari: I don't know.
Cathy: —being? Again, you don't know?
Divakari: (Moving head side to side).
Cathy: And you're the president of the organization?
Divakari: Yes.
Cathy: Pass the witness.

Counting the day's five witnesses, the defence would call a total of twelve witnesses – ten devotees or relatives of devotees and two others – before they were done.

Day Six

The 'Star Witness' for the Defence

Tuesday, 1 March 2011

THE DAY STARTED with Kate being recalled to the stand by Gates – who then tried to trap her in incriminating testimony.

Gates: Did you say during that conversation to your sister Prabhakari that you were tired of being treated second to Barsana Dham and Swami Ji?

Kate: No.
Gates: Did you threaten your sister and tell her that you were going to bring Barsana Dham down if they did not leave?
Kate: No, because we already knew at that point that I could not even do – I was past the statute of limitations. And I said whatever Vesla and Shyama want to do, I will support them. So I can't – I can't even do anything about what happened to me, but I will support whatever Vesla and Shyama do.
Gates: So, specifically, Ms Tonnessen – the question is a specific question. Did you or did you not threaten your sister that you would take Barsana Dham down?
Kate: I – no, I did not.
Gates: Yes or no?
Kate: I absolutely could not even do that.

On cross-examination, Amy questioned Kate about her motivation and the high price she was paying to recount her story of abuse in a court of law.

Amy: And your only motivation for coming forward was to protect other children?
Kate: Yes.
Amy: And you could have lived your life without ever, ever thinking about him and what he did to you again, couldn't you have?
Kate: Yes.
Amy: Except for the fact that you knew you had to act?
Kate: I knew.
Amy: And, actually, the only thing these allegations have done is brought your life down and brought your family down?
Kate: It's horrible.
Amy: What's changed about your life since you've come forward?
Kate: I haven't seen my family. I don't – I'm scared when I come

> to Austin. We know that – I know that there's a whole huge room full of people that – I lost all my history. I don't know.
> Amy: What does it mean when you say you lost your history?
> Kate: I mean I lost all of my family, all of my childhood. I don't – besides my sister, I'm an orphan now. I don't have people.
> Amy: Why are you scared when you come to Austin?
> Kate: Because there's a very large group of people that are very mad at me for speaking out.
> Amy: Well, when Prabhakari came to visit you, she again tried to tell you why it is – that you don't understand what he did to you was – was a blessing or a grace, right?
> Kate: Uh-huh.
> Amy: And why is that something that you would be made to believe?
> Kate: I guess just as – as I was told when I was a child, because it was a test or that this man was so beyond the material plane that nothing he does is material; that sex acts aren't sexual if there's no sex in the mind of the person performing them, which, at the time when Prabhakari was visiting me, was ridiculous and I knew was nonsense. And why any man of any age of any spiritual rank would need to commit sex acts on children as a test was – I knew was absurd.

Next, the defence called three more witnesses: another female ashram resident, a process server and a religious teacher – all of whom gave underwhelming testimony.

By mid-afternoon, the defence called its 'star witness' – Prabhakari. She had taken the order of sanyas at the age of twenty-one under Prakash. From then on, she wore saffron saris and never again knew what it was like to have anyone tell her 'no' or hold her accountable for unreasonable actions. Even her mother and stepfather, as devotees, had to do as she commanded.

From the time she was twenty-six, she was the undisputed ruler of the Barsana Dham ashram in Prakash's absence. We were told that she was heading his defence strategy and managing his defence team. Now, in a court of law, she still seemed to expect that people would accept whatever she said as the truth, no matter how far-fetched.

However, catching people in inconsistent testimony is one of the primary goals of lawyers in criminal trials. Inconsistencies can look like lies to the jury, and often make them doubt the entire testimony of a witness. When Prabhakari got on the stand, her testimony revealed major inconsistencies. On her first day of testimony, through sporadic tears (which appeared on cue), Prabhakari responded to questions from Reagan Winn, Kearney's law partner.

> Winn: You had testified earlier that you had a grandmother that was living in Seattle. Is that right?
> Prabhakari: Near Seattle.
> Winn: Did something happen to her in the spring of 2008?
> Prabhakari: She passed away.
> Winn: Do you feel any emotions toward Kate and Vesla over the situation with your grandmother?
> Prabhakari: Yes, I do.
> Winn: What are those emotions?
> Prabhakari: They didn't let me say good-bye to her.
> Winn: How does that make you feel?
> Prabhakari: I don't have a word big enough.

Winn also questioned Prabhakari about her insinuation that Kate and the girls expected Hays County to 'lynch' Prakash when they spoke out about their abuse.

> Winn: Did – during this conversation, did she say to you, quote, I'm tired of being second to Barsana Dham and Swami Ji?
> Prabhakari: Yes, she did.
> Winn: During this conversation, did she say to you, quote, I'm bringing Barsana Dham down if you-all don't leave?
> Prabhakari: Yes, she did.

Winn: By 'you-all', who did you take that to mean?
Prabhakari: My father, my mother, my brother and myself.
Winn: How did that make you feel?
Prabhakari: Threatened.
Winn: Did she tell you that she would make an accusation against Swami Ji?
Prabhakari: Yes, she did.
Winn: Did she tell you that she thought the accusation would work because Swami Ji would get a lynching – and that's a quote – in Hays County?
Prabhakari: She did.

Amy's cross-examination of Prabhakari began that afternoon.

Amy: So you agree that you've been quoted a lot as kind of representing the position of Barsana Dham?
Prabhakari: Yeah. I've talked to the Statesman Record.
Amy: And that you've been very involved in the legal defence of this defendant?
Prabhakari: I've been at every hearing.
Amy: And you've been at most of the meetings with the attorneys that the defendant has been to, right?
Prabhakari: Not most of them. Some.
Amy: Now, in all this time where you – when you say that you have been participating in his defence, did you ever go to law enforcement to address your concerns with law enforcement that these girls are lying?
Prabhakari: No.
Amy: Have you ever told anyone in law enforcement this, your position that you've told this jury today?
Prabhakari: I don't think I've ever been interviewed. I can't remember ever being interviewed by anyone.
Amy: Did you ever voluntarily go to them and explain to law enforcement what the real story was?

Prabhakari: You mean like go to the police station?
Amy: Right.
Prabhakari: No.
Amy: Well, you don't think it would have been helpful to determining whether an offense were committed for the police to know that Kate had made all these threats against him?
Prabhakari: I was waiting for my day in court. That's what I thought I was supposed to do.
Amy: Well, if it could have been resolved three and a half years ago, wouldn't that have been better?
Prabhakari: Yes.

Day Seven

Nothing but Lies

Wednesday, 2 March 2011

THE NEXT DAY, Amy exposed another inconsistency in Prabhakari's story.

Amy: Now, you also said yesterday that Kate is the one who kept you from your grandmother's deathbed, essentially, right?
Prabhakari: It wasn't just Kate. There was my uncle – all three of my sisters were there, actually.
Amy: Were where?
Prabhakari: With my grandmother.
Amy: And this is during the month that she died?
Prabhakari: Yes.

Amy: So when did your grandmother die? In April of 2008? Is that right?
Prabhakari: It was March or April. I don't remember.
Amy: Did you know that Kate was on a month-long retreat in New Mexico and she wasn't even there with your grandmother when he – she died?
Prabhakari: No, I didn't.
Amy: Okay. But it was your testimony yesterday that Kate is the one who kept you away from her?
Prabhakari: I understood that all three of my sisters were there, but I only heard about it through my mother.

Interestingly, while Prabhakari radiated confidence and bravado on her first day of testimony, on this second day, she was glum and moody. My guess is that she got blasted by Prakash the night before for the obviously failing 'defence strategy'. It was all downhill from there for the defence.

Next, they called three more female devotees to the stand, each one worse than the previous one. Carol Bartos, who had cleaned Prakash's kitchen, claimed that no young girls or single women ever went into his room alone. Vishi claimed the same, as did the next witness, Michelle Paul, a long-time devotee who lived in Austin. But they all made unimpressive witnesses, as evidenced in the following excerpt from Cathy's exchange with Michelle.

Cathy: So that would be – it would be fair to say that at night or at any time when you weren't there that you didn't have any way to know what he was doing?
Michelle: Correct.
Cathy: So you don't have any way to tell this jury that you know for sure what he did with young girls in his room when you weren't out there?
Michelle: I know Swami Ji, and I know his behavior.

Cathy: You don't have any way to know what he was doing when you weren't there, do you?
Michelle: No.
Cathy: So for all you know, he could have been doing all sorts of other things that you didn't know about?
Michelle: I have no way of knowing.
Cathy: Pass the witness.

I was amazed at Cathy's cross-examination of the defence witnesses. She did a brilliant job of exposing their desperation to say whatever they thought might help get Prakash out of his jam.

The defence spent the rest of the day trying to get a paid 'expert witness' on the stand. A man with a PhD in psychology was supposed to make statements about false allegations of sexual abuse. But after the prosecution protested and interviewed him without the jury present, they brought case law to the judge and the man never made it in front of the jury. After calling only a fraction of the people listed on their 100-plus witness list, Prakash's entire defence was about to implode.

Day Eight

The Defence Rests, Abruptly

Thursday, 3 March 2011

AFTER A COUPLE of hours of intense examination and cross examination of the paid 'expert' about what he was actually an expert in and what insight he could provide in this trial, Judge Ramsay finally administered the coup de grace.

> Judge Ramsay: Do you have any studies that apply specifically to this case where the outcry is later when they're adults and not children? Because these are not children. These are all – all the alleged victims were adults. Do you have any studies about that?
> Witness: No, sir.
> Judge Ramsay: The State's objection [to this man testifying] is sustained.

Clearly, the loss of this witness was a major blow to the defence, because within half an hour Kearney stated, 'The defence rests, Your Honour.'

It was an extremely sudden decision, considering the length of their witness list, their assertion that the defence would need two to three weeks to make its case, and the fact that a few witnesses had been milling around the courthouse that morning, waiting to be called to the stand, including Kate and Vesla's brother, Akhilananda (formerly called Luke), who had been looking sick to his stomach and pacing in the hallway all morning, and another young woman who had grown up in the ashram and used to be close friends with the girls. This young woman had taken Prakash's side, likely because her mother was a staunch Prakash supporter.

Kate called me to give me the surprising news. 'You can come to the closing arguments tomorrow.'

I began making plans to get back over to Kathi's that evening, so I could drive to the courthouse in the morning.

After having waited in the witness room for so long, it would be my first day in the criminal trial of my former guru.

Day Nine (Part One)

Lawyer Interrupted

Friday, 4 March 2011

KATHI AND WAYNE decided to attend the trial too. So, the three of us left their home at 6:30 a.m. We needed to arrive at the courthouse early to ensure that we got seats in the famously packed courtroom full of devotees.

Kate called while we were en route: 'Are you guys on your way?'

'Yes, why?'

'Because Dylan's dad Larry is already there and he said a line has started forming.'

When we arrived, I parked behind the building and we hurried to the line. But devotees started cutting in front of us, joining others who were already there. The man in front of me, who had grown up in the ashram, was soon joined by his parents.

I looked at Kathi and Wayne in frustration. 'If one more person cuts in front of me, I'm going to go up to the front with Larry.' Sure enough, more devotees got in line.

'You can join me if you want,' I told Kathi and Wayne. Then I walked up to Larry, who was standing a couple of dozen people ahead of us.

'Hi, Larry.'

He looked at me curiously. We'd only met a couple of times.

'I'm Kate's friend, Karen.'

'Oh, hi,' he said and gave me a hug.

'A bunch of people have been cutting in front of us, so I decided to cut in front of them. I need to make sure we get seats.'

'Sounds good,' he said with a laugh. We chatted until the doors opened at 8:00 a.m.

We got through security and hurried into the courtroom. The devotees in front of us had already reserved chairs not only for themselves, but for others who were yet to arrive. In several rows, shawls were spread out over several of the chairs. I followed Larry to the prosecution side of the courtroom, where they were saving the first three rows for the girls and members of the prosecution team.

I quickly assessed the mad scramble for seats and put my purse and a notebook on the two seats next to me for Kathi and Wayne. Several minutes later, they entered the courtroom and I called them over.

We chatted for the next hour while we waited for the trial to start. More people entered the courtroom, looked around for seats, and had to leave. Eric Dexheimer got there about twenty minutes to 9:00 a.m. and took one of the saved seats in the first three rows. He waved to me and sat down.

A television reporter entered the courtroom a few minutes later. She made a fuss with one of the bailiffs over the lack of seats for the press. Finally, he got her a chair from somewhere else and put it in the front row on the defence side, right next to Prabhakari and her parents, Adolph and Sondra Tonnessen.

A few minutes before the hour, the defendant was rolled in. Prakash used the backs of the lawyers' chairs to make his way to his Lazy-Boy chair. Soon, the girls were escorted into the courtroom by Hays County officials and they took their seats in the first row. I watched Adolph Tonnessen stare at his two daughters, whom he had not seen in three years, including his newly pregnant youngest daughter, Vesla. He had always been close and loving with his children, but now he had abandoned two of them. He looked like a broken man, a shadow of his former self.

The lawyers took their seats and Judge Ramsay entered the room. He announced the start of the trial and said that each side would have forty minutes in which to make their final remarks to the jury. Each side divided that time between two lawyers. Amy would go first, followed by Gates and Kearney. Cathy would have the final word.

But first Kearney's partner, Winn, presented several of the defence's now-infamous mid-trial motions. One of the requests was for lesser charges since there was no 'proof of arousal' by the defendant during the 'indecency with a child' charges. The judge denied this motion and all the rest.

Finally, the jury entered. We all stood up as they took their seats. I appreciated the ritual of showing respect to the twelve men and women who would soon decide Prakash's fate.

Amy started the day by explaining how Prakash had used and abused his role as a spiritual leader to take advantage of innocent people and children.

> This is a simple case about exploitation of power and misuse of love. The defendant has used the power given to him as a religious leader, and he used the love and trust of his devotees to gain access to children. … so he could fulfill his sexual desires. And that's all that this case is about, a man exploiting the power given to him and abusing the love and the trust of families and children so he can get what he wants. And in the beginning when I told you that this trial was not going to be about religion and you will not be judging him for his religion or his devotees for what they believe, that still holds true. It doesn't matter what religion he is. We only ask the people about their beliefs to show you that he had the power and the authority and that he had their love and trust. So that's how he committed the crimes.

She used slides to review each of the twenty counts of indecency with a child by sexual contact that he was accused of committing with Shyama and Vesla. Amy guessed that the defence would stress the lack of evidence in their final remarks. She reminded the jury that they had all agreed that they could convict someone based on the 'one witness rule'. She added, 'It should be no surprise to anyone that our evidence is the testimonies of the girls.'

Amy went through all the defence witnesses and commented, with specific references, on how untrustworthy everyone's testimony was.

> I want to talk quickly about their witnesses and the defence in this case. What did the defence witnesses come here to tell you? He's never alone with these girls, and they're liars. Okay? But look at who is telling you that. These are people who are still completely devoted to him. These are people who are still in service to him. These are people that still love him and trust him and believe in him. What those witnesses are, are just more proof that he is willing to use the love and trust of others to benefit himself.

She closed her remarks by saying:

> These girls were brave to stand up for the truth. They endured threats, invasion of privacy, practically went into hiding, and lost their families. They spoke out because they knew if they didn't they would be just as bad as the people who didn't say anything. All they wanted was for it to stop. We are asking you to finish our fight for us. We did our job. The girls did their job. There is no one left to hold him responsible. We request that you convict him of everything he did. Tell them they matter. That what they endured was not for nothing. Tell them their choice to do something about it was worth something.

As Amy had predicted, Kearney went right to the lack of evidence: 'You have a duty to require them to provide evidence.' He cited a long list of 'evidence' that the defence had supplied, including several people who said that the girls were known to be liars. He claimed that the girls' stories contradicted each other, and accused them of conspiring to make up the story to get back at their parents. He also made some comment about the impossibility of Prakash unhooking one of the girl's bras with one hand.

He concluded by saying, 'Maybe these girls really didn't tell the truth ... then you have a reasonable doubt.' He added: 'We have done the best we could in representing Swamiji Ji, and we have, for the last some time, had his future in our hands. When Ms Gates sits down, it's going to be in your hands, and I trust he's in good hands.'

After carefully refreshing her lipstick, Gates got up and wrote 'EVIDENCE' on a white board. She then turned to the jury and talked about how no one had supplied any evidence in the case – despite the fact that the prosecution had already made it clear that they had no hard evidence to offer and that they were basing the trial on the one-witness rule, meaning that the girls' testimonies *were* the evidence.

Then Cathy presented her final comments to the jury.

> Don't you hate it when people treat you like you are stupid? And when they use parlor tricks and patronize you?
>
> They are acting like the defendant is the only one who matters. They are saying the accusers are conspirators, as if they are the ones on trial. It's a parlor trick. These are the victims and they are not the ones on trial.
>
> The defence has attempted to baffle you with a bunch of BS [bull shit] that doesn't matter. It's circular logic. To believe them, you would have to believe that Kate is an evil mastermind who is capable of controlling the two other women. These women are not dumb. If they created a big nefarious plan to bring down a religion, they could have come up with a better story than he touched their breasts.
>
> A measure of the truth is the cost it took to bring it. What in the world have these girls gained? And what has been the cost to them? They've run the gauntlet even to get up here, enduring threats from people who once professed to love them.

Throughout Cathy's closing arguments, Prabhakari sat next to her parents with a sour expression, her lips pursed like she had smelt something bad. Periodically, she would shake her head, as if to say, 'No that's not right.'

But Kearney was not as subtle in his disapproval. Every few minutes he interrupted with some objection, and the judge would deny it.

Intermittently, with his head hanging down, he would mumble: 'Request for mistrial, your honour.' In fact, Kearney asked for a mistrial a total of five times. Judge Ramsay denied every one.

Finally, in exasperation, Cathy beseeched the judge: 'Your Honour, Mr Kearney is using up my time with his repeated objections. Can I have extra time to get through my comments?'

'We'll see,' was the answer.

Kearney continued his interruptions – clearly trying to waste Cathy's time, throw her off her game, or perhaps by some miracle get Judge Ramsay to grant a mistrial.

Finally, Cathy was out of time.

'Can I have one more sentence, Your Honour?'

The judge nodded.

She faced the jury and gave one final admonition: 'Please find this man guilty. You will not be telling him a thing he doesn't already know.'

Day Nine (Part Two)

Beyond a Shadow of a Doubt

Friday, 4 March 2011, 5:30 p.m.

LAWYERS ON BOTH sides of a criminal trial get nervous when a jury returns with a verdict in under two hours.

At about 4:30 p.m., several of us were waiting in the DA's office, wondering how long it will take the jury to reach a verdict. Judge Ramsay had dismissed the jury members to deliberate at about 3:00 p.m.

At 5:05 p.m., I overheard someone in the hallway say, 'They have a verdict?'

I stood up and rushed to the bathroom, where Kate was standing before the mirror. 'Oh my god. I wonder what they've decided.'

'Whatever it is, they are very sure about their decision,' she replied in her typical wise-beyond-her-years way.

I hurried towards the courtroom. As I approached the doors, I saw a mass of devotees huddled in a circle off to one side. Those on the outer edge were leaning in with their arms around each other to hear what someone at the centre of the circle was saying.

When I entered the courtroom, I saw Kathi and Wayne in their seats, and a few others scattered around the room. 'The jury has a verdict,' I said.

'We know,' Kathi said. 'One of the bailiffs just told us.'

'There's a mass of devotees out in the hallway.'

'They were all in here and the lawyers took them out a few minutes ago,' Kathi said. 'I walked by them on the way to the bathroom and overheard his lawyers say, "Do not have any reaction."'

Kearney was no doubt prepping them for whichever verdict the jurors had reached – including a guilty one.

I was not as prepared. I wanted to hear one verdict and one verdict only. I had waited three years for this moment. Now that it was here, I thought I was going to faint. I was almost hyperventilating. Luckily, Kathi had a bottle of Rescue Remedy in her purse and held a dropperful out to me.

I opened my mouth like a baby bird and the tincture trickled down my throat. But it didn't seem to help – my leg was shaking and my foot was tapping uncontrollably.

My brain raced and my eyes scanned the courtroom for any clue to the decision that would either vindicate the past three years of my life and my efforts to support the women and expose the guru and his organization, or turn me into the target of Barsana Dham's attacks as a troublemaker and worse.

I studied three of the four defence lawyers for clues as to what they were thinking. Kearney was sitting at the table with his head down.

Gates was pacing – snapping her fingers and clicking her heels with every step. Winn was pacing with smaller steps and puffing out air with each turn. They were all clearly worried. The devotees sat stone-faced, facing forward and not talking to each other.

Kate told me later that Cathy and Amy had given the girls a brief talk in the back room. 'Cathy was really worried about how fast the jury had made their decision. She looked pretty miserable.'

The minutes ticked by with excruciating slowness. Finally, at 5:25 p.m., Judge Ramsay entered the courtroom. 'Bring in the jury,' he instructed the bailiff in his deep, resounding southern accent.

The jury members entered with their poker faces firmly in place. I searched their faces for clues. And there it was: one woman looked towards the girls and gave the tiniest of smiles – so fleeting it was gone almost before I saw it.

The jury foreman handed the paperwork to the bailiff, who handed it to the judge. 'Is this your decision? Say so by saying "yes."'

'Yes,' they all said.

Judge Ramsay looked down at the paper. I grabbed Wayne's thigh and squeezed it, leaning into him. Time was standing still. My whole body was shaking. I grabbed him by the shoulders and squeezed him harder.

Then Judge Ramsay finally read the verdict on the first count: 'The verdict of the jury in Count I, We, the jury, find the defendant, Swami Ji, guilty of the offense of indecency with a child by sexual contact as alleged in Count I of the indictment.'

'Guilty!' He was guilty!

Never had a single word sounded sweeter. I took a huge gasp of air and tears of relief and happiness and pain streamed down my cheeks. I looked at the three girls who had been sitting rigidly in the front row between the two husbands and a brother. All three dropped their shoulders in a simultaneous expulsion of air. I could tell they were crying. I began sobbing loudly, squeezing Wayne even harder.

Judge Ramsay continued reading the verdict:

> … and guilty as to Count II, guilty as Count III, guilty as to Count IV, guilty as to Count V and VI and VII and VIII and IX and X. That was in Cause Number 272. In Cause Number 273, the verdict is guilty in Count I and Count II, Count III, Count IV, Count V, Count VI, VII, VIII, IX, and X.

I glanced at the devotees. They were stones, sitting motionless, looking forward. There seemed to be a special effect that made them all appear to have a shadow, like a black cloud, over them. The defence lawyers stood up and helped Prakash into his wheelchair. As they wheeled him down the aisle, I looked into the face of the man I had called 'guru' for fifteen years. He displayed no emotion whatsoever. In fact, he appeared oblivious to the fact that he was leaving the courtroom as a convicted child sex offender.

Justice may have been delayed (over and over again) in the criminal trial of Prakashanand Saraswati, but in the end, it was not denied. Prakash was released on his own recognizance that evening to await sentencing on Monday.

Weekend Negotiations

A Low Blow

Sunday, 6 March 2011

AFTER THE VERDICT, the girls had planned to take a much-needed break over the weekend. On Friday evening, they enjoyed dinner out in a San Marcos restaurant and posted photos of themselves with the biggest smiles I'd seen on their faces in a long time. But there was something different about these smiles. They projected an interesting mix of innocence – and power. These three women were happy and proud of what they had accomplished.

But their happiness was short-lived.

I planned to meet them, but when I called Kate to figure out where we should meet, she was upset. 'You'll never guess what happened! My father called us.'

'What?'

'About a half-hour ago, he called my phone. I refused to talk to him. But Vesla did. He begged us to ask the jury to give Prakash probation. In fact, the defence lawyers have been calling Cathy all weekend, trying to negotiate an offer of probation. We said no.'

I met Kate in the park and we continued to talk about this low blow by their father. Apparently, when the lawyers couldn't make a deal with Cathy, the Barsana Dham team decided to use the father to try and influence his daughters. This was the first time he had spoken to either of them in almost three years. He had never met his first grandchild, Kate's one-and-a-half-year-old daughter. And he had just learnt that Vesla was five months pregnant with her first child, also a girl. And now he was calling to beg them to show leniency to their abuser. Talk about manipulation!

'You're hurting the person I love the most in the whole world,' he implored. Vesla told him that was too bad, and hung up.

For the entire time that they were waiting for the trial, Vesla had held out hope that her father would one day wake up, see the truth and leave the man who had sexually abused her as a child. After she hung up on her father that day, she knew that would never happen. It was time to accept the harsh truth – her father would never abandon Prakash the way he had abandoned her and her sister.

Day Ten

And Then He Was Gone

Monday, 7 March 2011

AT 9:10 A.M., Prakash was not in the courtroom for the sentencing.

I had already noticed that there were far fewer devotees in the courtroom than usual. I started watching the devotees more closely. Some were talking to each other, some were sitting quietly. A few were reading. Overall, their demeanour seemed odd, considering the gravity of the situation.

By 9:40 a.m., it was clear that Prakash would not show up. Cathy walked over to me and said, 'It looks like we are missing one swami.'

Hays County officials called all the area hospitals and issued a warrant for his arrest.

While we were waiting for Judge Ramsay, I called Eric Dexheimer, who was also absent from the courtroom. After the initial pleasantries, I informed him about the no-show. He asked me to keep him posted.

I also called my insider friend who said there had been a meeting the night before at Marsha's house, where Prakash had been staying. All the devotees had gone to his dinner at about 5:00 p.m. This piece of critical information gave us his last known time and location.

Many times during the three-year wait for his trial, I imagined Prakash not showing up. And now, when he was finally a convicted felon, he was on the run.

When Judge Ramsay arrived, Cathy requested that the trial proceed in absentia, but Kearney, who was the spokesman for the morning's drama, made a fuss about his client being involuntarily missing.

Kearney: We have not located our client, Your Honor, and we

> don't know the reason for his absence at this time. We're still trying to determine that. You know, we don't know if he's lying in a ditch somewhere. We don't know where he is, and so we're certainly not in a position to say that he has voluntarily elected not to be here. We have no information to that effect, and we're trying to locate him.
>
> Cathy countered: Well, the alternative is you don't know either whether he just took a one-way flight to India, right?

Kearney tried to shift the blame to the prosecution.

As the heated discussion between the lawyers waged on, Judge Ramsay requested their presence in chambers and we were all dismissed until after lunch. I got calls from Eric and my insider source, who told me that the story was headline news on the *Statesman* website.

All the local television stations picked up on Eric's breaking news update. When we returned to the courthouse, there were five news trucks in the parking lot – one for every news station in the area. When we walked up to the courtroom doors, Eric held them open for us. I smiled at him: 'You made it.'

Although Cathy and Amy fought to have the trial proceed as intended, Judge Ramsay made the final decision.

> Judge Ramsay: The Court's plan is to release the jury on the defence request until nine o'clock in the morning. We'll proceed at nine o'clock in the morning. And you have a motion?
>
> Kearney: Yes, Your Honor. In view of all of the media and far-reaching press coverage on the fact that our client did not show up this morning – it's all over the Internet. It's on every news station. It's everywhere that – we would ask the Court to sequester the jury just out of an abundance of caution. It's so easy for some family member or friend or neighbour to mention to them what they saw, and there's no way to undo that. And so just because of the extensive media coverage, we're asking that you sequester the jury.

> Judge Ramsay: Request is denied. Bring the jury in, please.
> Cathy: And, Your Honor, just for the record, we will ask that – we will call Prabhakari Devi tomorrow as our first witness. So if you can let her know she needs to be here, with or without her attorney.
> Kearney: Which one do you think it will be?
> Cathy: I'm guessing probably the former. The real question is who it's going to be. That's the question.

As he was leaving the courthouse, Kearney stopped to talk to KXAN television news reporter Chris Sadeghi.

> Sadeghi: It has been a bizarre day. We were supposed to hear testimony to start the sentencing phase of this trial, but instead, we ended up hearing testimony from a detective on the attempts to locate Swamiji. Now, the argument becomes is the eighty-two-year-old man unable to make it, or is he on the run? The question on everyone's mind is where is Swamiji? His attorney could only wonder, like everyone else.
> Kearney: He's been real sick this last weekend and we have an eighty-two-year-old client [with] severe, you know, health issues.

To me, the most striking aspect of the surreal day was that not a single devotee looked the least bit concerned about Prakash's sudden disappearance.

Day Eleven

Fugitive from Justice

Tuesday, 8 March 2011

EVEN THOUGH CATHY had made it clear that she wanted to put Prabhakari on the stand to question her about Prakash's disappearance, she never got the chance. Overnight, Prabhakari and Peter S. had hired lawyers, each of whom requested immunity from prosecution for their clients. Hays County gave immunity only to Peter. They weren't going to let Prabhakari skate away scot-free.

However, Peter's testimony turned out to be completely useless, as was the case with the testimonies of the two other witnesses the defence trotted out that day. One was a Hispanic male devotee who was brought to the stand for an obvious reason – to appeal to the Hispanic members of the jury. I even thought I saw one of the Hispanic men on the jury roll his eyes at the ploy. Their second witness was an Indian doctor from Oklahoma who detailed a litany of illnesses that supposedly afflicted Prakash. He was a staunch Kripalu devotee and was not Prakash's doctor.

However, it hardly mattered who was on the witness stand or what they said, because the fact remained that Prakash was not there. His lawyers had the audacity to continue fighting for probation, even though their client was now a fugitive.

Amy Lockhart said it best:

> I never thought I'd see it. Never thought I would see someone stand up here and ask a jury to give a fugitive probation, let alone someone who's been convicted of 20 felonies who – what does he do right after? Goes out and commits more felonies. And he

> wants to ask you for probation, and by doing it he tells you that, well, God, how's he going to defend himself in prison, like he thinks you're dumb enough to think that they're going to put an 82-year-old ailing man in general population with people that are going to hurt him; that this State of Texas is crazy enough and doesn't have the sense to have a special ward for geriatric patients, for people who need medical attention. And you think somebody with as much money and lawyers as he has access to is going to be stuck in a place where he can't defend himself and where he can't get the proper medical needs? Please. There's a place for people like him.
>
> But you know what? Even if he was still sitting there in that recliner, we would be up here asking you to sentence him to prison. That was the plan all along. Even if he was still there (pointing), we'd be asking you to – for him to go to prison because the very same people that are helping him hide, the very same people who aren't even bothering looking for him, who are on the line for $11 million and can't even bother to call him to see if he'll answer his call – those very same people who are helping him hide would be the very same people who would be helping him do whatever he wants to do while he's on probation.

Prakash's charges of indecency with a child carried a jail sentence of two to twenty years per charge. Cathy had said all along that she would request jail time, and that she would ask for at least eleven years. However, now that Prakash was on the run, she asked the jury to give him all 400 years.

Amy also made a devastating statement that cut right to the heart of the matter – the pain of being sexually violated as young girls by this man, whom they once thought of as their grandfather, was a life sentence for the girls.

> For the rest of their lives, will they have to stop themselves from recoiling from the touch of their partners because – every time

> they reach to caress their breasts, will they think of him? He'll always be there. When Shyama finally finds love, she's going to have to explain to him, 'I was molested as a child.' It's always going to be there for her. When Vesla brings her newborn child to her breast to feed it, will she see his face? Every milestone for the rest of their lives, they will see him, and they will remember his touch, and they will remember what he did to them, and it will never leave them. When he acted on his sexual desire for these girls when they were children, he gave them a life sentence. All we're asking you to do is sentence him to 20 years. And, besides, for a fugitive from justice, he shouldn't get anything less.

The jury deliberated for one hour and gave Prakash fourteen years per count for a total of 280 years. Judge Ramsay ruled that the penalty per charge would run concurrently, instead of consecutively, which meant that Prakash would serve just fourteen years in a penitentiary. However, he would now be facing additional charges as a fugitive from justice. Whether it was fourteen years or 400, the once-glorified guru was going to jail – if the US Marshals could find him, that is.

The Wicked Flee

A Run for the Border

US MARSHALS QUICKLY found that Prakash had crossed the border into Mexico at Nuevo Laredo on Sunday, the evening before his sentencing – and that he was neither alone, nor broke.

The *Austin American-Statesman* ran an article on 1 April 2011, under the headline, 'Guru Still in Mexico, Say U.S. Marshals':

> The U.S. Marshals Service is reasonably confident that convicted guru Prakashanand Saraswati is still 'hunkered down' in Nuevo Laredo, Tamaulipas, according to Hector Gomez, supervising deputy marshal of the agency's Austin office. 'I really think we've got him landlocked now.'
>
> He declined to identify how the marshals knew Prakashanand was hiding out in the border city, but he said the latest hard evidence of the guru's location was reliable as of about a week ago.
>
> Gomez also said the agency has evidence that Prakashanand left the country 'with loads of cash', presumably to use to bribe a pilot to fly him out of Mexico, probably to India.

Two women close to Prakash were also missing – his assistant Vishi and a woman named Allison, who went by the Hindi name, Chittra. Allison was fluent in Spanish, so it made sense that Prakash would take her. And of course Vishi was his long-time servant. Why he did not want Prabhakari is anyone's guess. Perhaps they had a falling out over the failed defence strategy. Or maybe he assumed she would continue to run Barsana Dham.

But Kripalu had other ideas. Within ten days of Prakash's run for the border, he kicked Prabhakari and her family out of Barsana Dham, ostensibly to go to New Jersey and run a JKP centre. But that did not pan out and all four Tonnessens, including the son, Luke, moved to Colorado.

Kripalu also created a new management team that included only two of the former members: Divakari and Katie W. He added three Indian men to the team, naming one of them as the new president and instructed devotees to remove photographs of Prakash from the prayer hall at Barsana Dham. And – the oddest thing of all – he changed the name of the ashram to Radha Madhav Dham. Later in the summer, he reportedly performed a death ritual in India for Prakash. As Kripalu's partner in crime for nearly sixty years, Prakash had become a serious liability – and Kripalu now wanted to disown him publicly.

PART SEVEN

In Hindsight

Deconstructing the Gurus' Con Game

'No lie can live forever.'
– Martin Luther King Jr, American civil rights activist

'I once was lost, but now am found,
Was blind, but now I see.'
– John Newton, English poet and clergyman

Cult-Proof?

Resisting the Irresistible Lure

IN THE FIRST JKP lecture I ever attended, Prabhakari told the audience that a person needs three things to find God: the desire, a human body and a God-realized saint.

In hindsight, I now know that people need at least three things to be lured into a cult: a sense of meaninglessness in their lives, a deep desire for something specific (and usually difficult to achieve) like God, and the introduction of a charismatic leader who claims to have all the answers.

Joining a cult gives a person three main things: a feeling of purpose, a feeling of superiority, and an 'all-powerful' leader who purports to know all the answers.

In actuality, having a distorted and excessive relationship with a 'guru' is a way to abdicate the responsibility of your life. In the cultic relationship, the person regresses and becomes like an infant, doing exactly what the leader (the 'all-knowing adult') tells them to do. Strangely, this path can be very seductive, even for accomplished grown-ups, for it feeds a primal need to be taken care of and to not have to work for what you want.

Many people think that they cannot be lured into the clutches of a cult. I know I thought that. In fact, at seventeen, I believed I was cult-proof though I grew up in the age of cults. In fact, there was an incident when two smooth-talking, glassy-eyed members of a cult tried to scope me out and I managed to escape their clutches – an incident that made me even more confident about my ability to outsmart any mumbo-jumbo plying recruiter.

An Accumulation of Evidence

Is Kripalu God or an Unstoppable Madman?

AFTER LEARNING THE truth about JKP, I started to wonder about Kripalu Maharaj – who was he, really?

Among his devotees, he is considered the incarnation of Radha-Krishna, the reincarnation of Lord Chaitanya Mahaprabhu, and the fifth Jagadguru with some extraordinary mythology surrounding his birth and growing-up years.

But of course it is all a lie. So who is Kripalu? My first clue came when I began learning about a personality disorder called psychopathy or sociopathy that is, according to Wikipedia, characterized by 'a lack of empathy and remorse, shallow emotions, egocentricity and deceptiveness. Psychopaths are highly prone to antisocial behaviour and abusive treatment of others.' After continued research, I came to the conclusion that Kripalu was a textbook psychopath.

My studies led me to what is widely considered to be the seminal book for laypeople on the subject: *Without Conscience: The Disturbing World of the Psychopaths Among Us*, by Robert D. Hare, the world's leading expert on psychopathology. Dr Hare identified the twelve most common characteristics of psychopaths.

I am not a trained psychologist and cannot provide a definite diagnosis of Kripalu, but based on my years as a follower, I can say with complete confidence that he exhibits all twelve characteristics, from being 'glib and superficial' to showing signs of 'poor behaviour control' to displaying 'adult antisocial behaviour'. I also found a description of Kripalu's early life in an article that talked about his arrest on charges of raping three underage girls in India. It shed interesting light on his origins – including the fact that he had studied tantric yoga from a tantric yogi. This fact is very enlightening for two reasons: 1) Kripalu claims to never have had a guru, and 2) tantric yoga is closely associated with the 'dark arts'.

It's no surprise that Kripalu's official back story is a complete fabrication, because being an accomplished liar goes hand in hand with being a textbook psychopath.

Liar, Liar

Who is Prakashanand Saraswati?

PRAKASHANAND SARASWATI, THE man in saffron who came to the US in the 1980s, led a relatively small group of followers and built a huge temple in Austin, Texas, was not just your average, everyday guru – at least according to him.

His 'official' biography claims that at the age of twenty-three he was offered the prestigious religious position of Jagadguru Shankaracharya of Joshimath, considered one of the four principle religious positions in India. There is only one problem with his lofty claim: it's completely bogus. In fact, most of Prakash's professed history is a lie. He was not born into a 'respected Brahmin family (typically meaning a family of preachers)', he did not wander in forests and live in caves for eighteen years, nor was he asked to be the successor of Brahmananda Saraswati (known familiarly as Guru Dev).

We may never know the whole truth about him, but the facts we do know reveal much about the man behind the mask.

For starters, one of his closest followers who had worshipped him for twenty-five years confirmed that Prakash was 'just some village boy', which explains why no one from Prakahs's past ever visited him and why there was never any mention of his parents or any family member.

His claim to have wandered in forests and lived in caves is equally false. For many years as a young sadhu he lived in a small building atop a hill near Barsana, India, where the footprints of Krishna were said to be imprinted into a rock. I've seen the place. It was a tiny room, but it was definitely not a cave. And he did not have to worry about food, because the villagers surrounding the area brought daily meals to the sadhus who lived there. They even brought food to the group of devotees I was with when we visited the location.

There is also no evidence to support the claim that Guru Dev wanted Prakash to be next in line for his title. In fact, I found long dissertations online examining the complexities of succession that arose after Guru Dev's death in 1952, because there were several potential candidates, many of whom had been Guru Dev's long-time disciples. Prakash's name only shows up as a footnote, as someone who 'claims to have been offered the seat of Shankaracharya of Joshimath'.

Glaringly absent from Prakash's biography is the tremendous future influence that Guru Dev's personal secretary, a man named Mahesh Prasad Varma, would have on him. Three years after Guru Dev's death, Varma assumed a new name – Maharishi Mahesh Yogi and introduced a path of yoga called Transcendental Meditation© (TM), which was supposedly based on the teachings of Guru Dev.

The Maharishi found an eager audience in the growing numbers of westerners seeking Eastern mysticism. The TM programme became famous worldwide in the 1960s when The Beatles spent some time with the Maharishi in India – before becoming disillusioned and leaving. The Maharishi became one of the most successful Hindu gurus to ever land on the US shores, and this did not go unnoticed by Prakash. In fact, Prakash's footsteps to the US show a man interested in emulating the Maharishi's success.

Sometime in his late twenties, Prakash met Kripalu.

Prakash's biography also claims that when he was about forty-five, 'the Divine Will of Shree Radha inspired him to come back into the world, help the souls looking for God realization, and rejuvenate and spread the path of raganuga bhakti in the world'. Since Prakash claimed that Kripalu was Radha in an earthly form, it follows that he left India to go out preaching at Kripalu's bidding. In fact, it wasn't until the 1970s that Prakash started travelling abroad and working in earnest to gather a following. He started in Fiji, Singapore and New Zealand, ultimately visiting the US for the first time in the late 1970s.

It appears that Prakash planned to tap into the wealth of westerners interested in Eastern religions, because he made a beeline for Fairfield, Iowa – a stronghold of Maharishi's followers. Like some kind of Hindu guru pirate, Prakash seemed intent on plundering the Maharishi's booty of devotees. While there, Prakash gave lectures and actively sought out people who had become disgruntled with TM for whatever reason – people who were ripe, easy-picking for the fledgling guru. Prakash even ran ads in the local newspaper denouncing the Maharishi and claiming that he was an atheist.

By joining Prakash, the former TM followers gained one thing many had craved for years – close proximity to a guru. Maharishi's following was large enough that personal contact with the guru was rare. Prakash gave these people a chance to finally become members of a guru's inner circle.

Prakash's claim to have been offered the seat of Shankaracharya of Joshimath played heavily into his strategy to pilfer the Maharishi's followers, because they had been taught to worship Guru Dev. However, for all his wheeling and dealing, Prakash only ever gained a few dozen former TM followers.

Interestingly, TM was not the only organization that Prakash poached from. He also brazenly copied the name of another successful Hindu spiritual organization that had been operating in the West since the 1960s – the International Society for Krishna Consciousness (ISKCON). Prakash named his organization the International Society for Divine Love Consciousness (ISDL). He even started reproducing several of ISKCON's famous paintings of Radha–Krishna, until he received a cease-and-desist letter for copyright infringement.

Years later I discovered that he had also stolen from his own guru, Kripalu, by plagiarizing one of his books and claiming that he had written it. This was Prakash's first book, *The Science of Devotion and Grace*, which is an almost verbatim copy of *Prem Ras Siddhant,* one of Kripalu's books, which was available only in Hindi for many years. Although he claimed to have authored many books, most are simply compilations of his speeches, while others are merely piecemeal ramblings with whole sections plagiarized from other sources.

Before long, Prakash had enough devotees with enough available money to purchase a large house in the outskirts of Philadelphia, where he ran his US centre for years. But what he longed for was a large plot of land where he could build his own temple.

One of Prakash's followers brought to his attention 200 acres for sale south-west of Austin, Texas, which was adjacent to acreage owned by the TM organization.

While living in the ashram, I had got to know the details of how the land was purchased by Dennis Wagner, one of Prakash's devotees, and transferred to Prakash the very next day. The purchase and immediate transfer was uncovered by Jeannie Ralston, the writer of the 1995 *Texas Monthly* article about Prakash.

Was it a coincidence that Prakash gathered as many former TM followers as he could find and then bought property just north of the establishment of his old nemesis? And what was his inspiration when he instructed his followers who lived in Los Angeles to 'find celebrities to become devotees'? Was the Maharishi's well-publicized contact with The Beatles the inspiration for Prakash's desire for his own 'star power'? In fact, Prakash wanted a similar celebrity endorsement to give him a public relations boost. However, the Los Angeles devotees were unable to entice any big stars to the Barsana Dham ashram. The best they could do was invite Lindsay Wagner (who played the Bionic Woman in the 1970s television show) to Barsana Dham. She stayed for only a few days and chose to spend most of the time in her room by herself, doing yoga.

When the Maharishi died in February 2008, Prakash made a last-ditch attempt to attract more TM followers and instructed his former TM followers to contact anyone they had known from TM *who had money* and invite them to a special seminar in New York. The seminar was scheduled for the first weekend of May 2008, and the response was promising. But in the end, it backfired stupendously. Prakash was arrested in Washington DC on 24 April. He refused to cancel the seminar. The rich attendees were angry and disgusted to discover that their host was an accused child molester.

Thus ended Prakash's inglorious attempt to follow in the footsteps of Maharishi Mahesh Yogi.

Unholy Union

A Deal between Devils

ONCE I REALIZED the true nature of this organization, I wondered about the relationship between these two criminally minded men. Obviously, something was very off in their odd association. Prakash appeared to worship Kripalu to an excessive degree, fawning over him at every turn. But whenever Kripalu was not around, Prakash wanted to be worshipped in a similar way by his own devotees. To his face, Kripalu would praise Prakash, but regularly take mean-spirited verbal swipes at him behind his back.

There was something very twisted going on between these two. The relationship hinted of a sado-masochistic dynamic between psychopaths. Dr Hare makes an interesting point about co-dependent psychopaths in his book *Without Conscience*, which I believe speaks directly to the relationship between these two men:

> Psychopaths usually don't get along well with one another. The last thing an egocentric, selfish, demanding, callous person wants is someone just like him. Two stars is one too many. Occasionally, however, psychopaths become temporary partners in crime – a grim symbiosis with unfortunate consequences for other people. Generally, one member of the pair is a 'talker' who gets his or her way through charm, deceit, and manipulation, whereas the other is a 'doer' who prefers direct action – intimidation and force. As long as their interests are complementary, they make a formidable pair.

Kripalu was the talker with charisma, while Prakash was the heavy-lifter, the one who made things happen. Some have described him as the 'businessman' of the pair. The two letters described earlier clearly show that they had a business relationship – contrary to the purely 'devotional' one they faked in public.

My guess is that back in the 1950s, both fake gurus were floundering by themselves – Kripalu as the aimless charmer and Prakash as the ambitious wannabe with a Napoleon complex. When they met, they sized each other up and realized that they could be more successful together than they had been on their own.

So what exactly was Prakash up to after he hitched his wagon to Kripalu's cart in the 1950s? Obviously he wasn't preaching, because he did not collect any devotees before the 1980s. I believe he was devising a plan that would appeal to Kripalu – one that involved creating their own form of mysticism. His letter to Kripalu is proof that they had devised a plan to 'gain millions of dollars' from westerners. All they needed now was a clever new angle on Hinduism and a mystical back story, which took a little time to concoct.

Eventually they settled into a holy-man tag-team approach, like a king and his trusty sidekick. They concocted a unique and clever twist on worshipping Radha–Krishna that involved a guru providing intimate 'divine love' to devotees on earth in the way that Krishna supposedly gave intimate divine love in the divine world.

My understanding of the relationship between the two men and the creation of their unusual sect crystallized one day while I was reading Prakash's derogatory book about Christianity: *Formation of the New Testament and the History of Christianity.* In one passage, I realized that he was describing events with such an authoritarian tone, not because he was a scholar of Christianity, but because he was actually describing the relationship and plans made between himself and Kripalu:

> Paul (c. AD 10–67) ... was an ambitious man and liked leadership ... Peter discovered he has found the right man whose skilled oratory and passionate enthusiasm could be used for promotion of their desired religion. Thus both joined as a team and ... got busy deciding the central theme of their mission which could divert the people towards their side.

If you reread this passage with Paul as Prakash and Kripalu as Simon Peter, and replace Hinduism with Christianity in the text, it takes on a whole new meaning.

False Profits

Is JKP's 'Charity Work' a Scam?

FROM THE TIME I joined JKP in 1991 up until 2004, I never heard anyone talk about doing charity work – it was simply not part of the organization's mission. In fact, once, when Sureshwari was attending the Parliament of World Religions in Chicago in the 1990s, she called to ask Prakash: 'What should I say when people ask me what kind of good works we do?' His answer? 'Tell them we provide prayer services and books that enrich people's spiritual lives.' The response was, of course, ridiculous.

While I was in the organization, there was no focus whatsoever on charity. Later I discovered that Kripalu had established a girls' school – which, in hindsight, was a highly suspicious enterprise.

Also, Kripalu would periodically put on a show of charity. For example, one year, during his annual Intensive in India, devotees in attendance were asked to purchase bicycles for the poor people in the village. Each time a devotee purchased a bike, Kripalu would have his photo taken with the bike and its lucky recipient – and JKP announced that *Kripalu* was donating bicycles to poor villagers.

The first I ever heard about JKP establishing any hospitals was in 2004, when I was in India. One of the preachers asked me to help prepare a brochure she could use to collect donations for the hospitals that JKP was about to build. However, it wasn't until after Kripalu's arrest that they started talking about the hospitals as if they were going to erect huge, modern, multi-storey facilities to care for thousands of poor patients in India. No such hospital was ever built by JKP. There were only small clinics – offering minimal services and treatment and often staffed by devotees – set up at each of the ashram locations. One Indian doctor told me that he had been planning to spend three months in India working in one of the clinics – until he learnt about the true nature of JKP from 'The Truth Project' Facebook page.

JKP's 'charity work' was nothing more than a giant smokescreen designed to provide it with yet another way to collect millions of dollars.

The Guru–Devotee Dance of Narcissism

Are Their Followers Drinking the Kool-Aid™?

THE ONE QUESTION I've been asked more than any other since I left the JKP cult is this: Why would *anyone* stay in that organization considering the depravity of the fake gurus?

It's a good question and a logical one that any normal, law-abiding person would ask. Unfortunately, I do not have any easy answers. For one thing, it is a mystery to me why anyone would continue staying in an organization in which the leaders have been accused repeatedly of sexual abuse and where one was convicted on charges of indecency with children.

The simple answer is that the people who have not left JKP are so entrenched in the concept of worshipping the gurus that they can only believe one of three things: first, that anyone who accuses the gurus of bad behaviour are wrong and out to persecute the mystic men; secondly, that any action of a saint is 'gracious'; finally, several people, mostly women, had to know exactly what the gurus were up to and they willingly participated. I consider the last group to be willing members of a Hindu sex cult. (In fact, a female devotee who was in the inner circle of the women and girls who had sex with Kripalu, told me: '*Way* more than *several* knew exactly what was going on. It's true. We were willing members of a sex cult. Because we believed he was God, so anything God does must be okay. Pretty sick, huh?')

The first and foremost falsehood put forth by the gurus was that they were saints. If one could accept that, it was easier to swallow the next lie – and the next, et cetera.

In an article 'Why We Forget' on Salon.com, neuroscientist David Disalvo made the following statement that relates to the hold the gurus had on the devotees in the beginning of the process:

> ... [C]ognitive psychology studies have made clear ... that humans can be exceptionally gullible. With a little push, we're prone to developing false beliefs not only about others but also about ourselves with equal prowess – and the results can be, well, hard to believe.

Kripalu said that the guru was more important than God in a devotee's pursuit of the divine. He cited scriptural references extensively to prove his point. I never truly took these teachings to heart, largely because I was never deeply attracted to the gurus. I wanted God in his divine form, not these men who seemed to be uncommonly attached to their physical comforts and the attention they garnered from besotted followers. Maybe that's why it was easier for me and a handful of others to detach ourselves from the organization once the gurus' secrets came to light.

In the years since I left the ashram, I've had more time to consider the dysfunctional dynamic between devotees and their guru and have considered why, in the face of all common sense and logic, many followers just keep drinking the Kool-Aid. The psychology of the guru–devotee relationship is complex. Developed over years of careful conditioning by the gurus, it culminates in a shared narcissism. The guru play-acts as if he or she is God incarnate and the devotees narcissistically believe that they are among the chosen few selected to follow this supreme form of God on earth. For these people, to leave the guru and no longer be 'special' is a pain worse than the sting of admitting that you are following a conman. So the diehard devotees perform whatever mental gymnastics are necessary to continue living their lives in lockstep with the guru.

I found this quote from Alexis Sanderson, Spalding professor of eastern religions and ethics, University of Oxford, that describes how easy it is to wander into such cults and how difficult to disengage from them.

> The pressure of the Guru and his favourite acolytes can be

> overwhelming even in less obviously coercive groups, and recovery, if it ever comes, is likely to be an extremely painful process involving grief, self-loathing, and rage.

Sanderson is right. When I left the cult, the grief and self-loathing nearly destroyed me. I went through a bleak phase of self-recrimination until I finally started to heal and rebuild a new life for myself. It took four years for me to feel like I had moved beyond my past life and to become passionate about new things.

Like so many others with similar experiences, I needed to understand why anyone would ever choose to stay in a self-limiting and abusive virtual prison, such as those created by the gurus. After much honest introspection and consideration of explanations from self-help books, professionals and other former cult members, and a great deal of brutally honest introspection, I settled on one particular theory that makes more sense to me than anything else. I am sure it will be controversial, even blasphemous to some, but, for me, it speaks more strongly to the twisted world of the guru–devotee dance of narcissism than anything else. I believe that the guru–devotee relationship shares a commonality with the fetish known as BDSM (bondage, discipline and sadomasochism).

Bondage and Discipline

Spiritual Masters or Slave Masters?

IT'S AMAZING HOW similar the guru–disciple relationship is to the master–slave relationship in the fetish subculture called BDSM, which practises bondage, discipline and sadomasochism.

When I was a new devotee, I watched a woman prepare flowers for the altar. When I bent down for a whiff of the beautiful fresh flowers, the woman reproached me: 'Those are for Swamiji to enjoy. He should be the first to enjoy their fragrance.'

This odd and obsessive reaction to something so mundane was the norm, not the exception, in the life of the JKP masters. Devotees believed that everything was done for the gurus, that our relationships with them were primary, and that even if they were not thinking about us, we should be thinking about them. This is exactly how the subordinate party in a master–slave relationship is conditioned to think.

I knew nothing about BDSM until I left the cult. In one of those online surfing experiences where you start clicking on links and wind up on some completely unexpected website, I ended up on a page where a woman was describing her BDSM relationship as a 'slave' to a 'master'. The more I read, the more I realized that it sounded like the relationships between JKP devotees and the gurus – who are even *called* 'masters'.

In BDSM relationships, slaves worship their masters, surrender to them and do exactly as they are told, with no questions asked, which is exactly what devotees did for the gurus in JKP. While most BDSM relationships include a sexual component, not all of them do. So was the case with JKP.

There is a book in the BDSM community called *SlaveCraft*, written by 'a grateful slave', which clarified the psychology of this lifestyle. The book details what it means to be a good submissive slave and serve a dominant master. Several passages – especially those on the concepts of surrendering to the master, serving him/her, and remaining humble around him/her – sound incredibly similar to concepts Kripalu and Prakash spoke and wrote about. According to the book, to remain 'blissfully happy' as a slave, one must allow the 'Master's will' to prevail over one's own; obedience 'is an opportunity to demonstrate to [the master] the sincerity of the slave's craving for surrender'; and as the submission deepens, 'the feeling of being connected to our Master expands', leading to the slave falling in love with the master who becomes the slave's 'lifeline', which lets the slave enter a space where he/she longs 'to deny Him [the master] nothing – nothing at all'.

Even when Dr Gordon Warme, author of *Daggers of the Mind*, visited Kripalu's ashram in Mangarh for a few days as part of his research on different cultures' healing methods, he picked up on the sadomasochistic relationship Kripalu had with his followers. Compared to the utter submission of the others around the god-man, Warme's 'polite conversation probably looked irreverent', he notes. Maharajji 'nagged his devotees' to carry out his instructions such as taking notes when he lectured or 'to come forward and dance', and had two cameras record his every public movement.

Dr Warme could see that Maharajji's followers aimed at utter subservience, denying their own interests. They lived vicariously as the guru led an enviable life, a hypothesis that was verified by one of his followers who agreed: 'We live through him.'

Of the devotees, he observed that they had given up their souls and are 'reborn in him, like those reborn in Christ', with some being so involved that they ate and slept and conducted their ablutions and prayed at the same time as he did. 'The devotees are examples of the cure by rebirth of the soul – but in this instance, reborn in their leader, not in themselves.'

I'm sure the majority of the JKP devotees do not consciously believe that they are in sadomasochistic relationships with their gurus; but then they wouldn't because, as some cult researchers point out, cult relationships are so restrictive and controlling that they promote a kind of psychopathology that blinds people to the truth.

The $10 Million Question

Where is Prakashanand Saraswati?

THE LAST KNOWN whereabouts of Prakashanand Saraswati, according to news reports, was Mexico. A worldwide manhunt was launched for him after Judge Ramsay issued a warrant for his arrest and ordered the forfeiture of his $1 million bond. It was widely speculated that he had made an exit using a false passport.

And what about the $10 million bond? After Prakash's trial, Peter S., the devotee who put up the money, hired four of the best bail-bond lawyers in Texas and got out of paying the bond. The only money paid to Hays County was the forfeited 1 million dollars in cash, which had been given to keep Prakash out of jail immediately after his arrest, and an extra $200,000, which was the amount charged to Prakash for the penalty phase of his trial.

With Prakash still at large and the loss of the anticipated bail bond, the best that can be said about this situation is that Prakash no longer enjoys the fame he so desperately craved. In fact, his and Kripalu's sordid con game is finally being exposed for exactly what it is. He no longer gets to visit the man he had a sixty-year-long masochistic relationship with, playing the faithful slave to Kripalu's dominating master. Neither does he get to surround himself with his adoring devotees.

It's no coincidence that while I was in India for the new year in 2004, Prakash was busy finalizing the creation of several JKP trusts for which Kripalu's daughters were named as administrators. After Kripalu's arrest in Trinidad, lawyers in the US researched JKP's funds on behalf of a woman who was raped by Kripalu as a child and found that JKP's money was hidden in a 'complicated network of India-based trusts', no doubt the very ones that Prakash had set up. This clever pre-planning makes it extremely difficult for anyone to hold Kripalu, Prakash or the organization financially accountable for any criminal actions of the gurus.

However, I have not given up hope that Prakash will someday be caught and sent to spend the remainder of his life in jail.

Cult-Proof

How to Steer Clear of Fake Gurus and Other Con Games

NOW THAT I'M finally out of the cult – body, mind and soul – I am happy in the knowledge that I will never again allow myself to be conned. I will never let a conman or woman or organization swindle me out of my precious time, money and self-respect.

About a year after I left the JKP cult, I had a dream in which I angrily confronted Prakash, shaking with rage as I yelled in his face: 'What the hell do you think you were doing?' His response cut right to the heart of the matter: 'I only told you what you wanted to hear.'

I knew this was my inner wisdom speaking to me – and warning me to be on alert, to watch out for false prophets bearing gifts, especially ones that I was looking for.

In my case, I was looking for the way to God. I thought that I needed to receive a divine message that would allow my soul to snip the rope tying me to the material world, so that I could ascend to the divine world and dwell with God forever. This is what everyone in the cult seemed to want too. And this is exactly what the fake gurus promised. And that's the crux of the problem – the conmen's uncanny ability to tell us exactly what we want or need to hear.

If I've learnt anything from this experience, it's how to spot a con. It's easy once you know what to look for. But you have to be on your guard and question everything. What's more, if you think you've found someone bearing the answers to your prayers, you must demand legitimate, verifiable proof that they are who they say they are and that they can provide what they are promising. If you do this, you will quickly spot a con, because a conman or woman will fail the first test.

On my way to processing the fact that I was conned, I read many great books which helped me see the truth of the matter. It also taught me that I am not the first to be conned by a cult and, sadly, I won't be the last.

One of the books that helped me is titled *Take Back Your Life: Recovering from Cults and Abusive Relationships*, by Janja Lalich and Madeleine Tobias. It points out the common socio-structural, socio-psychological, and interpersonal behavioural patterns commonly found in cultic environments.

The book says that an unquestioning commitment to a leader is a huge red flag. If you come across this situation, just turn around and bolt! No one has all the answers – and if they say they do, they are lying, plain and simple. In this case, if you request verifiable proof, you will be rebuffed, for questioning is never allowed in controlling organizations. Also along these lines, watch out if the group claims the leader is a messiah, avatar or God incarnate, and if he or she is not accountable to anyone.

Other troublesome indicators of a cult, according to the authors, are mind-altering practices, like excessive and routinized meditation and chanting; a preoccupation with attracting new people and collecting money; regular dictates from the leader prescribing what to wear, how to raise children, or to participate in unethical behaviour and a polarizing us-versus-them mentality. Other warning signs the authors share include the following:

- The leadership induces feelings of shame and/or guilt in order to influence and/or control members.

- Subservience to the leader or group requires members to cut ties with family and friends, and radically alter their personal goals.
- The most loyal members (the 'true believers') feel there can be no life outside the context of the group.

I also gained great insight and clarity from a list of the eight criteria for mind control from the book *Thought Reform and the Psychology of Totalism* by Robert Jay Lifton, which explains the psychology of cultic manipulation. It provides clear insight on what to watch out for, such as this point:

> **Mystical Manipulation**. The manipulation of experiences that appears spontaneous but is, in fact, planned and orchestrated by the group or its leaders in order to demonstrate divine authority, spiritual advancement, or some exceptional talent or insight that sets the leader and/or group apart from humanity, and that allows reinterpretation of historical events, scripture, and other experiences.

I had certainly experienced this – in spades! My fake gurus easily manipulated their group of followers. Looking back, I realize how easy it was. They could say *any* illogical thing and the people would just nod their heads. No one seemed to question anything. I imagine the gurus thinking: 'You stupid cows. I can tell you anything and you'll fall for it.' Kripalu was in the habit of calling people donkeys using the derogatory Hindi word for 'ass'. People thought it was endearing. But now I don't think so. I think it was one of the few times he was being honest.

Other warning signs of a controlling group, according to the author, are impossible demands for perfection (such as being perfect before you can be divinized); forcing members to confess their sins; creating unique verbiage to describe the leader's world view; and a tendency to say that the outside world is wrong and the group is right.

I also like the 'Checklist of 20 Ways to Resist Unwanted Social Influence' by Philip Zimbardo, PhD, and Susan Andersen, PhD, in the book *Understanding Mind Control*, because they provide a proactive way to gauge the brainwashing and mind-control tactics of any organization that makes you suspicious. Here are a few of their tips for testing the veracity of anyone or any organization:

- Insist on an understandable explanation, without double-speak.
- Remember there is no such thing as instant, unconditional love from strangers.
- Avoid 'total situations' that are unfamiliar and in which you have little control and freedom.
- Greed and ego-flattering will get mind control manipulators and con agents far, but only if you allow yourself to be seduced.

As I said at the beginning of this chapter, I will never again be conned. But it saddens me to know that there are still many people who will be. Because as long as there are gullible people who don't question authority figures, through intimidation, fear or an all-consuming desire to buy what the scam artists are selling, there will always be conmen and women preying on the weak. Like many problems of our age, true change in the area of cult control can only happen when the people supporting the con games make the firm decision to say 'no' and walk away. And hopefully they reach out and take a few others with them.

My utmost desire is that this book made you, like me, cult-proof. And I hope you'll share this with family and friends, especially if you are ever afraid that being conned is a real possibility for someone you care about.

Making the decision to remain cult-free is an empowering action that will truly set you free. I am here to tell you that this is a greater power than anything any power-mongering, know-it-all 'leader' can ever promise you. Your God-given inner wisdom is your true guru: honour it, listen to it and let it lead the way.

EPILOGUE

My Next Chapter

Life after a Cult

IT'S COMMON PRACTICE to try to find the upside of any traumatic event. The lesson. The silver lining. The point. But in the years after I left the cult, I felt only robbed – of my money, my time and my life.

Two years after I left, I was having lunch with a woman who would later become my life coach.

'What is the main thing you learnt during your fifteen years in the ashram?' she asked.

I thought about that for a moment and said, 'I learnt to cook really delicious Indian food.'

Her eyes widened and she burst out laughing. 'I thought you would tell me about some profound spiritual revelations.'

In fact, the profound spiritual lessons I thought I was learning in the ashram were, in reality, just the twisted ruminations of two fake gurus hell-bent on glorifying themselves and satisfying their own worldly desires. How could anything they taught translate into deep and meaningful spiritual lessons? I could not credit them for anything 'good' that came out of my years in their cult.

However, if I remove them from the equation and think about God and his or her plan for me, I can say this: that if you long for God realization to such an extent that you are willing to give up everything else in the world, including the love of another human being, it could mean that God will choose you for a purpose that you never saw coming – and which you might not have accepted if you had known about it in the beginning. If, in fact, God did make use of my dedication towards finding him or her, I think it was for this purpose: to use me as a witness to live the horror of this fake spiritual enterprise so that I could one day write this book and expose the truth of it as a warning to others.

It is a heavy burden and, if I am entirely honest, my years with these gurus is an experience that I regret – one I would take back if there were such a thing as an 'undo' button in life. There is no way around the fact that my blind faith robbed me of fifteen years of my life. Instead of 'surrendering' to these men's twisted world view, I should have been living, loving and experiencing this world – as, I now believe, God intends us all to do.

Many people ask some version of the same question: how did you not realize for fifteen years that this place was a cult? It's a tough question. But I finally realized the answer. When I joined the cult, I was quite depressed. I had lost my entire family and was divorced from one man and not in love with the other man whom I agreed to marry.

A therapist once showed me a chart that illustrated how much depression can narrow a person's vision compared to when one is happy and content. At the most depressed, our vision is at about 10 per cent of normal, which leaves us at risk of ignoring the important details that help one avoid certain danger. This is what happened to me.

But at least I finally got out. Many poor souls have had their vision impaired permanently and will die in the cult.

The primary goal of my wonderful new life now is to live as fully as possible, experience as much as possible and enjoy the world as much as I can. The one thing I know for sure is that God did not put us on earth to renounce the world's miracles, beauty or bounty but to live, laugh, love and enjoy, and to understand that we are already one with him.

For the rest of my life, I will have relationships with men, eat whatever I want, enjoy the theatre and the arts, revel in the natural beauty of this world, embrace the mysteries of life, read good books, write more books and be good to people. Instead of a God 'out there somewhere', I have found God within me. In my years outside the cult, I have discovered my innate wisdom which I always possessed but didn't recognize. And that inner wisdom contains the higher power that I've been seeking all along.

This is my religion now.

Follow the Story

It's Not Over Yet

THE STORY OF the two fake gurus abusing innocent people is not over.

Kripalu died in November 2013. However, the crimes of Jagadguru Kripalu Parishat have not ended with Kripalu's death. Though he has finally been restrained from harming people, his daughters – who have learnt everything from him directly over the past several decades – have inherited the organization. (I discovered soon after that his death was highly suspicious and took place after an argument with two men who have managed his finances for years, and who were involved in the death of the man who had been Kripalu's driver for about twenty-five years.)

His preachers will live on to help recruit new warm bodies to provide the cash they crave and the women that others have been groomed to 'grace'. JKP's preachers are located in many countries around the world, and have started new organizations with different names, such as JKP Yog and Radha Madhav Society. They've all been well trained by the master conman, Kripalu, and they will all work to continue propagating the con game. (In May 2014, one of JKP's followers was arrested while attempting to travel from Nepal to India with almost $80,000 in cash. Ferrying cash between countries is presumed to be one of JKP's methods to transfer cash donations into India from around the world.)

As of May 2014, Prakashanand Saraswati has not been caught –

and he is likely never to be, unless the citizens of India complain that a convicted child molester is free in their country – because JKP is probably paying off government officials to keep Prakash a free man. The devotees who aided and abetted his escape have not yet been held accountable for helping a convicted felon to flee and hide. (The US marshals have not given up on capturing Prakash. They know where he is hiding in India, but need the cooperation of the Indian government to arrest him. At the time of the publication of this book, assistance was still awaited.)

As long as the organization exists and as long as I am alive, I will continue to provide updates about this cult to the public at large, and advise people to steer clear. You could follow the ongoing story on Facebook at RishikaXcult. I had been writing on a blog (www.rishikaxcult.com) where I provided the truth of JKP, but it was cyber-bombed in mid-2013. I have relaunched the blog, so that it can, along with the website of my book, stand as a beacon of truth about the darkness that is JKP.

AFTERWORD

The Authentic Guru–Disciple Tradition in Hinduism

Commentary by Dr Madhu P. Godsay, Austin, Texas

IN THE PRECEDING pages, you read the story of the Barsana Dham ashram and the experiences of the author of this book. It is natural to feel disappointed, angry and frustrated when we meet people possessing demonic dispositions. It is our misfortune when we fatefully get involved with such people, who will stop at nothing when it comes to lust, power, insatiable desires and money. These types of people strive to amass, by unfair means, hoards of money and other things for the enjoyment of their sensual pleasures.

All religious traditions suffer from such perverted people, who constantly deceive people and prey on the innocent and gullible. The exploitation goes on, be it in a religion or any other organization. These people, posing as 'gurus', are beyond ethics and morals. In most cases, therefore, it is not the tradition that is at fault but their personalities, which exploit traditions to deceive the innocent.

It is my intention to describe, briefly, the authentic guru–shishya parampara (guru–disciple tradition), which dates back to thousands of years in India and which is still alive and well in the country. However, this tradition is not monopolized by India. The Western world has also seen the epoch of teacher–student relationships, which existed in

Greece in the fourth century BC, an example being the famous triad of Socrates, Plato and Aristotle.

Although the word 'guru' is used very loosely today to denote an expert in any particular field, it is mainly related to spirituality. In Sanskrit, the letter 'gu' stands for darkness (in other words, ignorance) and the letter 'ru' means that which removes the darkness. Thus, a guru is a teacher who removes the ignorance of his disciple and helps him evolve into a person with appropriate spiritual knowledge.

'Shishya' means disciple. The root of this Sanskrit word is 'shas' meaning to teach, instruct, or provide discipline. Traditionally, the student is seeking knowledge, particularly spiritual knowledge. He or she desires knowledge and is ready and willing to follow the teacher's instructions and discipline. The teacher, on the other hand, is the well-wisher of the disciple, is capable of imparting knowledge, and is of clean character and above worldly affairs. The place where teaching takes place is called an ashram, which should be a quiet, simple place, away from the city and conducive to spiritual development. Typically, the teacher and student are celibates. No material exchange and transactions of any kind take place between them. This fact is a very important aspect of this relationship in Hindu tradition. Otherwise, it opens the door for exploitation of the student by the teacher.

The student should never put his trust and devotion in a teacher who requests anything, which could be money, possessions or anything physical. The student can have confidence in the teacher's capability and show respect for his knowledge only if he is free of material desires and if he is not self-serving. This relationship must remain pure for the entire duration of the imparting of knowledge.

The student's 'surrender' to the guru should be based on the secure knowledge that he or she is not being taken advantage of or exploited. What's more, it's important to understand that the student's trust and devotion are not supposed to be based on blind faith or an expectation of miracles from the guru. Trust in the guru is supposed to be verifiable. In other words, there must be clear proof that the teacher actually possesses spiritual knowledge and is capable of imparting it. Without veracity, a person posing as a guru is worthless.

There are many famous guru–shishya pairs in Hindu mythology. In the Upanishads, one finds many philosophical dialogues between teachers and students. For instance, in the *Mundakopanishad*, the creator teaches his son Atharva, and Atharva teaches his disciple Angiva, and so on and so forth. Another famous scriptural pair is Lord Krishna and his disciple Arjuna in the Bhagavadgita. In modern India, various saints, such as Ramakrishna Paramahansa, Ramana Maharshi, Swami Chinmayananda, Swami Dayanand, etc., have imparted knowledge to hundreds of their disciples.

Hindu children are taught that their parents are their first gurus. Then other gurus follow throughout their lives, including a spiritual guru. The highest guru is the one who teaches and gives the experience of 'tat twam asi', meaning, 'You are Brahman (God)'. Guru Dattatreya was once asked by King Yadu the secret of his happiness and the name of his guru. He said atman (self) is my guru, yet I imbibed wisdom from nature.

Gurus can be roughly divided into two main classes – those who teach the bhakti tradition and those who follow the gyan tradition:

1. Bhakti tradition is related to loving a form of God.
2. Gyan (knowledge) tradition is related to impersonal devotion.

The bhakti form of the guru–shishya relationship generally incorporates:

- Devotion to the guru as a divine figure.
- The belief that such a guru will eventually impart moksha, peace, or divine power to the shishya.
- The belief that the shishya, with strong devotion and preparedness, will gain the merit.

The danger of the bhakti tradition lies in the choice of guru. There is real danger that ignorance and blind faith will mislead a shishya from what he or she is really seeking. In the gyan-based relationship, there is less danger of deceit, because the student does not worship the guru as God.

Some learned and God-realized people, like J. Krishnamurti and Lahiri Mahasaya, refused to allow their followers to form any kind of organization or sampradaya around them. Their relationship was strictly based on the exchange of knowledge. The guru's only goal is to help the shishya accomplish his or her spiritual advancement via his or her own ability to look within from a healthy, unattached perspective.

In the annals of guru–shishya tradition there are various types of sampradayas. There are the demonic types – such as people like Bernie-Maddox (an infamous man in the US who ran an investment con game and stole millions of dollars from investors), who prey on people's innocence, beliefs and gullibility. This is what we witnessed with the Barsana Dham episode, and its fake gurus, who were clearly only interested in exploiting people.

However, despite the people with ulterior motives acting as gurus, having wrong intentions, and no true knowledge to impart, the tradition of the teacher–student relationship in spiritual advancement has endured over thousands of years – and will continue to endure long into the future. With so many calling themselves gurus today, it is of paramount importance that every student seeking a guru hold that guru up to the standards that have endured through the ages: true knowledge, right motivation and pure intentions.

Om Shanti, Shanti, Shanti

Peace, Peace, Peace

For more information, or if you have questions about Dr Godsay's commentary, please contact him at mpgodsay@yahoo.com.

Acknowledgements

I AM GRATEFUL to so many people for helping me recover from the traumatic experience in the cult and tell my story. I hope I remember everyone.

First of all, to the group of ex-devotees and friends whom I leaned on heavily for support during my first few years out of the cult: Kathi, Wayne, Deepak, Sushma and Sue.

To the ex-devotees who told me their stories. People who spilled Jagadguru Kripalu Parishat's secrets online. The women and girls who spoke out about being raped by Kripalu Maharaj.

To the three young women who spoke out and faced down Prakashanand Saraswati in a criminal trial (two of whom lost their families, as a result): Kate Tonnessen, Shyama Rose and Vesla Tonnessen. You three are the bravest women I will ever know. Without you, these gurus would never have been held accountable for any of their crimes.

To the Hays County prosecution team that faced incredible odds to prosecute Prakashanand for his sex crimes against children: Cathy Compton (lead prosecutor), Amy Madison (assistant prosecutor), Sherri Tibbe (district attorney), Allison Ott Jordon and Leticia Nino (victims' advocates) and Jeri Skrocki (investigator of this case).

To the US marshals who continue to search for this fugitive from justice.

To the journalists who covered this story, especially Eric Dexheimer, who uncovered deep secrets of Jagadguru Kripalu Parishat and published them in the *Austin American-Statesman* and who followed this story from the beginning. Also to Jeannie Ralston, who uncovered many of Prakashanand's secrets in the mid-1990s, when few were willing to tell them and wrote an article that was published in the *Texas Monthly* magazine.

To all of the people who donated the money we needed to purchase the transcripts from Prakashanand's criminal trial, especially Sandeep, Rajiv and Vijay.

To the people who read my book in the early stages and gave me feedback. First and foremost, my best friend 'in the world', Karen Roller, who pushed me through three drafts of my book and helped me finally find my voice and (hopefully) tell my story in the most compelling way possible. To my book readers who read my final draft and gave me invaluable feedback: Sheridan, Suzy, Kathi, Kate, Raj, Milan and Sandeep.

And finally to God who, in the end, put me exactly where he or she wanted me to be.